Key Concepts in
Developmental Psychology

Key Concepts in
Developmental Psychology

H. Rudolph Schaffer

Los Angeles • London • New Delhi • Singapore

First published 2006

Reprinted 2008

SAGE Publications Ltd
1 Oliver's Yard
55 City Road
London EC1Y 1SP

SAGE Publications Inc.
2455 Teller Road
Thousand Oaks, California 91320

SAGE Publications India Pvt Ltd
B 1/l 1 Mohan Cooperative Industrial Area
Mathura Road, New Delhi 110 044
India

SAGE Publications Asia-Pacific Pte Ltd
33 Pekin Street #02-01
Far East Square
Singapore 048763

British Library Cataloguing in Publication data

A catalogue record for this book is available
from the British Library

ISBN-13 978-0-7619-4345-7
ISBN-13 978-0-7619-4346-4

Library of Congress control number: 2006923680

Typeset by C&M Digitals (P) Ltd., Chennai, India
Printed on paper from sustainable resources
Printed and bound in Great Britain by TJ International Ltd, Padstow, Cornwall

CONTENTS

INTRODUCTION

Why this book?

Every scientific discipline makes use of its own language in order to do justice to the particular phenomena with which it is concerned. For newcomers it is important that they learn this language, and especially the theoretical concepts employed for purposes of description and explanation. Developmental psychology is no exception to the prevalence of such concepts, and an essential part of finding out what the subject has to offer is to become acquainted with these terms. What, for example, is meant by **modularity**? Or **epigenesis**? Or **goodness of fit**? (terms in bold refer to concepts described in this book). This book sets out to make the more important concepts presently in use in developmental psychology readily accessible to students, by defining, analysing and discussing each in much greater detail than is usually done in textbooks. As I found out myself in writing an introductory textbook (Schaffer, 2004), it is rarely feasible to do full justice to the meaning, origins and usage of these terms; a special source of reference is therefore required which will hopefully not only help students to learn the relevant language but will also be used as a basis for discussion and serve as a spur for further consultation of the literature.

At the same time it is hoped that 'old hands' in developmental psychology will also find the book of help in checking their own ideas about particular concepts. It is highly desirable that we all share the same meaning attached to these terms, for one of the functions of a concept is to act as a communicative device in conveying certain theoretical propositions. However, it is by no means uncommon that different people give a somewhat different gloss to a term; moreover, the meaning attached to a concept is not necessarily static and set in stone for evermore; theoretical shifts may bring about a somewhat different usage even though the same term is retained. As far as possible therefore we need to avoid conflict and confusion, and it is intended that this book will be a means of pinpointing the reasons why such problems of definition arise in certain cases. Sharing meanings becomes even more important when we consider that concepts are not merely used by academics in theorizing about their data; they may also become part of the vocabulary used by practitioners – as seen, for example, in the use of the term **scaffolding** by teachers, of **bonding** by paediatricians and of **identity crisis** by psychiatrists and social workers. It is thus all the more necessary that we take care in the way we use language: terms need to be defined carefully so as to avoid misunderstanding which might then spill over into the kind of action taken by professionals.

A review of concepts is especially timely now because of the very considerable changes that have taken place in developmental psychology over the past two or three decades. In part, these changes reflect the great expansion of research activity we have seen over this period and the consequent increase in data calling for explanation. Even quite new topics have been added to the research agenda: **theory of mind**, for example, surfaced only in the 1980s but quickly grew into one of the busiest areas of study. New methodologies, such as those associated with **connectionist networks**, have surfaced recently, and the rapid advances of neuropsychology and behavioural genetics have also increased greatly the need for additional or, in some cases, revised theorizing.

However, the changes have not just been quantitative but also qualitative, in that the way we think about, explain and study development have in certain quite fundamental respects been transformed. For example, the prevalence of cross-sectional studies to investigate development is increasingly giving way to longitudinal designs, calling attention to the need for a **life-span** perspective and giving rise to such new concepts as **equifinality** and **multifinality**. Just as significant is the abandoning of simple, single-variable explanations for many developmental phenomena and their replacement by multivariate models that do far greater justice to the complexity of children's lives. Investigating the effects of maternal employment, for example, is no longer a matter of merely comparing children of employed mothers with children of non-employed mothers; rather, a large range of mediating and moderating variables are also taken into account, reflecting the many child, parent, family and social characteristics that also have to be incorporated into explanatory models. And to mention just one other change: developmental psychology has become less compartmentalized, in that it has become increasingly apparent that the traditional rigid division into areas such as cognitive, affective and social aspects does not serve us well in describing real-life behaviour. Again there are implications for the use of concepts: it may be, for example, that instead of having two concepts referring respectively to **emotional competence** and **social competence** we require only one, namely affective-social competence. Once again we see the need for keeping the list of concepts currently in use under constant review and ensuring that the way they are employed is widely shared.

What are concepts?

Concepts are the mental tools with which we think about a topic. They help us to organize, categorize, analyse and explain; they enable us to impose meaning on a diversity of observable phenomena; and they are thus essential to the task of advancing knowledge. They are not observable themselves – Newton did not *see* gravity but found it a useful device for explaining falling bodies. Freud too did not directly perceive the unconscious, but used it to account for a variety of mental phenomena such as dreams, neurotic symptoms and slips of the tongue. And similarly in developmental psychology: we do not, for example, *see* **internal working models**, but infer them from what we do see and find them of help in explaining what is out there in the real world – 'a useful fiction', as they have been described.

Concepts vary in how near they are to observable facts: **temperament**, for instance, is a lot nearer to the kind of behaviour the term refers to than such a much more abstract term as **deep structure**. Every concept, however, is tied to some specific set of empirical phenomena, and the limits of this set is therefore part of the specification of the concept. In fact, some concepts are rather more fuzzy than others, at least in their early stages of development, and it is then up to further work to ensure that their boundaries of reference become clarified. Let us also note that some concepts are really only summary labels for a group of phenomena: the term intelligence, for example, is really nothing more than an umbrella term or short-hand device used in referring to certain kinds of behaviour. Other concepts, however, go beyond their descriptive function and derive their value from being able to explain and make sense of our experience. Their contribution is heuristic: they serve to impose meaning and to lead to new insights. If they fail adequately to do so they will in due course be discarded and replaced by other concepts. The distinction between purely descriptive and explanatory concepts is sometimes difficult to make; nevertheless, in this book I have attempted to confine myself to the latter kind: umbrella terms like attention or sibling relationships are thus not included, nor are terms referring to methods and procedures such as Strange Situation or sociometry, however closely they may be associated with certain theoretical frameworks and however much they merit mention as procedures for generating data relevant to certain concepts.

Most concepts do not exist in isolation, but together with other concepts form part of a network that is encompassed in a general theory. Freud's psychoanalytic theory provides a good example: concepts such as the unconscious, regression, oedipal fixation and libido are all related to each other and form the building blocks of the theoretical framework. All the major theories that have been applied to developmental phenomena, such as Piagetian theory, social learning theory and information processing theory, similarly require the use of a range of concepts. Thus on the one hand a concept has a formal relationship to some particular set of observable phenomena, and on the other hand it is related to various other concepts forming part of the same theoretical framework. Both kinds of relationships need to be spelled out by the proponents of theories.

What are *key* concepts?

Some concepts clearly play a more significant part than others. Thus **attachment** has come to be widely recognized as central to our understanding of many facets of children's and also adults' socio-emotional life, and any list of key concepts is likely to include it. However, such near-universal agreement is rare: ask any dozen developmental psychologists to nominate their preferred key concepts and you are likely to come up with a dozen different lists. There will be a fair amount of overlap, but given the differences in people's theoretical orientations and in their special interests within developmental psychology it is inevitable that their nominations will not be identical.

In compiling my list I was very much aware of this dilemma and tried at least to minimize the subjective element. I consulted a large number of textbooks, many of which contain useful glossaries or lists of key concepts attached to individual chapters, in order to get some measure of consensus. However, it was interesting to note that even among texts covering one specific area, for example language acquisition, certain terms were given prominence by some authors while others did not even mention them. I also consulted the curricula for developmental courses as taught by different psychology departments and as set for nation-wide examinations. However, I am under no illusion that I have pleased everybody with my selection; my own preferences and biases no doubt played a part in what is on offer here. But such a subjective element is unavoidable; after all, when a Professor of Moral Philosophy at Princeton University decides that a whole book should be devoted to the discussion of just one concept, namely bullshit (Frankfurt, 2005), a certain latitude must be allowed for personal idiosyncrasy.

How to use the book

It is intended that the book will act as a source of reference for its readers, in that it offers definition, description and discussion for each of the concepts selected. It is not like a dictionary, in which the items are listed alphabetically; rather the concepts are arranged thematically, grouped in nine sections with titles corresponding to the kind of chapter headings usually found in textbooks. The entry for each concept contains three parts:

1 *Meaning.* A definition of the concept is offered here, but also some comments on how the term is used. In some cases the meaning is clearly understood and widely shared; that of others (and not necessarily the most recent ones) is rather more controversial, in that different people use them in somewhat different ways. Mention is also made in those cases where several different terms are used to designate the same concept.

2 *Origins.* Some concepts made their first appearance quite recently, signalling the emergence of a new field of knowledge (e.g. **gene–environment interaction**) or of a new theoretical perspective (e.g. **dynamic systems**). In such cases one can pinpoint their emergence with a fair amount of precision. This is not so with a surprisingly large number of other concepts, many of which have been in use for centuries, even since the days of Ancient Greece, when they made their first appearance in the writings of philosophers (**temperament** is one example). The precise origins are then much more difficult to identify; any historical changes that may have taken place in their use can, however, be described.

3 *Current status.* Many concepts come and go; being mental tools they will be discarded if found wanting. Quite a few of Freud's terms but also some forming part of Piagetian theory are examples that come to mind. This book focuses on those in current use, but where relevant to do so, mention is made of doubts that at least some people have as to how helpful the concept is. Sometimes, as a result of further work, it has become apparent that further refinement in the meaning of a concept is required. In quite a few cases, for example, it is clear that the concept is not the unitary entity it was thought to be and that it is therefore necessary to break it down into several components (e.g. **egocentrism**). A particularly important issue is the impact a concept has on present-day research, and an attempt is therefore made briefly to summarize the kinds of questions the concept has stimulated and the answers that have emerged from research.

In so far as some concepts are closely associated with other concepts, I felt it preferable to keep their presentation together under one entry. **Attachment**, for example, is tightly linked to the concepts of **internal working models**, **secure base** and **goal corrected behaviour**, and to discuss each under a separate entry would make it difficult to convey their interrelationship.

There are two main ways in which the book can be used. One is as a means of learning about some specific concept: thus students may want to consult the book in conjunction with a textbook in order to find out in depth what function the concept serves and why it is regarded as helpful. Anyone interested in a particular concept can go straight to it by locating it either in the Contents list or in the Index; for those wishing to study a topic in more detail than is possible in a book aiming to be concise, there are suggestions for further reading at the end of each entry.

However, the aim is also to make the book readable as a whole, with a narrative style that will make it possible to peruse it from cover to cover and so get a sense of how concepts in general are employed in present-day developmental psychology. Also, each of the nine sections of the book can function as a unit, and by means of the cross-references given at the end of the entry for each concept the reader will be able to pursue some general area of interest and get a sense of how any one concept fits into the general picture.

CONCEPTIONS OF DEVELOPMENT 1

ONE

How do we think about psychological development? Initially, the idea may conjure up an image of a curve progessively climbing upwards throughout childhood, levelling off thereafter and then remaining steady until it starts to decline in old age – somewhat along the lines of physical growth. In fact, even physical growth is a rather more complex phenomenon than such an image suggests, and when it comes to psychological development the complications increase greatly, giving rise to all sorts of questions that need to be settled if we are to understand it. For instance, is it right to think of psychological functions as developing in a steadily upward manner, or is it more a matter of spurts and plateaus? Does the pattern of change, as well as its rate, vary from one individual to another and from one function to another? Does development indeed stop once the individual has reached adulthood? And, for that matter, is it justified to see psychological development in terms of quantitative change or are there qualitative changes too?

The core of development is change over age – a change that is not haphazard, not temporary and not easily reversible. To document change it is necessary to accumulate empirical information about such matters as age norms, sequences, trajectories and transitions, and then to discern the patterns which underlie such factual information. For this purpose a variety of concepts have been employed, of which the following are singled out and described below:

LIFE-SPAN DEVELOPMENT
DEVELOPMENTAL CONTINUITY
DEVELOPMENTAL TRAJECTORIES
and: **Transition points**
    Equifinality and Multifinality
DEVELOPMENTAL STAGES
DOMAIN SPECIFICITY
and: **Modularity**
CONTEXT
and: **Ecological systems perspective**
    Developmental niche

LIFE-SPAN DEVELOPMENT

MEANING Psychological development is not just something that happens to children, but is a process common to all ages. Additionally, it refers to all types of change – not just to acquisition but also to decline. This is the basic message conveyed by the concept of life-span development, which we can formally define as –

> *the process of change associated with age which characterizes all human beings from conception to death.*

A life-span perspective does not refer to a single, coherent theory but to a particular orientation to the study of psychological development. It draws attention to the importance of not drawing an arbitrary line at some particular age point, such as the transition from adolescence to adulthood. The study of development can be applied to all ages, and it follows that no particular age period is more worthy of our attention than any other: all play some part in individuals' lives.

ORIGINS Awareness of development as a life-long process emerged in systematic form only in the second half of the twentieth century. Before then attention was exclusively paid to childhood and adolescence; the idea that *development* can occur in *mature* individuals seemed a contradiction in terms. A few exceptions did occur; for example, G. Stanley Hall, one of the founding fathers of developmental psychology, became interested in the possibility of adult change as he himself aged, and in 1922 published a book with the provocative title *Senescence: the last half of life*. However, it was not till the 1960s that interest in adult development and ageing became systematized and that these topics gradually grew into major areas of research (e.g. Birren & Schaie, 1977); and it was later still that attempts first began to combine findings obtained from separately investigated age periods and integrate them into one coherent body of knowledge about development.

There are several reasons for the growing popularity of a life-span orientation in the past few decades. One is demographic: the population is ageing, and the very fact that there are more elderly people about creates a demand for knowledge about the psychological characteristics found at the end of an increasingly drawn-out life cycle. Initially the field of gerontology developed separately from the study of childhood; however, insofar as both are concerned with the nature of change over age it seemed sense to ask whether lessons learned in one field could be applied to the other and whether it would not be of benefit to develop concepts applicable to all ages. In the second place, there was the opportunity afforded by a number of longitudinal studies launched from the Institute of Human Development at the University of California several decades ago to examine the question of psychological continuity from early childhood into adulthood. The original aim of these studies was confined to providing information about the childhood years; however, the availability of the participants in adulthood tempted a number of investigators (e.g. Block, 1971; Elder, 1974) to follow them up and trace their developmental pathways over a much wider span than had previously been attempted. And finally, a variety of methodological advances (summarized by Schaie, 2002) in conducting longitudinal studies and interpreting their findings have brought increasing sophistication to research on life-span trends, making it possible, for example, to separate out individual patterns of change from the average growth curves that had previously been the sole source of information about developmental phenomena. It is mainly as a consequence of these three sets of influences that life-span issues are now widely recognized as legitimate concerns and as constituting important areas of enquiry.

In general terms the basic message of the life-span perspective is widely accepted: change occurs at all ages and we should therefore replace child-based accounts of development with models applicable to the total age range. In particular, there is agreement that change is not synonymous with growth (the curve going upward); as has now been amply demonstrated, development is far more varied than suggested by some single index of increase in size or knowledge or competence. Paul Baltes (1987; Smith & Baltes, 1999), who has been one of the major contributors to this field, has proposed the terms *multidimensionality* and *multidirectionality* to characterize the nature of development: the former to indicate that different aspects of behaviour (such as various components of memory) may simultaneously show distinct courses of developmental change (see **domain specificity**); the latter to stress that decline of some functions may go hand in hand with stability or even improvement of other functions (something particularly evident among the aged). Thus development takes many different forms: already in childhood certain aspects of behaviour decline or drop out altogether, such as seen in the palmar reflex which is present only in the early weeks of life, or in the loss of the ability during infancy to detect certain sound contrasts in languages other than those in the child's native language. Other functions, on the other hand, such as the capacity of the sensory register in the memory store, remain virtually constant throughout life.

CURRENT STATUS

Given the comparatively recent origins of the life-span perspective it is perhaps not surprising that more precise theoretical formulations of what happens during the total developmental course are as yet sparse. While the need for concepts of development that have relevance beyond childhood and so perform an integrative function is generally acknowledged, only a few are at present available (though see below for the concepts of **developmental trajectories** and **transition points**). However, some useful proposals as to how we may think about the life course as a whole have been put forward; thus Shiner & Caspi (2003) have suggested a threefold classification of the kind of descriptive approach that can be taken:

1 an *organizational-adaptive* approach, which sees the life course primarily in terms of the various challenges that people encounter at different ages and asks how these are met by individuals with different personalities;

2 a *socio-cultural* approach, which gives prominence to the sequence of culturally defined, age-graded roles that each person encounters over time;

3 an *evolutionary-psychology* perspective, which describes the life course in terms of the series of adaptations human beings have had repeatedly to contend with in the history of the species (see **evolution**).

Such a taxonomy is useful in drawing attention to the complexity of the concept of life-span; equally useful is a classification proposed by Baltes, Linderberger & Standinger (1998) of the factors that steer the course of life-long development, namely *age-graded* influences, i.e. those that are commonly encountered within a particular age range (e.g. school entry, puberty); *history-graded* influences, which are specific to certain time periods (e.g. the start of World War II, the advent of television); and *non-normative* influences, which affect only some individuals and may occur at any age (e.g. an accident, emigration). Age-graded influences have received most attention from developmental psychologists; however, one of the contributions of a life-span perspective is to draw attention to the role that historical events play in people's lives (see **context**), and the inclusion of non-normative influences reminds us that the developmental course is far from standardized and that some incidents unique to a specific individual may have considerable implications for that person's subsequent development.

Research inspired by the life-span perspective has steadily increased in amount and gone through a number of phases. In the first place, it stimulated a considerable number of studies specifically concerned with development at post-childhood ages, in particular among the aged (Schaie, 2002), which set out to trace change at that age but without any attempt to link up with change in earlier periods. Secondly, we have a large number of studies that did investigate such links by examining the continuity of psychological characteristics across age, including some ambitious efforts to follow up individuals from the very early years to maturity in order to determine whether adult characteristics can already be predicted in infancy (see **developmental continuity**). And finally and more recently, efforts have begun to be made to pinpoint the *processes* responsible for stability and change, i.e. to go beyond merely establishing continuities and ask *how* these come about (see, for example, Caspi, Elder & Bem's 1987 investigation of individuals who both as children and as adults were characterized by an 'explosive style', that is, showed excessive temper tantrums and irritability).

Further reading
Baltes, P.B., Lindenberger, U., & Standinger, U. (1998). Life-span theory in developmental psychology. In W. Damon, (Ed.), *Handbook of child psychology* (5th ed)., vol. 1 (R.M. Lerner, Ed.). New York: Wiley. A detailed and fairly technical account of the ideas behind the life-span perspective and the empirical work it has generated.

Smith, J., & Baltes, P.B. (1999). Life-span perspectives on development. In M.H. Bornstein & M.E. Lamb (Eds.), *Developmental psychology: an advanced textbook,* (4th ed.). Mahwah, NJ: Erlbaum. Somewhat less detailed than the above, but also more geared to readers new to the topic, with an account of the questions asked and methods used by life-span psychologists.

See also **developmental continuity; developmental trajectories**

DEVELOPMENTAL CONTINUITY

MEANING

One of the major issues in developmental psychology is the extent to which individual characteristics remain constant across age, as opposed to becoming transformed in the course of development. No one can doubt that both trends occur: there must be continuity in some sense, for intuitively at least we feel basically as though we are the same individuals from childhood to old age; at the same time the very notion of development implies that there is change.

Continuity may be defined as –

> *the preservation of individual characteristics over age.*

Let us note, however, that this does not necessarily mean phenomenological sameness: an individual may remain highly aggressive from early childhood to adulthood, yet express aggression in very different ways at older than at younger ages. Continuity is thus not a matter of identical behaviour but rather of the kinds of connections that exist among age points: are these such that we can predict later characteristics from early ones? Prediction is at the core of continuity; if psychological attributes in some sense remain the same over time, expressing identical processes even though in different overt form, it should be possible to foretell the nature of future development, with considerable implications for intervention and help.

ORIGINS

The issue of continuity and change has been of long-standing interest, but in the past was debated more on the basis of dogma than empirical evidence. On the whole a strong belief existed in continuity, based on one of two assumptions. The first was that we are born with certain characteristics fixed once and for all by our genetic endowment: whatever experiences we encounter will not affect what has been handed down to us by our inheritance. This argument was mostly applied to intelligence, which was viewed as an attribute constant over time so that, in theory at least, one should be able to use IQs obtained in infancy to predict intellectual performance in adulthood. Evidence to the contrary was for a long time simply disregarded, and it was only in the middle of the last century, on the basis of a large body of findings, that it was accepted that fluctuations in measured intelligence do occur and that prediction over age is therefore not the simple matter it was formerly thought to be (Hunt, 1961).

The other assumption underlying the belief in continuity was that experience in the earliest years leaves irreversible effects on our personality, and that our individuality is thus shaped for good by whatever events we encounter at that impressionable time. This is an argument put forward by writers as diverse as John B. Watson, the father of behaviourism, and Sigmund Freud, who for different reasons were both convinced that we are victims of our past, in that experiences absorbed in the first few years are of a foundational nature and thus likely to determine the course of personality growth once and for all. Again it follows that one should be able to predict outcome in maturity from infancy on: the impact of trauma and deprivation, for example, was said at that time to have life-long consequences that cannot be changed. However, this view too has had to be changed in the light of subsequent evidence: the effects of early experiences have not been found to be permanent under all conditions, however early and however severe they may be. As follow-up studies have repeatedly shown, some degree of change can be brought about in the psychological functioning of even quite badly affected children by appropriate measures: for example, some (though not all) children severely deprived as a result of spending their early years in grossly depriving orphanages can make up marked degrees of both physical and psychological deprivation if placed in caring, adoptive homes (Rutter and the ERA Study Team, 1998; Rutter, Kreppner & O'connor, 2001). As is now widely acknowledged, continuity in this respect too is therefore not as absolute as had once been thought (Schaffer, 2002).

CURRENT STATUS Ascertaining the nature and extent of psychological continuity has become a most lively topic of research. This has been brought about, in part at least, by methodological advances in carrying out longitudinal studies, both of a prospective and a retrospective nature. However, what is now clear is that the concept of continuity is a highly complex one, involving several different meanings distinguished largely by different ways of measuring continuity (see Caspi, 1998, for an extended discussion). Two in particular need to be differentiated:

1 *Relative continuity*, which is based on the extent to which individuals retain their rank order in a particular sample from one assessment point to another, as measured by the correlation coefficient for the scores obtained at the two ages. Continuity in this sense thus refers to individuals' standing relative to other members of the sample; it does not, however, say anything about the actual level of individuals' scores and whether that changes between ages.

2 *Absolute continuity*, which refers to the extent to which some particular attribute remains stable in individuals over time. It is thus concerned with the constancy of test results in the course of development, and is assessed by comparing the actual scores of individuals as found at different ages.

The majority of investigations to which the concept of continuity has given rise have taken the first of these two forms. They have concerned themselves with a range of psychological attributes and asked a variety of questions. For instance: Can the origins of mature personality be traced back to temperamental qualities evident in infancy (e.g. Caspi, 2000)? Do the most salient aspects of personality, such as the so-called Big Five (e.g. Agreeableness, see Laursen, Pulkkinen & Adams, 2002) have specific antecedents in the behaviour patterns of young children? What about aggression: do aggressive children become aggressive adults or, for that matter, were aggressive adults also aggressive children (e.g. Huesmann, Eron & Lefkowitz, 1984)? Similarly with shyness: is this an enduring quality, so that one can predict from the behaviour of babies confronted by a stranger their behaviour in social situations in later years (e.g. Kagan, Snidman & Arcus, 1998)? Or, to take an example of great practical importance, does maladjustment in the early years necessarily signify maladjustment at subsequent ages (e.g. Caspi & Moffitt, 1995)? And finally, taking the psychological quality where this debate originally started, is intelligence predictable from one age to another (e.g. Slater, Carrick, Bell & Roberts, 1999)?

Three basic questions underlie the research efforts that have been undertaken in this area. The first is concerned with establishing the sheer amount of continuity – the extent to which prediction is feasible for particular attributes and particular age spans. Secondly, there is the problem of the conditions under which continuity or discontinuity can be found – conditions such as individual differences in children's dispositions, their family circumstances and their life experiences generally. And third, what are the mechanisms responsible for bringing about continuity: is it, for example, a matter of genetic processes that function similarly at different ages, or is it determined by environmental influences which promote continuity of personality functioning because they themselves remain stable? Although research on the topic of continuity is still a relatively new field of endeavour, a number of conclusions can be stated with confidence. To summarize:

1 Continuity of psychological characteristics, as expressed by correlation coefficients between ages, is rarely more than moderate. Discontinuities do occur, making prediction hazardous. It is only at the extremes of the distribution (the very shy, say, or the highly aggressive) that it is possible to predict with any certainty.

2 The degree of continuity depends in part on a combination of age and interval: the older the individual the more likely it is that attributes remain stable, and the shorter the interval between assessments the greater will be the extent of continuity.

11

3 Continuity also varies from one behavioural domain to another. It is, for example, especially marked for emotional maladjustment (Rutter & Rutter, 1993): if present at age 3 there is a three-fold increase in the risk of its presence at age 8.

4 It is essential to take into account the degree of continuity of the child's environment: drastic changes in life experience may well disrupt established patterns of behaviour, as seen, for example, in fluctuations of attachment security under conditions of family disturbance (Goldberg, 2000).

5 Continuity is basically not a matter of carrying forward identical response patterns, nor can it necessarily be assessed by performance on similar tests. For example, IQs obtained from tests administered to infants bear virtually no relationship to IQs obtained from the same children at older ages; on the other hand measures of infants' information processing capacity, as obtained from habituation tasks, are much more likely to predict later intelligence (Slater et al., 1999). The same underlying predisposition may manifest itself in different ways at different ages: similarity at a conceptual rather than a behavioural level provides the link.

Further reading

Caspi, A. (1998). Personality development across the life course. In W. Damon (Ed.), *Handbook of child psychology* (5th ed.), vol. 3 (N. Eisenberg, Ed.). New York: Wiley. A general overview of research on personality development that contains a section on continuity across the life-span.

Rutter, M. (1987). Continuities and discontinuities from infancy. In J.D. Osofsky (Ed.), *Handbook of infant development* (2nd ed.). New York: Wiley. Especially valuable for clearly outlining the methodological and conceptual complexities involved in finding answers to the problem of continuity.

See also **developmental stages; developmental trajectories; life-span developent**

DEVELOPMENTAL TRAJECTORIES
and: TRANSITION POINTS
EQUIFINALITY and MULTIFINALITY

MEANING Also sometimes referred to as *developmental pathways* or *life course patterns*, trajectories are –

the paths that individuals follow in the course of development, including the long-term patterns of behaviour adopted, the challenges encountered and the manner of meeting them, and the implications that particular courses have for long-term adjustment.

Thus, given a particular starting point such as a high level of antisocial behaviour at age 7, by what specific steps do some children turn into law-abiding adults while others retain their previous ways of behaviour? Are there certain crucial events that account for change and certain ages when this is more likely to occur? Trajectories take very many different forms, for they are affected both by individuals' make-up and by life experiences, and they serve thus to draw attention to the great range of individual differences to be found in the developmental course, even when individuals have similar starts or encounter identical events during their formative years. Instead of regarding these early experiences as determining once and for all outcome in maturity, the concept of trajectory draws attention to the fact that development should be thought of as (to quote Clarke & Clarke, 2000) 'a series of linkages in which characteristics in each period have a probability of linking with those in another period. But probabilities are not certainties, and deflections of the life path, for good or ill, are possible ...'. The impact of any particular experience, that is, needs to be seen in the context of each individual's total life path, and attention must therefore be paid to the modifying role of other events, both before and after.

To a considerable extent trajectories are determined by the way in which an individual negotiates the **TRANSITION POINTS** that everyone encounters from time to time in the course of development. A transition point is basically concerned with the possibility of change of trajectory; it is a form of change which may occur more or less abruptly at some particular point of development, and can thus be defined as –

the choice confronting an individual in the course of development as to which of several alternative pathways to follow, resulting in some instances in a radical alteration of life circumstances.

To stay on at school or to leave; to obtain an unskilled job or to undertake further study or training; to marry one individual or another – these are some of the alternatives with which people may be confronted, with considerable implications for further development. The choices are by no means always free but can be forced upon individuals by situational pressures; nevertheless, whatever pathway is taken may well reinforce or, on the contrary, minimize the consequences of previous experiences and determine the future direction of the trajectory.

ORIGINS   The concept of trajectories is closely related to the work on continuity and change described earlier. As that work has demonstrated, it is rarely possible to find direct, one-to-one links between early characteristics or events and future outcome; research that jumps straight from early to later ages is therefore of limited use and needs to be extended by studies of the intervening period in order to spell out how individuals can develop so differently after the same early start. The notion of developmental trajectories was therefore adopted as a way of thinking about continuity and change by drawing attention to the need to investigate all the relevant links involved in the life path.

As a consequence, recent work has come to pay far more attention to individual differences in children's psychological development rather than emphasize uniformities. Recognition has been given, that is, to the diversity of trajectories to be found in different individuals – illustrated, for example, by the fact that early trauma does not inevitably result in later pathology and that survivors as well as victims emerge from such experiences. It follows that attempts to explain the processes involved usually require a highly ambitious undertaking, in which individuals are followed up longitudinally and repeated assessments are made of both their psychological characteristics and their life circumstances. An excellent example of such an undertaking is the Christchurch Health and Development Study – a prospective longitudinal investigation carried out in New Zealand, based on a representative sample of more than 1,200 children who were followed up from birth to early adulthood and assessed repeatedly during this interval. Research such as this can give rise to a wealth of findings about the nature of developmental trajectories, the sequence of steps that make up different kinds of trajectories and the mechanisms underlying continuities in behavioural development (for examples of some specific reports, see Fergusson & Horwood, 1998; Fergusson, Horwood & Lynskey, 1992; Fergusson & Lynskey, 1997). Such studies are costly and time-consuming and therefore still few in number, but they have already shown a considerable potential for adding to our knowledge about developmental processes.

CURRENT STATUS   A variety of purposes underlie research on developmental trajectories. In the first place, studies have aimed to provide detailed description of the course of particular traits. Instead of assessments carried out on just two occasions, once early on and then again many years later, they have filled the gap with repeated assessments, especially at ages thought to be crucial in the development of that particular characteristic. To quote an example from a report by the NICHD Early Childhood Research Network (2004): when the course of aggression in a sample of over 1,000 children was traced over the age period 2–8 years by means of repeated assessments, five different trajectories were identified on the basis of level of aggression and the kind of changes that occurred in this level. In this way it was possible not just to provide a detailed account of the development of physical aggression in general but also to do justice to individual variation.

In the second place, an important lesson has been learned by investigating trajectories – a lesson summarized by the concepts of **EQUIFINALITY** and **MULTIFINALITY**. Equifinality refers to the fact that –

> *there is more than one developmental pathway to a given outcome.*

Take antisocial behaviour: individuals manifesting severe levels of conduct disorder or delinquency have been found to be quite heterogeneous in the developmental course leading up to such behaviour (e.g. Frick, Cornell, Bodir, Dane, Barry & Loney, 2003). Thus relevant aetiological factors such as genetic predisposition, parental rearing patterns, educational opportunities and peer group pressures may operate in different combinations to produce identical results.

Multifinality indicates that –

> *identical early experiences do not necessarily result in the same outcome.*

As, for example, the literature on early deprivation has repeatedly shown (Schaffer, 2002), it is impossible to predict individuals' adjustment and competence as adults on the basis of the deprivation experience alone – heterogeneity is the rule. Thus both equifinality and multifinality present a very different view to that which ties antecedents to outcome in a one-to-one correspondence.

Thirdly, attention to the intervening period makes it possible to pinpoint the factors that are associated with change of course. For example, Ge, Lorenz, Conger, Elder & Simmons (1994) explored the manifestation of depression at annual intervals from age 9 to 20, and noted a sharp increase among girls, though not among boys, around 13 years. When examining the factors that covary with this change they found that the increase was linked to a rise in life stresses of one kind or another, but especially so among girls who received little warmth and support from their mothers. It appeared therefore that particular combinations of gender, stress and family relationships can account for the various patterns of change observed in the trajectory of depression in children at this age.

Finally, there are studies that focus specifically on the transition points that are such a prominent feature of all developmental trajectories. For example, Rutter, Quinton & Hill (1990) set out to investigate the link between deprivation in childhood and becoming a depriving parent in adulthood. A group of mothers who had spent a major part of their early years in institutions were indeed found to be markedly impaired in their sensitivity and warmth with their children; however, not all members of the group were so affected in that some of the mothers functioned perfectly well in their parental role (an example of multifinality). The reason for the different outcome was found to lie in the kinds of intervening experiences encountered by the mothers; above all, getting married to a supportive and well-adjusted partner enabled the women to function generally well and in particular to establish sound relationships with their children; choice of an unsatisfactory partner, on the other hand, was more likely to reinforce a woman's previous patterns of malfunctioning and result in inadequate parenting. The fact that this did not occur till adulthood did not detract from the influence exerted in counteracting trajectories followed during the childhood years.

Further reading

Elder, G.H. (1985). *Life course dynamics: trajectories and transitions*. Ithaca, NY.: Cornell University Press. Written by one of the main contributors to this topic, the book illustrates the kinds of findings obtained from follow-up research.

Elder, G.H. (1998). The life course as developmental theory. *Child Development*, *69*, 1–12. A brief but useful outline.

Rutter, M. (1996). Transitions and turning points in developmental psychopathology. *International Journal of Behavioral Development*, *19*, 603–626. A detailed analysis of the concept of transition points, showing by reference to research findings the role these play in development.

See also **developmental continuity**

DEVELOPMENTAL STAGES

MEANING How should we characterize the course of development – as a constantly rising curve or as a step-like structure? In terms of steady quantitative accretion or as a series of leaps? Both models have had their adherents, with the debate for a long time based on the assumption that it had to be one or the other – accretion or stages.

A stage can be defined as –

> *a distinct phase of life characterized by a unique set of mental characteristics.*

Three principal criteria have been proposed to identify a stage (Flavell, Miller & Miller, 1993):

1 *Reorganization*: developmental change is heralded by the appearance of a qualitatively different form of functioning; in other words it is not so much a matter of getting better but rather of acting in a distinctive new manner.

2 *Abruptness*: the transition from one stage to another takes place relatively speedily and suddenly.

3 *Concurrence*: change occurs simultaneously and in a similar manner across a wide range of mental functions.

Stage theories appear in many different versions. In some of these the concept of stage is not 'real' but merely a descriptive device: for convenience sake, that is, a continuous progression is more or less arbitrarily cut up into segments, thereby making it easier to describe the change taking place. The most influential stage accounts, however, do conceive of stages as distinctive shifts, brought about in a predetermined manner common to all members of the human species and appearing in an invariant order, so that skipping any one of them is impossible.

ORIGINS

For much of the twentieth century the two contrasting views, stage models and accretion models, existed side by side, though espoused by adherents of opposing theoretical orientations, depending mostly on whether they saw the source of developmental change as located primarily in the organism or in the environment – as stemming from maturation or from the effects of experience. Advocates of maturation found stage language congenial as a way of describing the periodic reorganizations that they believed to be built into the organism as part of its biological inheritance; the experiential view, on the other hand, appealed to adherents of the various learning theories who saw change as resulting from the gradual shaping of the individual in the course of encounters with the environment. Little attempt was initially made to settle the issue by examining directly the course of developmental change; the debate was conducted instead on a global theoretical plane.

Stage theories were espoused by many of the most influential writers on developmental psychology in the last century, though there were considerable differences between them in the psychological domains described, the number and nature of the stages proposed and the age ranges assigned to them. Consider the distinctive approaches adopted by Freud, Erikson, Gesell and Piaget. Freud's (1949) aim was to trace human beings' psychosexual development, which he described as passing through a series of five stages (oral, anal, phallic, latency and genital), each based on different libidinal needs occurring in sequence from infancy to maturity. Erik Erikson (1950), though also a psychoanalyst, put forward a very different developmental scheme, concerned with psychosocial adjustment in general and the formation of personal identity in particular, and encompassing eight stages, each confronting the individual with a particular developmental task. Easily the most enthusiastic proponent of a stage approach, however, was Gesell (1954): his concern was to document in very great detail the emergence and manifestation of the numerous perceptual, motor, verbal and personal-social abilities that appear in the early years – a task for which he found stage a useful, indeed essential device. As Thelen and Adolph (1994) put it, he thereby 'raised stage theory to an unparalleled degree of refinement. Who before or since has had the tenacity to describe 58 stages of pellet behaviour, 53 stages of rattle behaviour, and so on for 40 different behavioural series?' Gesell was convinced, however, that stages serve not only a descriptive but also an explanatory function, in that they represent the outward manifestation of human beings' biological equipment and thus account for the orderly change so characteristic of early behavioural development (further described under **maturation**).

It was Piagetian theory, however, that stimulated most discussion about the uses and misuses of stages. Piaget saw his four major stages (sensori-motor, preoperational, concrete operational and formal operational) as representing sequential levels of adaptation, in each of which children's thinking is characterized by a particular kind of mental organization, giving rise to a fundamentally distinctive view of the world. The stages appear in an invariant order, each replacing its predecessor, and while Piaget, unlike Gesell, did not see their emergence as an automatic unfolding but as dependent on nurture as well as nature, he was convinced that the same sequence characterizes all members of the human species. Piaget (again unlike Gesell) was not interested in providing norms of development; his concern rather was to characterize the dominant mental approach to problem solving that can be found at various ages, and for this purpose a structure of successive stages appeared to him to be well suited.

CURRENT STATUS
Since about the 1970s, stage models, have been on the wane. Increasingly it has become necessary to acknowledge that the picture of human development they provide is inaccurate. To a large extent the disillusionment stemmed from efforts to replicate Piaget's account of the way children's thinking progresses over age, for unlike much of the rest of Piaget's theorizing his stage notions have come to attract a considerable body of criticism. That criticism centred in the first place on the age of transition between stages given by Piaget, albeit usually in approximate terms. As Donaldson (1978) and others have pointed out, the age when a child is judged to become capable of a new cognitive achievement depends not merely on the readiness of the appropriate mental structure (as Piaget believed) but also on the demands imposed by the assessment task, that is, on the complexity of the procedures and the nature of the instructions employed. By devising tests that were simpler in nature than traditional Piagetian ones and did not rely unduly on verbal instructions and answers, much younger children were found to be capable of performing at a higher level. Piaget, it appeared, had grossly underestimated young children's cognitive abilities.

If it were merely a matter of shifting age of attainment downwards the stage concept would remain intact. However, doubts have also been raised about the extent to which children's cognitive development proceeds as the three criteria for stages listed above would lead one to expect:

1 *Reorganization.* There is no doubt that periodic changes involving the qualitative nature of mental organization do occur, each resulting in a very different style of thinking and problem solving – see, for example, the attainment of object permanence taking place towards the end of the first year, or the transition from sensori-motor functioning to representational action in the middle of the second year. Yet there is also wide agreement that to characterize development solely in these terms is inaccurate: continuous quantitative changes occur too, as seen in aspects of children's information processing capacity such as speed and span. The sharp dichotomy between stage models and accretion models has been abandoned; instead of arguing for one *or* the other the search is on for ways of describing the interplay between the two kinds of change.

2 *Abruptness.* This criterion too is not as straightforward as once thought. Much depends on how a new achievement is assessed. Object permanence, for example, appears to develop relatively suddenly if the measure is the child's ability to retrieve an object that has just been hidden under a single cover; yet, as Piaget himself pointed out, much goes on in the preceding months to bring about this step and in the following months to elaborate upon it. Similarly with conservation and indeed with most other cognitive developments: detailed examination indicates that these rarely if ever appear suddenly and that gradual and slow change is the rule.

3 *Concurrence.* This stage criterion has become the major arena for debate in recent years. Are developmental changes as pervasive, across-the-board as the Piagetian account appears to suggest, or does change occur independently, in terms of timing and/or nature, in different areas of cognition? In fact Piaget is often misrepresented in this respect: as his account of conservation shows, he did make allowance for different content areas developing according to different timetables, and specifically used the concept of *horizontal decalage* to stress that children learn to conserve an aspect like substance years earlier than they are able to conserve volume. And yet, with respect to many other cognitive characteristics he made no allowance for variation according to content area, thus asserting his belief in a degree of coherence of mental functions that further evidence has not been able to confirm. **Egocentrism** is a particularly notable example: instead of giving way at the same age with respect to all aspects of mental functioning (as Piaget believed) it is now apparent that there are marked differences between the perceptual, affective and cognitive domains – that is, when children realize that others may see or hear things differently, feel about things differently and have different knowledge about things. Thus far greater diversity in developmental pattern is to be found among specific cognitive functions than stage theories allow (see **domain specificity** for further discussion).

It is now widely accepted that cognitive development does not proceed as uniformly stage-like as had once been thought, and that in some respects at least accounts dressed in stage terms confuse and mislead by oversimplifying the nature of development. What has not been settled, however, is whether the concept of stage should be abandoned altogether (as some advocate), or whether (as others argue) stage-like changes are specific to particular aspects of cognitive functioning, though intertwined with overall quantitative advances.

Further reading

Fischer, K.W., & Silvern, L. (1985). Stages and individual differences in cognitive development. *Annual Review of Psychology, 36,* 613–648. Sets out to disentangle the arguments for and against stages by drawing on research on cognitive development.

Miller, P.H. (2002). *Theories of developmental psychology* (4th ed.). New York: Worth Publishers. This useful book contains some detailed discussions of the concept of stage as applied in the theories of Freud, Piaget and Erikson.

See also **domain specificity; maturation**

DOMAIN SPECIFICITY
and: MODULARITY

MEANING Domain specific views of development stand in sharp contrast to domain general views. Both have been employed primarily in relation to cognitive development, but whereas domain general views assume that all aspects of cognition are controlled by the same set of mental mechanisms, domain specificity refers to –

> *the proposition that each mental domain is served by its own specific mechanisms and that development in any one domain therefore takes place independently of development in any other.*

Underlying this discussion is the question of how the mind is constructed. According to some (and Piaget is the best known example), human beings are endowed with a general set of mental mechanisms, limited in number, that operate in a uniform manner across all areas of psychological functioning and that account for all types of developmental change. Others, however, on the basis of increasing evidence that such uniformity is illusory, have concluded that the mind appears to be far more compartmentalized than the domain general view allows, and that it is therefore necessary to postulate the existence of different mental mechanisms for different cognitive domains.

As more research on a range of specific cognitive abilities came to be carried out in post-Piagetian years, it became evident that far more discrepancies in developmental patterns occur than domain general theories allow for. Take the following lines of evidence:

ORIGINS

1 The clearest examples are to be found in cases of pathology. Autistic children develop normally with respect to a wide range of cognitive functions, yet are severely impaired in all tasks involving the understanding of mental states. On the other hand, children with Williams Syndrome (another congenital disorder) show marked deficits in areas such as planning and spatial and numerical reasoning but function well with respect to language and social cognition. An even sharper contrast is presented by idiots-savants, who are severely retarded right across the board except for one specific skill such as drawing, where they may be quite outstanding (Karmiloff-Smith, 1992).

2 Disparities in performance, though of lesser scale, are apparent in most children's cognitive functions. For example, the mental skills employed to understand the three domains of physical, biological and psychological phenomena have been found to develop independently and at different rates, the intra-individual variations occurring in all children (see **theory theory** for more details).

3 Competence may also vary according to individual children's acquired knowledge. To quote a classical example (Chi, 1978): expert chess players aged 10 years were able to remember the layout of a chess board far better than adults with no such expertise, yet the children's memory for digit strings showed no such advance. Memory, that is, does not develop in domain general fashion; it is tied to specific experience rather than to general intelligence.

4 According to Gardner (1984), there is now sufficient evidence to abandon the idea of general intelligence altogether and substitute a package of multiple intelligences, such as linguistic, musical, logico-mathematical, spatial, bodily kinaesthetic and personal intelligence. Each is conceived as a discrete information processing operation, with its own separate brain-based location.

Historically of most importance, however, are Chomsky's ideas about the nature of the human language system, for these represent the first coherent account of domain specificity (see **universal grammar**). In contrast to Piaget's assertion that language is an integral part of general intelligence and develops in common with other aspects of symbolic representation such as pretend play, and in contrast also to Skinner's belief that general learning principles can explain children's linguistic development, Chomsky (1988) saw language as an independent mental organ distinct in structure and function from other aspects of the mind, operating according to a set of biologically specified rules that differ from those on which other systems such as vision and numeracy are based. The mind, that is, must be seen as consisting of a series of separate domains, the working of each of which requires investigation in its own right. The details of Chomsky's views on language development have encountered considerable criticism; his influence on subsequent accounts of the domain specific nature of the mind, however, cannot be disputed.

One of the most important attempts to formalize a domain specific view of cognitive functions was made by the philosopher Jerry Fodor (1983), who proposed the concept of **MODULARITY** to indicate that –

> *different aspects of cognition are represented in the brain by inbuilt structures, each of which functions on its own as a processor of some specific types of input from the environment.*

These modules, as he referred to them, are part of each individual's neural network, innate in origin and adapted in the course of evolution to perform only certain quite specific cognitive tasks: the processing of spoken language, the recognition of faces and of voices, the perception of colour, the analysis of shape, and so forth. Each module is pretuned to process only one particular distinctive kind of information from the environment, responding to such data in an automatic, speedy, highly constrained manner and functioning quite independently of any other part of the mental apparatus. As Karmiloff-Smith (1992) put it, this layer refers to 'the parts of the human mind that are inflexible and unintelligent', representing 'the stupidity of the machine'. However, the output of the modules is then passed on to another layer, functioning as a central information processor, which uses the information to perform higher conceptual functions such as coordinating, re-arranging and planning. The human mind, according to Fodor, should thus be seen as an organ basically composed of a set of fixed, domain specific structures, though presided over by a much more flexible domain general mechanism.

CURRENT STATUS Considering the frequency with which the concept of domain is mentioned in the research literature, it is ironic that there is still so much confusion as to what domains are – their nature, their developmental origin, their content and how to identify them. The term has been used in several quite different senses (Wellman & Gelman, 1992), in particular:

1 as innately specified neural devices, i.e. as identical to modules;

2 as limited areas of knowledge, thus distinguishing them according to their content;

3 as distinctive sets of mental processes, using the particular operations performed for purposes of definition;

4 as specific cognitive tasks, such as classification or seriation.

Just to identify domains and specify their boundaries is thus a matter of controversy (Keil, 2002): for example, a domain may designate some highly localized area of expertise such as knowledge of chess; on the other hand, it may also be used to refer to certain widely encompassing realms such as those of physical, biological and psychological knowledge (mentioned above) about which children are said to develop early but quite distinctive theories. This issue in turn has implications for the sheer number of domains said to exist: in the former case there are thousands that could qualify while in the latter there are very few. Even when, say, language is regarded as an area in its own right there is disagreement as to its make-up: should it be seen as a unitary domain or as a series of distinct, more narrowly defined domains involving aspects such as syntax, phonology and lexicon? Even such a strictly delimited function as pronoun acquisition has been designated as a domain. As yet, no agreement has been reached on how to choose candidates for the designation of domain.

However domains are conceptualized, few now believe that an unqualified domain general view of development can be justified. The evidence that cognition is made up of a considerable variety of abilities specialized for handling different kinds of information is too convincing for that. Yet it has also become apparent that it is not a matter of *either* domain generality *or* domain specificity – that only one type of operation is possible and that therefore a choice has to be made between the two. There are indications that domain general processes co-occur with domain specific ones: for instance, speed of information processing shows developmental advances in an across-the-board fashion underlying a whole range of domain specific abilities; similarly the capacity of working memory influences a large number of specific cognitive skills. Thus one type of mechanism need not preclude the existence of the other; it seems more likely that development depends on both. A more meaningful question to address therefore is how the two interact (see Case, 1992, for one attempt to bring about such a reconciliation).

The concept of modularity has also come in for some lively discussion, especially with respect to Fodor's belief that modules are innately fixed and remain unchanged throughout development. Thus Karmiloff-Smith (1992) has argued that the more pre-determined the cognitive system is in its functioning the less room there would be for the high degree of flexibility of thought and creativity that are the hallmarks of the human mind. The view she advocates is a more epigenetic one (see **epigenesis**), in that she agrees with Fodor that modules have an innate origin but that they are no more than predispositions which can be changed in the course of an individual's development. They are thus a product of both endowment and experience – a joint process which Karmiloff-Smith refers to as *modularization*. The debate is by no means settled, though recent evidence from neurocognitive studies supports on balance the epigenetic view as the more likely (Mareschal, Johnson & Grayson, 2004).

Further reading
Hirschfeld, L.A., & Gelman, S.A. (1994). *Mapping the mind: domain specificity in cognition and culture.* Cambridge: Cambridge University Press. Contains a wealth

of different approaches to the topic of domain specificity, with a particularly useful introduction by the editors.

Karmiloff-Smith, A. (1992). *Beyond modularity: a developmental perspective on developmental science.* Cambridge, MA: MIT Press. Influential discussion of the way the human mind is organized and the extent to which a modular view can contribute to our understanding.

Mareschal, D., Johnson, M.H., & Grayson, A. (2004). Brain and cognitive development. In J. Oates & A. Grayson (Eds.), *Cognitive and language development in children.* Oxford: Blackwell. A brief but authoritative outline of the main issues concerning domain specificity and modularity.

See also **cognitive architecture; developmental stages; epigenesis; theory theory**

CONTEXT
and: ECOLOGICAL SYSTEMS PERSPECTIVE
DEVELOPMENTAL NICHE

MEANING It is widely agreed nowadays that it is insufficient to look for explanations of development solely within individuals; rather, that it is essential also to take into account the wider context in which individuals function. Yet more often than not the meaning of the term *context* is taken for granted, on the assumption that it refers to the external situation in which individuals find themselves and is thus equivalent to *environment*, with no further effort made to define and analyse it. However, in the light of those studies where such efforts have been made the most useful definition of context to emerge is –

> *the multi-layered setting in which an individual's behaviour takes place, as perceived by that individual.*

Let us comment on the various parts of that definition:

1 'Multi-layered' draws attention to the fact that at any one moment of time individuals function in a complex system of different types of contexts, among which physical, interpersonal, cultural and historical settings can usefully be distinguished. According to some writers these operate as a hierarchy, and various proposals have been put forward as to ways of conceptualizing such a hierarchy (e.g. Bronfenbrenner & Morris, 1998; Hinde, 1992).

2 'Setting' is used rather than environment, as the latter tends to be thought of only as the individual's physical surroundings and thus neglects the other types of context. In addition it is important to stress that the setting in which development takes place is often far from static, as implied by the term 'environment'; much of early learning, for example, occurs in interpersonal contexts in which an adult may well be continuously adjusting the kind of guidance given in the light of the latter's changing understanding (see **scaffolding**).

3 The phrase 'as perceived by that individual' indicates the vital role which the child plays in evaluating and interpreting the setting. In other words, the traditional dichotomy between individual and context, between 'inner' and 'outer', is much too sharp: the 'outer' can become part of the 'inner', with the two aspects forming one total system. This is well reflected in Mercer's (1992) assertion that 'what counts as context for learners ... is *whatever they consider relevant*' (emphasis added).

ORIGINS

It is true that some of the pioneers of child psychology, such as James Mark Baldwin and John Dewey, already argued for the importance of not considering children in a vacuum but relating their behaviour to contextual variables. Yet whatever general agreement this assertion elicited, it was rarely applied to the practice of research. More often than not investigations took place under laboratory conditions, the laboratory being regarded as 'neutral' and therefore not worth considering as a possible source of influence. Instead, explanations were individual-based and context-free, the assumption being that findings so obtained could be generalized across all settings.

This changed as part of the disenchantment with Piagetian theory. For one thing, Margaret Donaldson (1978) demonstrated empirically that context does matter, that children's performance even on traditional Piagetian tasks is affected by the extent to which the task is made meaningful and that all reasoning should therefore be seen as embedded in particular settings. And for another, Vygotsky's writings were belatedly discovered and translated (1962, 1978), with their emphasis on the interpersonal and cultural context of development and the importance of not seeing the child as a lone learner but as a participant in joint, culturally determined problem solving exchanges with others (see **zone of proximal development**). As a result, instead of explaining cognitive development wholly in terms of mechanisms operating within the individual it came to be recognized that processes such as attention, memory and learning are affected by what is 'outside' the child, giving rise to the idea of *situated cognition* and the adoption of a social-contextual perspective in the investigation of 'internal' processes (Gauvain, 2001). And at the same time it was realized that laboratory-based studies, if used exclusively, may in some respects be misleading and that investigations of children's behaviour in real-world settings play an essential part too.

CURRENT STATUS

A large body of evidence is now available to show that children's learning abilities and task performance are indeed a function of context. To give a few examples:

1 Preschool children show more advanced conversational skills at home with their mothers than at nursery school with their teachers (Tizard & Hughes, 2002).

2 Children aged 9–15 working in street markets in Brazil made complicated arithmetical calculations more effectively at their 'real-world' market stalls than they did in their classrooms (Carraher, Carraher & Schlieman, 1985).

3 Children and adolescents, asked to arrive at a judgement concerning some social issue, used different forms of reasoning according to the context (peer group, friendship and school) to which the issue applied (Killen, Lee-Kim, McGlothlin & Stangor, 2002).

4 Aboriginal children, living in the wilds of central Australia where navigational skills for finding the way in almost featureless desert landscapes are essential, performed much more competently on spatial memory tasks than on other types of memory tasks. White children living in urban environments, on the other hand, were inferior to Aboriginal children on spatial but superior to them on other tasks, their performance on the two kinds of problems being more or less at the same level (Kearins, 1986).

Merely to show that behaviour varies according to context is, of course, not enough. It is also necessary to unpack the concept of context in order then to account for the part it plays in influencing the course of development. By far the most sophisticated conceptual scheme that has been put forward in this respect is that by Urie Bronfenbrenner (1979, 1988), whose **ecological systems perspective** represents –

> *a framework for systematically arranging the influences from the multiple settings which children encounter, and for investigating the interaction between these influences and the individual over the life course.*

According to Bronfenbrenner, settings can be viewed as a set of nested systems, each inside the next, rather like a set of Russian dolls. The following layers can usefully be distinguished:

1 *Microsystems*, that is, the part of the environment with which children are directly in contact. Home, school and peer group are examples; it is here that children have most opportunities to become involved in face-to-face contact with the people who can initiate behavioural change.

2 *Mesosystems* are the links between microsystems, for example the home–school link or the family–peer group link. Such relationships need to be taken into account, because what happens in one microsystem may well affect what happens in another.

3 *Exosystems* are settings in which the child does not directly participate but which nevertheless affect development. An example is a parent's work experience: what happens there may well spill over into the home and influence the child via the relationship with the parent.

4 *Macrosystems* refer to the overarching structures of the particular culture in which children live. They include the lifestyles, belief systems, customs and opportunity structures of each society, which determine what happens at the lower levels.

5 *Chronosystems* are a more recent addition to the scheme. They represent the time dimension of children's experiences, thus acknowledging the fact that each individual's life course is embedded in a particular historical context – a period of economic depression, a war or sudden technological advance – that helps to determine the developmental course of children living through that time.

Each system can be studied in its own right, yet they are closely interdependent and exercise a reciprocal influence on each other. Research has concerned itself mostly with the impact on children of immediate contexts, especially that of the family, but it is the virtue of Bronfenbrenner's scheme that it reminds us of the role that more remote contexts also play (see the volume edited by Elder, Modell & Parke, 1993, entitled *Children in time and place*), and that it draws attention to contexts not previously investigated in relation to children's development such as historical time (e.g. Moen, Elder & Luscher, 1995). It is also to Bronfenbrenner's credit that he has increasingly emphasized the need to understand the *processes* whereby contexts produce developmental effects (Bronfenbrenner & Morris, 1998): instead of being merely content with what he calls the *social address model*, referring to global descriptive labels such as social class, parental education and maternal employment status, it is essential to explain *how* context can bring about change in individuals' functioning.

There have been other proposals for conceptualizing context, notably the notion of **DEVELOPMENTAL NICHE,** advanced by Super and Harkness (1986, 1997) – two cross-cultural psychologists keenly aware of the diversity of contexts that children experience in different societies. Developmental niche refers to –

> *a child's place within a particular community, as determined by the multiple cultural influences on child development prevalent in that community.*

According to Super and Harkness, it is useful to distinguish three types of such influences: (1) the physical and social settings in which the child lives, (2) the customs of child care as regulated by each culture and (3) the psychological characteristics of caretakers. The three sets operate together to mediate each individual's experience within their specific community, and it is their regular occurrences that provide children with the opportunities to learn the rules of their culture (see **gene–environment correlation** regarding 'niche picking', that is, children actively selecting or creating their own environments).

The general thesis, that accounts of development must not just be child-based but also consider contextual influences, is now widely accepted. In addition, there is agreement that context should not be left as just an amorphous mass but requires analysis and conceptual ordering and, what is more, that we need to go beyond merely identifying and describing contexts but must proceed to understand the *processes* that account for the reciprocal influences at work in the interaction of contexts and children. However, other than processes operative in family interaction settings and in peer groups, there is still a great deal of ignorance about the way in which contextual effects exert their influence; moreover, justice is rarely done to the fact that children are often exposed to a variety of contexts acting simultaneously – for example, the child at school who is confronted at one and the same time by the physical environment of the classroom, the interaction with the teacher, the presence of peers and beyond that the cultural setting that governs the nature of what is taught and how it is taught. As Bronfenbrenner's scheme makes clear, context is a multidimensional concept, and the dynamic interplay of the different components thus requires to be analysed.

Further reading

Bolger, N., Caspi, A., Downey, G., & Moorehouse, M. (Eds.) (1988). *Persons in context: developmental processes.* Cambridge: Cambridge University Press. The various contributors to this volume set out to show how the course of individual development is related to different environmental contexts, ranging from conditions affecting society as a whole to immediate interpersonal situations.

Gauvain, M. (2001). *The social context of cognitive development.* New York: Guilford. A detailed and persuasive argument for the need to take account of the social context in which cognitive growth occurs.

Light, P., & Butterworth, G. (Eds.) (1992). *Context and cognition.* London: Harvester. A number of authors discuss why context needs to be considered when explaining children's cognitive behaviour and what is meant by 'situational cognition'.

See also **individualism–collectivism; zone of proximal development**

MECHANISMS OF CHANGE

2

TWO

The concepts described above in Section 1 are primarily concerned with the *how* of development, i.e. with the way we can describe the course of change over age. In addition, however, there is also the *why* of development, namely the need to explain the mechanisms that account for change. Children in general become more competent with age; however, age itself is not an explanation but only an index of development, and a rough one at that. It covaries with both biological maturation and social experience, and to sort out the relative influence of these two sets of forces (nature and nurture respectively) has been one of the main preoccupations of developmental psychologists since the emergence of the discipline. Description and explanation are, of course, not wholly separate enterprises: thus the phenomena that an investigator chooses to observe may well be determined by pre-existing theoretical assumptions. Nevertheless, the distinctive aim of explanatory efforts is to incorporate descriptive data in a general theory, in order to give them a wider meaning and to derive certain general principles that can account for the way development takes place, including the conditions that set change in motion, the variables modifying its course and the reasons for individual differences in its nature. Concepts such as the following have been used for this purpose:

MATURATION
and: **Norms of development**
ENVIRONMENTAL LEARNING
and: **Observational learning**
CONSTRUCTIVISM
and: **Social constructivism**
DYNAMIC SYSTEMS
and: **Epigenesis**
    Self-organization
CONNECTIONIST NETWORKS

MATURATION
and NORMS OF DEVELOPMENT

MEANING Maturation is one of the devices that have been put forward to explain the mechanisms of development. It is at the opposite end of the nature–nurture debate to **environmental learning** (see below), in that it stresses innate rather than experiential influences and thus refers to –

> *the sequence of organismic changes occurring in the course of development that are governed by instructions in the genetic code.*

Although applicable to all aspects of development, the concept has been used in the past mainly in relation to motor functions and especially so with regard to infancy and early childhood.

ORIGINS The assumptions behind maturation have been around for a very long time, and were given explicit recognition by Rousseau (1762/1948) with his assertion that behaviour unfolds according to Nature's inner plan. However, it was not until the first half of the twentieth century that the assumptions were made explicit and incorporated in a formal *maturational theory*. This was very largely due to the efforts of one man – Arnold Gesell, a psychologist and paediatrician, who set out systematically and in the most painstaking detail to plot 'the course, the pattern and the rate of maturational growth in normal and exceptional children' (Gesell, 1928). In this way he aimed to establish **NORMS OF DEVELOPMENT**, that is –

> *the average ages and variabilities for the emergence of new behavioural characteristics.*

Gesell thus provided guidelines for parents and professional workers to enable them to compare the progress of individual children with the norm for their age group, and the test battery that he put together for this purpose (the Gesell Developmental Schedules, see Gesell & Amatruda, 1947) became enormously popular and the forerunner of a series of other, increasingly sophisticated developmental scales.

However, Gesell went well beyond merely collecting descriptive data, in that he also set out to derive various theoretical principles from his observations about the nature of developmental change – principles such as the proposal that development proceeds in a series of sequential changes (see **developmental stages**), and that motor skills emerge according to two directional trends, i.e. *cephalocaudal* (from head to foot) and *proximodistal* (from the centre of the body to the periphery). It was this orderly nature of development above all that convinced Gesell that the changes documented by him are instigated by an intrinsic, biological timetable that is part of our inheritance and common to all members of the species – that is to say, that developmental changes are maturationally determined. He agreed children need their social environment to realize their potential, but regarded this as essentially a secondary role, in that the sequence, timing and form of emerging action patterns are wholly determined by internal mechanisms regulated by the genes: As he put it:

> The original impulse to growth … is endogenous rather than exogenous. The so-called environment … does not generate the progression of development. Environmental factors support, inflect and specify, but they do not engender the basic forms and sequences of ontogenesis. (Gesell, 1954)

If these ideas are correct it follows that efforts to speed up the acquisition of motor skills by means of deliberate training should be unsuccessful. A number of studies, some carried out by Gesell himself, seemed to show that this is indeed the case: for example a pair of identical infant twins, one of whom was given the opportunity of practising such skills as crawling, climbing stairs and manipulating objects while the other one remained untrained, developed these abilities more or less at the same time. Age at acquisition, it was concluded, must therefore be controlled by an innate timetable and not by environmental factors. And while most of Gesell's work concerned motor development, he was convinced that the same conclusion applies to all other aspects of psychological development. As he put it: 'All his [the child's] capacities, including his morals, are subject to the laws of growth' (Gesell & Ilg, 1943).

CURRENT STATUS

Maturation plays a part in most of the major developmental theories, such as those of Freud, Erikson, Piaget and the ethologists, and moreover its role has received special recognition in certain accounts of language acquisition and perceptual development (Pinker, 2002). Little doubt exists that there is an inborn programme for the appearance of the basic developmental milestones in functions such as motor behaviour and cognition, the timing and rate of which are almost certainly largely laid down in the genes. What is also generally accepted, however, is that Gesell's reliance on maturation as the main, let alone sole vehicle for developmental change is misplaced. There is just too much evidence available to indicate that experience can slow down development, for instance in cases of malnutrition and deprivation (Rutter, 2002), though it is interesting to note that here too a *catch-up* phenomenon can occur whereby the individual returns to the original developmental schedule when restored to a normal environment. Even though the evidence for experience speeding up development is rather more equivocal (Spelke & Newport, 1998), it does seem highly likely that the environment can have a more direct and certainly a much more varied part to play than the merely supportive role which Gesell assigned to it. According to Gottlieb (1997), it is useful to distinguish four different roles which environmental stimulation serves in contributing to development:

- *Inductive*: stimulation that guides behaviour in one direction rather than another. For example, where children are brought up by English speakers they themselves will acquire English as their first language; in Chinese communities, on the other hand, they will learn Chinese.
- *Facilitative*: stimulation that influences when a new function appears. The speeding up or slowing down of motor behaviour by certain experiences is one example.
- *Maintenance*: stimulation that keeps on course already existing structures and functions; without it these would decay and be lost.
- *Canalizing*: a narrowing of responsiveness as a result of certain experiences. This is seen in infants' speech perception: the initial responsiveness to the full range of phonemes occurring in all languages gives way at the end of the first year to responsiveness only to those phonemes experienced by infants in their own language community (note that this is a different usage of *canalization* from the more common one associated with Waddington's, 1957, account).

Such a classification helps in analysing the highly complex interaction of innate and experiential forces, and makes the point that environmental stimulation can serve different purposes at different ages and for different aspects of development.

Even motor functions, the early development of which formed the main arena for maturational theory, are now known to depend on a far more intricate combination of internal and external influences than envisaged by Gesell. The theory was based on the assumption that infants cannot display skills such as reaching, standing and walking till the underlying neuromuscular structures have sufficiently matured to support these behaviour patterns, whereas more recent work has shown that giving children experience of the relevant bodily movements facilitates the development of the structures (Thelen, 2002) (see **dynamic systems**). Thus the relationship of structure and function must be seen as a reciprocal one and not based solely on the effect of the former on the latter. For instance, the more infants are held upright the more likely it is that they practise step movements, thereby stimulating the nervous and muscular structures on which walking depends and thus accelerating the development of walking skills. One of the fundamental tenets of maturational theory is therefore shown to be unfounded, though the concept of maturation itself can still be considered a useful one.

Further reading

Cairns, R.B. (1998). The making of developmental psychology. In W. Damon (Ed.), *Handbook of developmental psychology* (5th ed.), vol. 1 (R. M. Lerner, Ed.). New York: Wiley. Includes a brief but instructive description of the role of maturation as advocated by Gesell.

Thelen, E., & Adolph, K. (1994). Arnold L. Gesell: the paradox of nature and nurture. In R.D. Parke, P.A. Ornstein, J.J. Rieser & C. Zahn-Waxler (Eds.), *A century of developmental psychology.* Washington, DC: American Psychological Association. One of the best accounts available of Gesell's contribution to developmental psychology.

See also **developmental stages; environmental learning; epigenesis**

ENVIRONMENTAL LEARNING
and: OBSERVATIONAL LEARNING

The concept of environmental learning expresses a diametrically opposite point of view to that denoted by **maturation**, namely that –   **MEANING**

> *developmental change is brought about primarily by influences in the external environment and can be explained by mechanisms of learning.*

The emphasis is thus placed on experience, and especially so on the actions of adults who shape children's behaviour by means of rewards, punishment and example.

Environmental learning perspectives take three main forms: one based on Clark Hull's classical conditioning account, another on B.F. Skinner's operant conditioning model and the third on Albert Bandura's social learning theory – each distinctive in its view of human nature, its methodology and the mechanisms specified by it. The first of these is now of little more than historical interest while the second has only limited applicability, and it is therefore the third that will be our main focus.

The belief that learning mechanisms can account for all facets of psychological development goes back at least to John Locke (1693), who asserted that the mind is like a blank slate at birth which needs to be inscribed by experience provided by the child's parents in the form of learned associations and habits. Locke had little empirical evidence to offer for his ideas; however, in the first half of the twentieth century, under the influence of behaviourism and in the course of psychologists' attempts to make their discipline into a formal science, the emphasis on the all-powerful influence of learning experience was taken up again and systematized by Hull and Skinner. The former found a model in the work of Pavlov on the conditioned reflex in dogs: just as animals show a form of learning when initially neutral stimuli are associated with meaningful stimuli (the *classical conditioning* paradigm), so human behaviour too can be extended and transformed by such procedures. A large body of research, much of it on children, came into being as a result of   **ORIGINS**

Hull's proposal, showing that from infancy onwards behaviour can be conditioned and that it is possible to build up or to extinguish particular responses by applying the appropriate techniques. Yet the classical conditioning paradigm turned out to have minimal explanatory value when applied to developmental phenomena, in part because its laboratory-based findings were found to be difficult to generalize to other, real-life contexts, and in part because it became apparent that it is limited to just certain kinds of responses and certain kinds of stimuli – the result presumably of biological constraints operative in each species.

Skinner's *operant conditioning* model has fared rather better. Behaviour, according to this account, is controlled by its consequences: responses that are rewarded are thereby reinforced and become more frequent, whereas responses that are punished will be extinguished from the individual's repertoire. The learning sequence thus starts with the child's spontaneous behaviour, but is completed by whatever the environment supplies in the way of a reply: attention and affection when the child does something desirable, disapproval and anger when the act is considered undesirable. As numerous experiments have shown, this account can explain a range of behavioural phenomena in children, usefully drawing attention to the relationship between a child's actions and the specific ways in which adults respond to them. It is no wonder that the techniques of operant conditioning have been used for purposes of behaviour modification: thus there are claims that bedwetting, thumb sucking, shyness, even autistic symptoms have been eliminated by their use, and for a time the techniques were also applied to instructional methods, seen for example in the development of teaching machines.

Skinner's operant conditioning approach has continued to attract support (e.g. Gewirtz & Pelaez-Nogueras, 1992), yet its 'empty organism' view and neglect of cognitive processes increasingly made other alternatives more attractive, in particular the more widely encompassing perspective of Bandura's social learning theory in its various updated versions (see Bandura, 1977, 1986, 1997). Bandura's basic thesis was a straightforward one: most learning by children comes from watching and imitating other people, and as such has different characteristics from the trial-and-error learning referred to in the conditioning paradigms. **OBSERVATIONAL LEARNING**, as Bandura labelled it, is –

> *the acquisition of new behaviour patterns as a result of watching others perform them,*

and is distinguished by the following characteristics:

- It occurs mainly in social situations, where a model is available that the child can imitate.
- It can involve a whole sequence of responses in one go, as opposed to the bit-by-bit processes described in conditioning accounts.

- It can nevertheless take place very rapidly, often after just one exposure, and was therefore described by Bandura as *no-trial* learning – again in contrast to the gradual shaping entailed in conditioning.
- It does not require any reinforcement, in that responses can be acquired without being associated with a reward directly received by the child.

Bandura's account, like those of Hull and Skinner, was also originally based on the belief that development is fundamentally a matter of environmental learning. Nevertheless, it departed drastically in various respects from its predecessors, and in no way more so than in its assertion that reinforcement is not a necessary part of the learning process. *Vicarious learning*, that is, witnessing the rewards or punishments that follow when another person performs some action, can occur; so can *intrinsic reinforcement*, namely the internal feelings of pleasure or pride the child may experience on completing a task. Thus Bandura broadened the meaning of learning greatly to encompass a range of phenomena that had been neglected in other accounts, but without losing the conceptual and methodological rigour that characterized other learning perspectives.

CURRENT STATUS

The concept of observational learning stimulated a considerable body of research, carried out both by Bandura himself and by other investigators. In particular, a lot of effort went into closely examining the conditions under which observational learning occurs, such as the kind of models whom children choose to imitate; the manner of presenting a model, for example live or on television; the effect of symbolically coding a model's activity by, for example, verbally labelling it; and the extent to which the child's performance of observed behaviour can be deferred after observation (Bandura, 1977). In addition, the paradigm was applied to various areas of socialization, such as the acquisition of gender roles, the development of prosocial behaviour and the expression and control of aggression.

The flow of such research lessened from the 1980s on, in part because of concern that Bandura's account was not really a developmental one in that it had little to say about age-related changes in behaviour, and in part because the original version of the theory focused on overt behaviour and disregarded cognitive functions. The latter point, however, was met by Bandura in subsequent revisions (1986, 1997), when he set out to identify the mental processes that underlie observational learning, leaning heavily for this purpose on concepts borrowed from information-processing theory. In particular he singled out four groups of such processes, concerned respectively with attention, retention, production and motivation. As he acknowledged, any ability to reproduce some observed act on a later occasion must mean that the child is capable of symbolically coding that act in order to retain and subsequently retrieve it – a skill that comes increasingly to rely on verbal codes rather than on visual images as the child gets older. Similarly, instead of being tied to the observation of just specific instances of others' behaviour children with age become more and more adept at abstracting general rules from these instances and using these to guide their behaviour.

Statements such as these take us a long way from the mechanistic view of environmental learning: people are seen not as passive recipients of external stimulation but as 'self-organizing, proactive, self-reflective and self-regulating' (Bussey & Bandura, 1999). And with this change of emphasis it is also no wonder that Bandura came to refer to his account as 'social cognitive theory' rather than, as before, as 'social learning theory', thereby bringing it more in tune with the present *Zeitgeist*.

Further reading

Bandura, A. (1986). *Social foundations of thought and action: a social cognitive theory*. Englewood Cliffs, NJ: Prentice–Hall. One of Bandura's attempts to move beyond conventional learning theory accounts to a more cognitive, information theory-inspired statement.

Gewirtz, J.L., & Pelaez-Nogueras, M. (1992). B.F. Skinner's legacy in human infant behavior and development. *American Psychologist, 47*, 1411–1422. A fervent plea for the continuing usefulness of Skinner's ideas.

Grusec, J. (1994). Social learning theory and developmental psychology: the legacies of Robert R. Sears and Albert Bandura. In R.D. Parke, P.A. Ornstein, J.J. Rieser & C. Zahn-Waxler (Eds.), *A century of developmental psychology.* Washington, DC: American Psychological Association. Puts social learning theory in its historical context and critically evaluates its contribution to knowledge.

See also **epigenesis; maturation**

CONSTRUCTIVISM
and: SOCIAL CONSTRUCTIVISM

MEANING The essence of constructivism lies in its view of children as active participants in their own development. Accordingly, the explanation of change does not lie solely in some inborn programmed plan nor in whatever environmental forces the child encounters; instead, children help to determine their own fate by virtue of the meanings they impose on the world.

Constructivism can be defined as –

> the belief that the mind actively participates in assembling knowledge of the world in the process of interacting with the environment, rather than passively acquiring such knowledge through direct perception.

Our knowledge, that is, is not a simple mirror image of what is 'out there', but is the result of the mind selecting, interpreting and recreating sensory experience. The end result is thus a product of the interaction of subjective and environmental factors, the subjective factors including such aspects as cognitive level, stored experience, beliefs, motives and temperament. Knowledge acquired from a particular encounter may therefore take different forms in different individuals and in the same individual at different ages.

The view of the mind as a constructive organ goes back to the eighteenth-century philosopher Immanuel Kant, who argued against both the rationalist position that knowledge is derived from innate concepts and ideas and the extreme empiricist belief that the environment is the source of all we know. Instead, he put forward a synthesis of the two views, proposing that the mind is endowed with various structures ('categories of understanding') that enable all human beings to make sense of experience in a certain manner, but adding that these structures will only be mobilized when the relevant experiences are encountered. Knowledge, that is, is acquired during the individual's active interaction with the environment and takes shape as a result of the mind's efforts to assimilate experience (see **cognitive architecture**).

ORIGINS

In psychology the idea of the mind as a constructive organ was given prominence by Frederick Bartlett (1932), whose experiments on memorizing showed vividly that the act of remembering is basically a creative process: we rarely recall a message verbatim but rather remember its gist and in doing so transform it in the light of what we already know and expect. It was Piaget, however, who has come to be most closely associated with the idea that cognition is a constructive activity and as such a universal aspect of human development (e.g. Piaget, 1954). For him, knowledge is not a copy of objective reality, accumulated as a result of passively soaking up information. When children try to master their environment they actively select and interpret the information available by bringing to bear upon it what they already know and with the use of whatever cognitive strategies they possess at the time, and in the process they construct successively higher, more sophisticated levels of knowledge. In this sense children are their own agents of development: by struggling to understand their world they come to change that world as they perceive it.

For Piaget the world inhabited by children is largely composed of objects; other people play only a peripheral part in it. Vygotsky (1962, 1978), while also seeing children as actively involved in constructing their knowledge, put a different slant on this process by emphasising the social context in which it takes place. His version has been referred to as **SOCIAL CONSTRUCTIVISM**, which is –

> *the belief that the meanings attached to experience are socially assembled, depending on the culture in which the child is reared and on the child's caretakers.*

According to this view, the key to cognitive development lies not so much in the child's spontaneous discoveries while exploring inanimate objects as in the interpersonal processes that occur when the child interacts with more knowledgeable people. The attainment of higher intellectual functions is thus seen as essentially a social operation: the child's caretakers serve to pass on cultural values, highlight those aspects of the environment regarded as important, convey meanings to be attached to events, hand down tools for problem solving and support the child's efforts to master these. Development involves internalizing these social interactions – not on the basis of merely absorbing them but by actively processing them with the help of the adult's collaborative efforts. Vygotsky's emphasis on the role of language as used in adult–child dialogues, together with concepts such as **zone of proximal development** and **cultural tools**, has served to throw some light on the mechanisms involved in bringing this about and accounts for the rather greater attention now being given to Vygotsky's social constructivism over Piaget's biological constructivism.

CURRENT STATUS

The notion that children are active contributors to their own development, cognitive and social, has come to be generally accepted (see **child effects**). The form that this contribution takes varies greatly; it is seen most clearly in the often widely divergent ways in which children interpret and react to identical events and much research has gone into identifying the sources of these differences. Age, temperament, previous experience, emotional state, genetic endowment – these and other individual difference aspects show that the basic proposition of constructivism, that children view reality through a filter of their own making, can be accepted.

The actual process of construction, however, is still not fully understood. Mechanisms advanced by Piaget, such as **equilibration**, **assimilation** and **accommodation**, have proved to be too vague to be helpful; their appeal is to intuition rather than to research effort. On the other hand, the prominence given by Vygotsky to the role of language, especially that used in adult–child dialogue, has stimulated a considerable body of further work, designed to show how verbal exchanges can play a part in children's acquisition of the modes of thought customary in their society. This is well illustrated by work on *autobiographical memory* (e.g. Nelson, 1993a; Reese, 2002), which has provided detailed accounts of how young children are helped to give meaning to their past experiences in the course of discussing them with adults, thereby learning what is significant about the past, how to present it in narrative form and what events to incorporate in their self-history.

As to the theoretical underpinnings of constructivism, the anti-nativist position of Piagetian theory has increasingly encountered criticism. According to Piaget, the child arrives in the world with little more than a few sensori-motor reflexes, and by means of mechanisms such as assimilation and accommodation proceeds from there to build up the mental apparatus. A number of writers, collectively known as *neo-nativists* (e.g. Gopnik & Meltzoff, 1997; Karmiloff-Smith, 1992), while retaining the belief that cognitive development is largely dependent on the child's constructive efforts, consider that more account needs to be taken of the evidence now available that children are born with a variety of mechanisms that facilitate or constrain the acquisition of certain types of knowledge and that await only the appropriate sensory input to begin functioning. As a result (to quote Karmiloff-Smith), 'young infants have more of a headstart than Piaget granted them'; they are biologically prepared to make sense of the world in certain ways and to acquire particular kinds of knowledge (of human faces, language, space, objects, causation, etc.) that they can subsequently, by their own efforts, build up into more elaborate mental structures. There are disagreements as to the details of this process – just how much is innate and what form it takes (see **domain specificity**) – but the overall conclusion is that constructivism need not by any means be incompatible with nativism, a position that in certain respects takes us back more than two centuries to Kant.

Further reading

Fosnot, C.F. (Ed.) (1996). *Constructivism: theory, perspectives and practice.* New York: Teachers College, Columbia University. The first part of this multi-authored book provides succinct outlines of constructivism as formulated by both Piaget and Vygotsky, while the remainder examines the application of these concepts to teaching and learning.

Piaget, J. (1972). *The principles of genetic epistemology.* London: Routledge & Kegan Paul. Far from an easy read, but shows why Piaget adopted a cognitive constructive perspective.

See also **child effects; environmental learning; maturation**

DYNAMIC SYSTEMS
and: EPIGENESIS
SELF-ORGANIZATION

The term dynamic system is used to refer to –

MEANING

> *any complex organization that is composed of multiple parts, each with its own function but also involved in a pattern of reciprocal influences with other parts.*

Neural networks, embryos, mature human beings, families, industrial concerns, economic systems, cultures and galaxies may all be thought of as dynamic systems; the concept has also been used in physics and chemistry. Their potential for understanding human development has aroused considerable interest in recent years.

The basic principles that characterize the way dynamic systems operate are:

1 *Wholeness*. A system is an integrated whole that is greater than the sum of its parts. Its properties cannot be understood by merely studying the functioning of individual components; attention must also be given to the totality.

2 *Integrity of subsystems*. Complex systems are composed of subsystems, each of which can also be regarded as a system in its own right.

3 *Stability and change*. A system can be open to outside influences. A system may initially resist change in order to maintain stability; where this proves not possible the whole system has to change, even if the external influence affects first of all only one of the parts.

4 *Circularity of influence*. Within a system the pattern of influence is circular, not linear. The components are mutually interdependent; change in one has implications for the others.

The last of these characteristics deserves special emphasis when the systems view is applied to human beings. It is in contrast to the customary unidirectional view of causality which holds, for example, that genes cause structural change, that new structures bring about new functions, that parents direct their children's development, and so forth. Instead, change is always the result of *multiple* influences acting in *joint* fashion and therefore in a *non-linear* manner: new behaviour patterns, for example, can emerge from the interaction of many different parts of the system rather than by one single big push from some specific organismic or environmental source – the *emergent principle*, so-called.

Thus the dynamic systems view refers to the structure and organization of complex entities, but it also denotes a particular view of the way such systems change. When applied to development this is expressed by the concept of **EPIGENESIS**, which refers to –

> the idea that development involves the sequential emer-
> gence of new structures and functions as a consequence of
> the dynamic interaction among the different components of a
> system.

The organism, it is proposed, initially contains only a limited number of basic elements; all later structures and functions are the result of interaction of these original units with each other and with the environment. To understand development it is therefore necessary to shift the focus from the study of isolated elements to the question of how interactions occur, at either the same level (*horizontal* interactions, e.g.

gene–gene, cell–cell or organism–organism) or at different levels (*vertical* interactions, e.g. cell–tissue, behaviour–neural structure or organism–environment). Dynamic systems have thus also been referred to as *epigenetic systems* or *epigenetic hierarchical systems* (see Gottlieb, 1997; Gottlieb, Wahlsten & Lickliter, 1998).

The basic ideas behind dynamic systems have a long tradition, and this applies in particular to the concept of epigenesis. This goes back at least to the nineteenth century, when it was used by biologists as a counter to the belief in *preformationism* – the idea that development is wholly determined by innate structures, that in the fertilized egg there is already an adult-in-miniature (see Kitchener, 1978). It was mainly in the course of the twentieth century, however, that the epigenetic view was taken up by a group of developmental biologists, including such influential figures as Kuo (1967) and Schneirla (1957), and used as a theoretical framework to understand developmental processes in animals, with particular reference to embryological growth and so-called 'instinctive' behaviour patterns. Such behaviour, these scholars argued, does not in fact just appear automatically but as a consequence of multiple internal and external influences that shape the individual's history from conception onwards, indicating that 'instinctive' behaviour is really far more malleable than had previously been believed. A series of experiments, more recently continued by Gottlieb (1997) and mostly involving responses in birds such as pecking, vocalization and movement patterns, provided empirical support for these assertions and for the usefulness of adopting a systems view of mutually interacting influences to account for behavioural change rather than one relying simply on maturational push.

ORIGINS

The person generally credited with having first formalized the general principles underlying dynamic systems and demonstrated their wide applicability is von Bertalanffy (1933, 1968). An experimental embryologist himself, in his General Systems Theory he crossed the boundaries between biology, chemistry, physics, psychology, sociology and economics by arguing that the functioning of any multipart dynamic whole could be explained in terms very different from those of the customary 'machine theory', as he called it, which reduced everything to the properties of individual components and which therefore resulted in the hunt for ever-smaller units, whether in chemistry or in psychology. A system model, on the other hand, sees the essence of the whole to lie in the relationship of its parts, and it is this aspect, von Bertalanffy believed, that should be the focus of any study designed to understand the ability of the system both to maintain equilibrium and to bring about change. Systems thus have properties in their own right that cannot be deduced from the properties of their components; what is more, in a hierarchically arranged system each level is distinguished by its own properties: what happens at one level may not therefore explain what happens at another level – a child's motor action is not explained by reference to the constituent cells.

Von Bertalanffy's ideas received recognition among scientists concerned with many different kinds of systems, and a Society for General Systems Research was founded in

1954 to further his proposals and establish systems work as a distinct discipline. In psychology these views were somewhat slow to catch on: the prevalence of learning theory in particular ensured that a unidirectional way of thinking about causality continued to prevail. It is only comparatively recently that psychologists, including developmentalists, have begun to explore the usefulness of such an approach.

CURRENT STATUS

In recent years attention has focused on what is generally regarded as the essence of systems, namely that they are self-organizing. **SELF-ORGANIZATION** means that –

> *new structures and behaviour patterns emerge spontaneously in the course of development, without explicit instruction either from within the organism or from the environment, through processes intrinsic to the system itself.*

Such a view entails a marked shift of paradigm with respect to developmental issues. As Cairns (1998) has put it, the answer to the question 'What directs development?' is, simply stated, 'The organism'. Instead of looking to maturation or learning or even some combination of the two, systems theorists believe that it is a fundamental characteristic of living things for their constituent processes to change themselves. New patterns, that is, emerge spontaneously, without any explicit instruction from within the organism or from the environment. Thus, as a result of a series of small changes among the constituent parts a major reorganization in the system as a whole may be brought about, and following each such reorganization the organism will become increasingly complex and ordered. Self-organization, it is maintained, is thus the real source of developmental outcome.

Much of the research inspired by a systems view has been concerned with motor functioning in infancy, largely thanks to the efforts of Esther Thelen and her colleagues (Thelen, 2002; Thelen & Smith, 1994). As her work has demonstrated, a seemingly unitary behaviour pattern such as stepping is in fact composed of many subunits developing at different rates and sensitive to different organismic and environmental influences. Behavioural change can occur only when the system as a whole is ready to proceed to a new developmental level; locomotor development is thus a multidimensional process, dependent on the co-action of central nervous structures, bodily biomechanics and environmental supports and constraints. To explain such a development no one cause can be evoked; the baby's existing action patterns, the neural structures available, the nature of the task and its environmental setting, the child's past experience and present motivation – all play a part, and it is their interaction as a total configuration that brings about the eventual change.

Various other aspects of children's behaviour have also been investigated from a systems point of view, such as language (Smith, 1995), cognition (van Geert, 1993), emotion (Lewis & Granic, 2000), attachment (Laible & Thompson, 2000), dyadic communication (Fogel, 1993), infants' behavioural states (Wolff, 1987), psychopathology (Granic & Lamey, 2002) and antisocial behaviour (Granic & Dishion, 2003). However, it is in relation to family functioning that a systems perspective has gained most acceptance. A family is in many respects a particularly clear example of a dynamic system: it can be conceived as a three-level organization in that it is an entity in its own right, which is composed of two kinds of subsystems, namely individuals and the relationships between the individuals; it has properties that cannot be deduced from the properties of the components; and it is characterized by a highly complex, circular influence process that ensures that a change in any one of the components will have repercussions for all other components and for the system as a whole. Simple linear cause-and-effect statements cannot therefore do justice to the reality of the family situation; events such as marital conflict, the birth of another child, a father's unemployment or a mother's death have consequences that, according to a large number of studies, can more easily be understood if seen from a systems point of view (Cox & Paley, 1997).

There is still doubt in the minds of many regarding the extent to which all aspects of human behaviour and development can benefit from such an approach (e.g. Aslin, 1993). Others are more enthusiastic (e.g. Lewis, 2000), and there is certainly no question that the number of psychological functions to which the concept has been profitably applied is steadily increasing. In particular, a dynamic systems view is seen as having the potential of bringing unity to a field characterized by a great many mini-theories: it has the advantage that it includes many aspects of development and many levels of analysis, and so can provide a single explanatory framework applicable to a diversity of phenomena. The fact that the principles on which it is based can be extended to all types of complex organization is seen as an additional asset.

Further reading

Gottlieb, G. (1997). *Synthesizing nature–nurture.* Mahwah, NJ: Erlbaum. An informal account of the thinking and research underlying the idea of dynamic systems and associated concepts.

Lewis, M.D., & Granic, I. (Eds.) (2000). *Emotion, development and self-organization: dynamic systems approaches to emotional development.* Cambridge: Cambridge University Press. A collection of reports spanning a considerable range of work on developmental topics.

Thelen, E. (2002). Motor development as foundation and future of developmental psychology. In W.W. Hartup & R.K. Silbereisen (Eds.), *Growing points in developmental science.* Hove: Psychology Press. Useful as a succinct introduction by a leading dynamic systems researcher.

See also **connectionist networks; constructivism**

CONNECTIONIST NETWORKS

MEANING   Also referred to as *artificial neural networks* or *parallel distributed processing*, connectionist networks are –

> computer models loosely based on neural information processing, aimed at specifying the dynamics of cognitive processes and testing out models of development.

Connectionism is based on the belief that the traditional approach to cognition, as represented by information processing theory, is misleading in its emphasis on the *serial* processing of data. Instead, connectionist networks are seen as intricate systems of simple units (or nodes), generally arranged in layers serving such specific functions as input, processing and output, which handle information *in parallel* by means of a vast net of interconnections. While the units themselves merely fire or do not fire impulses and have no further meaning on their own, the total pattern of excitation created in the network by their activity can give rise to highly complex output patterns simulating human behaviour. Thus, instead of viewing cognition in terms of the manipulation of symbols as is common to other approaches, connectionists see it as a network of simple interconnected processing units functioning as a dynamic system which, supplied with some input, will spread a pattern of excitement and inhibition that accounts for mental activity. Connectionist modelling provides a computational methodology aimed at demonstrating this process and a means of evaluating alternative hypotheses concerning learning and development.

ORIGINS   While *connectionism* as a term goes back to Donald Hebb's writings in the 1940s, connectionist ideas did not become formalized until the mid-1980s. Two publications, edited by Rumelhart and McClelland (1986) and McClelland and Rumelhart (1986), are generally taken to be the point when connectionism started to be taken seriously. These two volumes spelled out in detail the principles and methods underlying the study of parallel distributed processing, and also demonstrated their applicability to specific aspects of cognition. For example, in one of the contributions to these volumes Rumelhart and McClelland developed one of the earliest connectionist models in order to investigate how children might be able to learn the past tense of English verbs and to differentiate between regular and irregular verbs. The computer model used by them was a fairly unsophisticated one, yet they were able to train it to perform in a manner similar to language-acquiring children and so demonstrate that a child's learning can occur in a relatively simple manner without the use of any rule-based mechanisms. They thus not only found a simulation technique for profitably investigating aspects of human behaviour but also showed that this could lead to new insights into the processes that bring about developmental change.

It subsequently became apparent that Rumelhart and McClelland's account was flawed in a number of ways and that their generalization to real children was in some respects unjustified. Other investigators in later years set out to improve on their methodology; however, the inspiration to use connectionist network modelling had been provided and, though initially slow to catch on, the technique has recently attracted interest from an increasing number of investigators.

Connectionist modelling has now been applied to a considerable range of topics, including problem solving, reasoning, memory, object permanence, vocabulary growth and syntax acquisition (see Elman, Bates, Johnson, Karmiloff-Smith, Parisi & Plunkett, 1996; Plunkett, Karmiloff-Smith, Bates, Elmon & Johnson, 1997 for details). As a consequence, the nature of connectionist networks and the uses to which they can be put have become greatly clarified. **CURRENT STATUS**

To summarize this work: connectionist networks can be computer simulated in a range of different forms and degrees of complexity, depending on the purpose of the investigator. All, however, contain certain basic ingredients, namely a large number of simple processing units (idealized brain neurons) that are interconnected via a network of pathways (like synapses). The most common form of network employed so far by investigators interested in modelling human behaviour involves the arrangement of units in three layers serving input, processing and output functions, respectively modelling sensory, central and motor processes. While units within any one layer are not interconnected, each unit at one layer is connected with every other unit at the next layer, enabling the processing of information to be carried on in parallel throughout the network.

Networks can be constructed to incorporate various constraints, representing individuals' inborn or age-related characteristics, and then be given 'tasks' in order to investigate the nature of the learning processes adopted by the system. Learning is said to occur as a result of changing the *weights* (i.e. strengths) of the connections between units in the different layers; during the learning process the weights change constantly until finally, as a result of the network comparing the pattern produced with some criterion (an external one such as the demands of a teacher or an internally generated goal), the connection strength becomes stable and learning is said to have been achieved. The assumption is that this represents a child's real-life experiences and provides insight into the precise characteristics of learning and developmental processes. Thus, by building in different initial constraints or by trying out various input–output patterns, all of which need to be precisely specified in constructing the computer model, it is possible to explore a range of different hypotheses as to the nature of developmental change (for detailed accounts see Mareschal, 2000; Plunkett, 2000).

Among the insights into the general nature of development claimed by connectionist workers the following stand out:

- Networks demonstrate stage-like changes in the nature of learning, but these are not the result of some new, qualitatively different mechanism suddenly clocking in as Piaget believed, but are brought about by a series of small, gradual increments in learning which, when some particular point is reached, can all at once lead to a drastic restructuring of overt behaviour. New behaviour, that is, does not necessarily mean new mechanisms.
- The acquisition of complex behaviour patterns in the course of development need not depend on the potential availability of complex learning devices from the start of development. These can *emerge* from the interaction of even a quite immature organism with a rich learning environment: it is the interaction that takes a complex form rather than the starting state of the organism.
- Some relatively simple networks are fixed in their structure from the beginning of life on, but others are *generative* in nature in that they change their structure as a result of learning experiences. They do so by creating additional hidden units, and in this way become capable of coping with tasks of increasing difficulty.
- Connectionist networks have been constructed that model a range of developmental disorders, including autism, dyslexia and specific language impairments. These show promise of throwing new light on the mechanisms responsible for different forms of psychopathology, challenging previously held assumptions and accepted views (for some further details see Thomas & Karmiloff-Smith, 2002).

As indicated, the most important point about connectionist networks is that they involve parallel as opposed to serial processing of information by the individual. For one thing, this is much more in keeping with what is now known about the functioning of the neural system; for another, it draws attention to the fact that connectionist networks share certain fundamental properties with **dynamic systems** – indeed, according to some writers they represent one particular type of such a system (for discussion see papers in a Special Issue of *Developmental Science*, introduced by Spencer & Thelen, 2003). Both approaches emphasize *non-linear* causation: that is, connectionist networks, too, are based on the assumption that the causation of behaviour is often not as obvious and straightforward as such earlier developmental theories as the various learning approaches believed (see **environmental learning**) – largely because the influence process is generally based on the joint functioning of multiple forces rather than on the pull–push model of linear causation. In addition, connectionist networks are like dynamic systems in being self-organizing in nature (see **self-organization**): changes in their make-up are not necessarily brought about by the action of external forces but by the network modifying itself spontaneously in the course of functioning. The two approaches have different histories and different vocabularies, but they share core assumptions and may well merge in the near future.

There has been something of a boom in research on connectionist networks in recent years as their potential for exploring ideas about development has become increasingly evident. This does not mean, however, that the approach has been without critics. Thelen and Smith (1994), for example, list a number of reservations, in particular the fact that connectionists do not acknowledge the diversity of brain structures and instead treat all processing units as homogeneous. Above all, however, one must bear in mind that the networks are not 'real' but simulated, having been put together by computer modellers and are for the most part of a degree of complexity vastly less than that of biological systems. Thus, the observation that a network can be trained to perform a particular task does not mean that children necessarily behave in the same way but only that they *may* be able to do so.

Further reading

Elman, J.L., Bates, E.A., Johnson, M.H., Karmiloff-Smith, A., Parisi, D., & Plunkett, K. (1996) *Rethinking innateness: a connectionist perspective on development.* Cambridge, MA: MIT Press. A book that has rapidly become a classic – not easy but foundational.

Mareschal, D. (2000). Connectionist modelling and infant development. In D. Muir and A. Slater (Eds.), *Infant development: essential readings.* Oxford: Blackwell. An overview of connectionist thinking, meant as an introduction to the topic.

Quinlan, P.T. (Ed.) (2003). *Connectionist models of development: developmental processes in real and artificial neural networks.* Hove: Psychology Press. Some knowledge of connectionist networks assumed, but gives good indication of the range of phenomena investigated with this approach.

See also **dynamic systems; self-organization**

3

THREE

BIOLOGICAL ASPECTS

The relationship of mind and body, of biological with psychological aspects, has been a topic of intense interest throughout the ages, but for long did not progress beyond the level of speculation on the part of theologians and philosophers. It was not until the end of the nineteenth century that attempts were made to introduce scientific methods to this area, and significantly they began in efforts to understand developmental aspects of humans. Thus Charles Darwin, in his book *The expression of emotion in man and animals*, published in 1872, included detailed systematic observations of the reactions of Doddy, his infant son, to various emotion-arousing situations, in order to bolster his argument that behavioural patterns such as children's facial expressions are of evolutionary significance and have their roots in our genetic inheritance. Darwin is sometimes, contentiously, credited with being the father of developmental psychology; what cannot be doubted is that he and various other scientists (mainly embryologists) working at that time gave a powerful boost to the view of development as a unitary process involving *both* biological and psychological aspects.

However, it was not until a century later that psychobiology (or, as some prefer it, biopsychology) emerged as a recognized discipline. It did so in part because of technological progress, as seen for instance in the availability of techniques such as magnetic resonance imaging which made it possible to observe brain activity in even quite young children and link these data to ongoing psychological activity. And in addition, conceptual advances such as the increasing use of **dynamic systems** models have helped in efforts to integrate biological with behavioural features: they have, for instance, made it easier to understand that bodily structures and psychological functioning are reciprocally related – that the growth of the former is rarely a simple 'cause' of development of the latter, in that biological structures (even genes) are activity-dependent and need to be used to reach their potential. To think of biological aspects as being the 'roots' or the 'basis' of psychological development is thus misleading.

Psychobiology refers to a range of fields, including evolutionary psychology, behaviour genetics, ethology and developmental neuroscience. The issue in all, as far as we are concerned, is the light they shed on the development of mental and behavioural aspects. To this end concepts such as the following have been employed:

EVOLUTION
FIXED ACTION PATTERNS
and: **Sign stimuli**
CRITICAL (SENSITIVE) PERIODS
and: **Experience-expectancy/Experience-dependency**
BRAIN PLASTICITY
GENE–ENVIRONMENT EFFECTS
and: **Gene–environment correlation**
  Gene–environment interaction

EVOLUTION

MEANING Largely due to Charles Darwin, evolution is the single most significant concept in the biological sciences – a concept, moreover, that has transformed the way human beings think of themselves. As Darwin saw it, evolution refers to –

> *the continuous changes that occur in the characteristics of animal species over successive generations as they adapt to their particular environment in order to ensure survival.*

Let us note two points about this definition. In the first place, it applies to human beings as well as to lower species; secondly, the characteristics referred to include not only physical organs and appearance but also mental functions and behaviour. It is the combination of these two points that has led to the formation of *evolutionary psychology*.

Evolutionary psychologists base their approach on the thesis that the behavioural patterns common to human beings have biological roots, which can be understood by considering how these patterns evolved in the history of the species. The nature of development examined thus concerns phylogenetic and not ontogenetic change – what transpired in the course of thousands of generations rather than in the life course of individuals. The goal is to identify the psychological attributes typical of human beings generally and to pinpoint the genetic and ecological mechanisms that shape the development of these attributes and ensure their adaptation to local conditions (Geary & Bjorklund, 2000). The concept of evolution is thus used to explain the origins of mind by examining our ancestors' adaptation to their environment, in the belief that a full understanding of human behaviour requires not only knowledge of the immediate conditions that underlie it but also of the distal forces that originally gave rise to it – ultimate explanations, that is, are required as well as proximal ones.

ORIGINS Darwin was by no means the first to put forward the idea of evolution. Rather his achievement, as seen in his monumental book *On the origin of species by means of natural selection or the preservation of favoured races in the struggle for life* (to give it its full title), published in 1859, was two-fold: first, in putting forward a comprehensive theory to account for evolutionary change, and second in assembling an impressively large body of observations to support the theory.

The principal mechanism employed by Darwinian theory was *natural selection* – the idea that each species evolves its particular attributes as a result of a process whereby those individuals best adapted to cope with environmental demands will survive and have offspring to whom these attributes are passed on. Thus among giraffes (to quote a popular example) it was the animals with the longest necks and hence the ability to reach the best leaves at the top of trees that were most likely to prosper in the distant past of the species; these animals had the greatest chance of survival and to produce most offspring similarly equipped, as a result of which a selection process took place over the course of generations that ensured the *survival of the fittest*, that is to say, those with the longest necks, which thus became a distinguishing feature of the species as a whole.

Darwin's work was based mainly on the study of the physical attributes of animals rather than human beings' psychological characteristics. Nevertheless, he was convinced that his general thesis held for the latter too – that the nature of intelligence, for example, can be explained because certain traits in our ancestors increased the chances of survival and were therefore retained while others were dropped. However, it was not until more than a century after the publication of *The origin of species* that the study of human behaviour from an evolutionary point of view became an endeavour in its own right, largely thanks to advances in the understanding of gene transmission and the writings of a number of individuals collectively known as the *Neo-Darwinians*, such as Hamilton (1964), Trivers (1972) and Wilson (1975).

Of these, Wilson's sociobiological theory is particularly relevant. As Wilson defined it, *sociobiology* is the study of all social behaviour, though his own focus was more on the structures of society such as its customs and institutions than on individuals and their interactions. The virtue of Wilson's approach was that it made a serious attempt to show how social and biological analyses could profitably be combined to make sense of human behaviour and the evolutionary functions it serves, using not just speculation but predictions that could be put to the test. In particular, sociobiologists addressed topics that classical Darwinism had failed to explain, such as the puzzle of altruistic and self-sacrificing behaviour – a puzzle because according to the original formulation such behaviour has no payoff for the individual. Sociobiologists, however, argued that individuals act not just to maximize their own fitness but to promote their *inclusive* fitness, that is, that of their kin as well. Darwin saw the production of offspring as the essential mechanism for species survival; sociobiologists, on the other hand, point out that other kin also share some of the individual's genes and that altruism, especially when directed at close kin, will therefore serve the same purpose. Far from dying out as a useless attribute, as Darwinism might expect, altruism is a widespread phenomenon throughout the animal kingdom, for according to sociobiologists evolution is about preserving the gene, not the individual, and any behaviour that ensures gene preservation will be selected even if the individual incurs costs, as long as it is of help to others who possess the same gene.

Sociobiology in its early stages aroused considerable controversy, much of it political rather than scientific, because it was perceived as arguing for biological determinism and so denying individual freedom. Some of Wilson's statements did indeed provide ammunition for such an impression (e.g. 'genes hold culture on a leash'), and one of the reasons for the emergence of evolutionary psychology was as a reaction to such determinism and to show that natural selection involves the *dynamic* interaction of organisms with their environment, where human beings actively select and adapt their environments rather than being passively compelled to adapt *to* the environment by forces beyond their control.

CURRENT STATUS

It is essential to bear in mind that evolutionary psychology does not seek to provide an *alternative* but rather an *additional* perspective in explaining the causes of behaviour. According to the ethologist Niko Tinbergen (1951), questions about the causes of behaviour fall into four categories:

1 *Immediate*: what are the immediate antecedents that bring about a particular behaviour pattern?

2 *Developmental*: what caused the individual to grow up to respond in such a way?

3 *Functional*: what is the adaptive value of the behaviour pattern?

4 *Evolutionary*: what are the forces that shaped the behaviour pattern in the historical course of the species?

Developmental psychologists have mostly concentrated on the first two of these questions; evolutionary psychologists, on the other hand, are primarily concerned with the last two. In particular, one of their main contributions has been to draw attention to the *functions* of behaviour, emphasizing the need to ask What is it for? when studying any one response pattern. Every pattern, it is proposed, at every stage of development, must have some adaptive value: even infants' immaturity is useful and should be seen in a positive light – limited visual capacities, for instance, serve to protect the young brain from overstimulation, and likewise a short auditory memory span serves to reduce the total amount of language processed and so ensures the individual's comprehension abilities are not overwhelmed (Geary & Bjorklund, 2000).

Considering the relatively recent origin of evolutionary psychology, the range of topics investigated from this perspective is impressive (as seen, for example, in the Handbook edited by Crawford & Krebs, 1998). Examples include socialization, attachment, sex roles, aggressiveness, moral behaviour, emotional expression, neighbourliness, child abuse, handedness, mating preferences, female attractiveness, rape, divorce, infant immaturity and age at puberty. Probably the best known of these is attachment, thanks largely to John Bowlby's (1969/1982) theory of the origins of attachment behaviour (see **attachment**). Bowlby was greatly influenced by Darwin's writings (it is noteworthy that his last publication was a biography of Darwin, published in 1990 just a few months before his death), and was especially attracted by the thesis that all structures of living organisms, including their behavioural equipment, are to be understood by reference to the contribution they make to the survival of the species in the natural environment of that species. Accordingly, he proposed that the young child's parental attachment system should be seen in its evolutionary context, namely as originating in humanity's distant past, at a time when predators spelled real danger and when a mechanism was required whereby offspring could keep close to their caregivers and so obtain protection, thus enhancing their chances of survival. As a result of evolutionary selection infants are equipped with various means of attracting and maintaining the attention of their parents, such as crying and smiling, and of staying within or regaining their proximity, such as clinging and following. The attachment system, that is, came into being because it served the biological function of survival, and has remained in the repertoire of the human species long after the original purpose of protection against predators largely disappeared.

Bowlby's ideas are highly stimulating, but they also illustrate one of the reasons why evolutionary psychology has encountered criticism regarding some of its arguments. Statements about origins, being post hoc, are hypotheses that are virtually impossible to verify; even those who find thinking in evolutionary terms congenial concede that one cannot obtain proof for the assertion that developmental phenomena are the product of natural selection (Belsky, Steinberg & Draper, 1991). Evolutionary psychologists are thus sometimes accused of being able to explain anything: suicide as well as appetite for life; parental abuse as well as parental care. And yet, in examining domain specific abilities like face and voice recognition (see **domain specificity** above), the evolutionary argument that these came into existence because of their usefulness and accordingly became an enduring characteristic of the human species sounds persuasive, albeit at an intuitive level and in the absence of conventional proof. There is an ongoing debate as to whether such ultimate explanations of the causes of behaviour require different criteria for acceptance compared with the proximal explanations generally favoured by psychologists (Crawford, 1998); what cannot be doubted is that consideration of both greatly widens our understanding, in that an evolutionary orientation opens up a new way of thinking about psychological phenomena and their development and poses questions not otherwise posed.

In general, the extent to which the concept of evolution is of use to psychologists is still subject to controversy. On the one hand there are the enthusiasts who have great faith in its explanatory power (e.g. Pinker, 1997); on the other hand there are the sceptics who pour scorn on the whole enterprise (e.g. Rose & Rose, 2000). Yet many now believe that a credible case has been made for adopting such an orientation, and that it is more a matter of how best to use the concept in explaining human behaviour than adopting a yes-or-no stance.

Further reading

Bjorklund, D.F., & Pelligrini, A.D. (2002). *The origins of human nature: evolutionary developmental psychology*. Washington, DC: American Association of Psychology. Firmly advocates the need for an evolutionary perspective for understanding the development of behaviour, and describes in detail the application of such a view to a range of topics studied by developmentalists.

Buss, D.M. (1999). *Evolutionary psychology: the new science of the mind*. Boston, MA: Allyn and Bacon. A comprehensive coverage of the whole area, with detailed explanations of the application of evolutionary thinking to a range of human functions, including child rearing, social living and culture.

Crawford, C., & Krebs, D.L. (Eds.) (1998). *Handbook of evolutionary psychology: ideas, issues and applications*. Mahwah, NJ: Erlbaum. See especially the chapter by Michele Surbey on developmental psychology.

See also **attachment; fixed action patterns; modularity**

FIXED ACTION PATTERNS
and: **SIGN STIMULI**

MEANING These two concepts form part of ethological theory. *Ethology* is the biological study of behaviour, and initially one of its aims was to compile an *ethogram* for each species, that is, to put together an inventory of the behaviour patterns that characterize a given species and that distinguish it from other species in the same way that its physical characteristics distinguish it. Such behaviour patterns are known as fixed action patterns, which can be defined as –

> *complex innate behavioural sequences of a species-typical nature.*

Fixed action patterns are complex in comparison with reflexes; they are innate in that they are common to all members of the species and have survival value; and the total array of these patterns, namely the ethogram, can be used to identify individual animals as belonging to a particular species.

Each pattern is triggered by a specific **SIGN STIMULUS**, that being –

> *the particular environmental feature that automatically releases a particular fixed action pattern.*

Also known as *releasers*, sign stimuli are to fixed action patterns what a key is to a lock – an analogy that describes well their functioning. They imply a selective responsiveness on the part of the animal to a specific environmental feature which is usually found from the very first exposure – for example, a moving object will release the following response in certain species of birds (the *imprinting* phenomenon); the red belly of a male stickleback fish will trigger a hostile response in another stickleback when seen in its own territory; and certain parts of the human face will automatically elicit a smile in very young babies. In each case the individual is preprogrammed to act in specific ways to specific stimuli, the connection having come about because in the course of evolution it helped to facilitate survival and ensure the individual's well-being. An evolutionary perspective is thus basic to ethological thinking (see **evolution**).

Ethology as a distinct perspective emerged in the 1930s, largely thanks to the work of **ORIGINS** two biologists, Konrad Lorenz and Niko Tinbergen (for a brief historical account see Smith, 1990). They argued that the behaviour of different species could best be understood in terms of the animal's adaptation to its natural environment, that each species was thus distinguished by its own behavioural patterns (named by them fixed action patterns), and that a primary task of biologists was to study these as they occur in the animal's natural habitat. Lorenz in particular was convinced that these patterns really are *fixed*, that is, that they are wholly innate and not modified by experience and that each is rigidly linked to a particular sign stimulus. He further proposed that this link operates through an *innate releasing mechanism* (IRM), a hypothetical internal structure which the sign stimulus activates and which in turn triggers the fixed action pattern through a release of energy – a 'flush toilet' conception, as it has been called. Generally, Lorenz thus tended to stress the more mechanistic, automatic side of behaviour, as seen in his focus on predetermined stimulus–response connections and genetically rooted timing of developmental events (see **critical periods**) – a view, however, which went out of favour in subsequent years, when it was found to be incompatible with more modern conceptions of the operation of the nervous system than those on which Lorenz based his theories in the 1930s and 1940s.

A more lasting contribution was the insistence by Lorenz (1950, 1965) and Tinbergen (1951) that behavioural studies must begin with a sit-and-watch phase. Instead of jumping straight into the laboratory, as psychologists tended to do until well into the second half of the twentieth century, they considered it essential first to observe individuals in their natural setting and provide precise descriptions of their behaviour and the circumstances under which it occurred. Only then is it meaningful to move to laboratory analysis and experimentation, using the real-life descriptive data for purposes of hypothesis generating. Much of early ethological work is thus of a descriptive nature, derived especially from birds and fish, and it was observation of their behaviour that gave rise to Lorenz's belief that the behavioural stream can be cut up into units, that is, fixed action patterns.

Many of the fixed action patterns described by Lorenz and Tinbergen serve to facilitate some aspect of social communication: courtship, threat gestures, affiliation, nurturance and so on, and in each case a particular sign stimulus serves to release the act. Take the fighting behaviour shown by male stickleback fish when another male stickleback invades its territory – an action described in detail by Tinbergen. In order to determine the precise nature of the sign stimulus involved, Tinbergen prepared models of fish that differed in various ways, and was thus able to demonstrate that the crucial feature was the stickleback's red belly: a model looking precisely like a stickleback but lacking the red belly elicited no fighting behaviour; a model only vaguely like a stickleback in shape but possessing the red belly did elicit it. Similarly with other fixed action patterns and their sign stimuli: the following response, observed in certain species of birds such as chicks, ducks and geese, is elicited by the first moving object the animal sees after hatching, but whereas this is normally the biologically 'correct' object, namely the parent, experiments with a wide range of other objects such as footballs, boxes pulled by string and even human beings show that the range of sign stimuli is much wider and involves anything large and mobile (Sluckin, 1972). And by similar experimental means it has been shown that *supernormal stimuli*, that is, those that exaggerate the crucial characteristic of the sign stimulus, are more effective: extra large eggs, for example, elicit gulls' egg retrieval response more readily than normal ones. In each case experimental analysis followed a natural history phase and was able to ask meaningful questions thanks to the availability of descriptive data.

CURRENT STATUS Research in more recent years has demonstrated that fixed action patterns are not as rigid in their operation even in birds and fish, let alone in higher species, as previously thought (Slater, 1985). For one thing, patterns may vary according to context, and rather more allowance must therefore be made for the influence of learning on their manifestation than is evident in Lorenz's writings. Also, Lorenz's claim that fixed action patterns do not differ from one individual to another has been shown to need amendment: while some of the simpler actions are very stereotyped other more complex patterns are only broadly similar in the way they are expressed by different members of the same species. In short, modern ethologists have become wary of putting too much emphasis on the fixed element of such acts in case too firm a line is drawn between what is innate and what is learned, and some have indeed dropped the term altogether in favour of *modal* action patterns (Hinde, 1982). In addition, it has become apparent that the term *innate* is by no means as straightforward in meaning as was once thought. According to Bateson (1998) there are at least seven different ways in which it is used: present at birth; a behavioural difference caused by a genetic difference; adapted over the course of evolution; unchanging throughout development; shared by all members of a species; present in the behavioural repertoire before it is functional; and not learned. Clearly, simply to label something as innate is not enough and can give rise to all sorts of confusion.

Despite reservations, the application of ethological thinking to human behaviour has become a major endeavour. By stressing the importance of observing people's behaviour in its natural setting, *human ethology* has brought into being a large body of descriptive data about the social interactions and play behaviour of children at home, at school, in the street and in playgrounds (for examples see Blurton Jones, 1972), and has attempted to make sense of such data by applying some of the concepts used by etholologists, including fixed action patterns and sign stimuli. The following are some examples of the topics investigated by human ethologists:

- *Social signalling devices* in early infancy, such as smiling and crying, can be seen as relatively simple and stereotyped actions that are activated by certain quite specific stimuli. They are evolutionarily based, functionally essential for survival and form part of the genetic endowment of all human beings. Descriptive studies have shown that even in the early weeks of life they are flexible in the form they take; nevertheless, they have been seen as essentially conforming to the notion of fixed action patterns.

- *Infants' 'cuteness'* has been described as a sign stimulus that elicits adults' affectional and caring behaviour. As experimental studies using pictures and dolls have shown, characteristics such as large eyes, bulging foreheads and chubby cheeks are the specific stimuli to which adults respond; infants who are deficient in this respect are less likely to call forth such behaviour (Sternglanz, Gray & Murakami, 1977).
- *Emotional expressions* provide another example of genetically determined responses that are common to all human beings. Every emotion is tied to a particular facial expression; basic emotions such as fear, anger or joy are present from very early on; and even blind babies have been found to manifest the appropriate expression. In addition, cross-cultural studies have shown that these patterns do not vary from one society to another (Eibl-Eibesfeldt, 1989). Again, the concept of fixed action pattern has been applied to these behavioural characteristics.
- *Preschool children's social interaction patterns* have been described and analysed in very great detail by human ethologists. Many of these investigations set out to establish ethograms for young children's behaviour, and thus resulted in large numbers of minutely observed lists of action patterns describing how children express such patterns as dominance assertion, appeasement and rough-and-tumble play (Smith & Connolly, 1972).

In general, the specific concepts generated by ethologists, such as fixed action patterns, sign stimuli, innate releasing mechanisms and **critical periods,** have been useful in drawing attention to the need to describe and analyse behaviour in great detail, and indeed ethological thinking was a major cause for the swing away from controlled experimentation to the observation of children's behaviour under natural conditions. In addition, these concepts served to emphasize the importance of considering the adaptive functions of developmental phenomena; answers to the question What are they for? helped to place phenomena such as attachment formation in a broader biological context and place overtly different behaviour patterns such as the following response of a duckling and the crying of a human baby under the same conceptual umbrella. However, it has to be concluded that in their own right the specific concepts are of rather less significance: their origins in rather mechanistic views of behaviour has meant that subsequently they either needed to be changed in certain respects to express a more flexible conception or that they had to be abandoned because they appeared to serve little purpose.

Further reading

Archer, J. (1992). *Ethology and human development.* Hemel Hempstead: Harvester–Wheatsheaf. Describes and evaluates the contribution which ethological theory and research can make to developmental psychology.

Eibl-Eibesfeldt, I. (1989). *Human ethology.* New York: de Gruyter. A big book! Presents detailed accounts of many ethological investigations into human behaviour, with emphasis on cross-cultural comparisons.

Kruuk, H. (2003). *Niko's nature: a life of Niko Tinbergen and the science of animal behaviour.* Oxford: Oxford University Press. Brings ethology to life by presenting a personal account of Tinbergen as seen by one of his students.

See also **critical (sensitive) periods; evolution**

CRITICAL (SENSITIVE) PERIODS
and: EXPERIENCE-EXPECTANCY/EXPERIENCE-DEPENDENCY

MEANING   One of the best-known concepts stemming from ethological theory, critical periods refer to –

> *biologically determined phases of development during which the individual is maximally ready to acquire a new behaviour pattern.*

In their original version critical periods were likened to the brief opening of a window: at that particular time the individual was said to be highly susceptible to certain specific experiences; if these do not take place then it is no longer possible to acquire the behaviour pattern called forth by that experience. The periods were regarded as critical because, first, they are *instantaneous* in producing an effect on the individual; secondly, because they are *immutable* in their timing during development; and thirdly because the effects they produce are *irreversible* in that they cannot be modified by later experience. However, because subsequent work challenged all three of these characteristics (the 'three is'), the term **SENSITIVE PERIODS** came to be preferred, denoting –

> *developmental phases at which the individual is more likely to acquire a new behaviour pattern than at other times.*

ORIGINS   Critical periods are generally associated with Lorenz and the phenomenon of imprinting. In fact, long before his time experimental embryologists had established that certain cell masses are affected by chemicals only during particular developmental stages; what is more, as long ago as 1873 Spalding had described imprinting-like behaviour in chicks and pointed out that this could only be elicited if the chick was exposed to its mother within the first three days after hatching: if this did not happen, the chick could never subsequently develop a bond with the mother. However, it was Konrad Lorenz, in a paper published in 1935, who was the first to give formal recognition to critical periods, going beyond the descriptive data of imprinting and conceptualizing critical periods as decisive developmental events with the quite essential characteristics of being instantaneous, immutable and irreversible. In addition, he subsequently claimed that the effect then produced could spread beyond the response affected to certain other behaviour systems: for example, if the following response in birds was elicited by a biologically 'wrong' object such as a member of another species then choice of mate would subsequently also be channelled to a member of that species. Lorenz thus had no doubt that these periods really are *critical*.

Following Lorenz, the concept of critical periods was applied to a wide range of species and aspects of behaviour. Thus imprinting-like phenomena confined to specific developmental periods were found in dogs, rats, sheep and goats and also in human beings. The latter is best illustrated by Bowlby's (1951) assertion that children are capable of forming attachments only at the very beginning of life and must therefore be given the opportunity to do so during this period: as he put it, 'even good mothering is almost useless if delayed until after the age of two and a half years'. The idea was extended to adults too: female goats, for example, were said to require contact with their newborns within the first five minutes after birth if they are to form an affectional bond with them; delayed contact results in the goat rejecting the young (Sluckin, Herbert, & Sluckin, 1983). Two paediatricians, Klaus and Kennell (1976), asserted that the same phenomenon exists in human mothers too: mothers who have limited contact with their babies in the first days after birth were found by them to have a less caring relationship with the baby than mothers with extended contact. As the difference between the two groups was still evident in subsequent years it was concluded that events in the immediate post-natal period had such decisive effects that they determined the nature of the mother–child relationship for a very long time (see **bonding**).

Yet other examples of critical periods in human beings have been described for sensori-motor functions and for language: for instance, in the case of binocular vision there is evidence that children need to have proper use of both eyes in the first three years or so; it is thus essential to correct strabismus (squint) at this time so that children learn to coordinate the two eyes at this early age (Banks, Aslin & Letson, 1975). Similarly, auditory experience before the first birthday has been found to exercise a decisive effect on auditory functioning: the sound characteristics of the language babies hear during this period will permanently affect their abilities to process linguistic information (Werker & Desjardins, 1995). The acquisition of language production has also been said to be constrained by developmental limits, Eric Lenneberg (1967) in particular arguing that a critical period for learning to speak ends around puberty. However, as the evidence for such an assertion depends mainly on children brought up under conditions of severe deprivation, it is difficult to arrive at firm conclusions as to whether biologically determined limits are operative or whether any of the many other factors associated with such an experience (malnutrition, cruelty, mental handicap resulting from deprivation, etc.) are the real determinants.

CURRENT STATUS
As happened with some other ethological concepts put forward by Lorenz, such as **fixed action patterns**, later work has found the original idea of critical periods to be in need of amendment. The main features characterizing critical periods (the 'three i's') have all turned out to be more flexible than was first thought: the acquisition of the new behaviour pattern is usually not *instantaneous*, requiring more than a brief exposure to the stimulus; the period need not be *immutable* but can be delayed within certain limits; and the effects produced may be modified by later environmental influences and are thus not necessarily *irreversible* (Bornstein, 1989). This applies to both animals and humans: in the latter, for example, attachment formation can be delayed well beyond the limit of 2½ years which Bowlby laid down: children reared under conditions of total deprivation until mid-childhood are still capable of forming close ties when subsequently adopted into normal families (Schaffer, 2002). As a result, the term **SENSITIVE PERIODS** is now preferred; it correctly expresses the belief that there are times during development when the individual is rather more susceptible to certain environmental influences than at other times, and it suggests that in thinking about this issue a mid-way position between total fixity and unlimited plasticity is the most appropriate one to adopt.

There are other respects in which the change of terminology from *critical* to *sensitive* has heralded a different approach. For example, a much more detailed, analytical attitude is now adopted in using the concept: thus Bornstein (1989) has listed 14 different parameters that need to be specified if it is to be adequately described, including such aspects as when and how often the period occurs, how long it lasts, the precise nature of the stimulation that is required to evoke responses during this time, the kind of contact the individual must have with such stimulation and the nature and duration of the behaviour pattern elicited. Moreover, it has become evident that there are great variations among different neuro-behavioural systems in the timing, duration and extent to which they are affected by environmental input, with the simpler, more 'physiological' systems such as sensori-motor functions less susceptible than the more complex 'psychological' ones such as language and attachment. Even within specific systems variations can occur from one aspect to another, as found when comparing the developmental vulnerabilities of grammatical and semantic language processing (Neville & Bavelier, 2002). Perhaps the most important change in thinking, however, concerns the general agreement that neither critical nor sensitive periods can be used as an explanatory device: to state that a particular outcome occurs *because* the individual is going through such a period is misleading, in that it does not have anything to say about the underlying mechanisms.

In an attempt to specify such mechanisms, Greenough, Black and Wallace (1986) proposed that it is necessary to distinguish between two ways in which experience acts on the brain to produce particular developmental outcomes, namely by means of **EXPERIENCE-EXPECTANT** and **EXPERIENCE-DEPENDENT** mechanisms:

- Experience-expectant mechanisms refer to species-typical experiences in environments that all members of a given species can expect at certain developmental periods. As a result they arrive in the world 'pre-wired' to respond in certain ways to certain stimuli at certain times: the chick, for example, by following parent-like objects in the period immediately after hatching, the human infant by smiling at certain facial features of their care-takers in the early weeks of life.

- Experience-dependent mechanisms in contrast are individual-specific. They involve experiences that are unique to particular individuals, such as the multitude of specific cognitive and linguistic stimuli that children encounter as they grow up, and which thus bring about the formation of new neural connections. Insofar as the timing, as well as the nature, of these experiences will differ from one individual to another the nervous system must be ready to incorporate the information at any time.

According to this view, sensitive periods are restricted to those aspects of development that are experience-expectant; the concept does not serve in explaining experience-dependent developments. Whatever the merits of this proposal, it does at least go beyond the merely descriptive use of sensitive periods in attempting to link these up with neural mechanisms, thus throwing light on what actually happens at such times.

Further reading
Bornstein, M. (1989). Sensitive periods in development: structural characteristics and causal interpretations. *Psychological Bulletin, 105*, 179–197. A very detailed look at precisely what is implied when descriptive or explanatory use is made of sensitive periods.

See also **attachment; bonding; developmental stages; fixed action patterns**

BRAIN PLASTICITY

This concept refers to –

MEANING

> the flexibility of brain organization, with particular reference to the ability of cortical areas to take over the functions of other areas.

When, for example, a human being suffers brain damage questions may be asked about the ease with which other areas can substitute for the damaged one. If particular areas are solely dedicated to some specific psychological function this will not be possible; if there is equipotentiality among areas recovery can occur. While much of the debate in the past concerning this issue has taken an either–or form, it is now apparent that we are in fact concerned with a continuum, in that it is the *degree* of functional plasticity of different areas of the brain that is the issue.

ORIGINS Interest in the localization of brain functions goes back many centuries, even to the days of the Ancient Greeks. For most of that time there was little doubt that the brain is rigidly divided into specific areas, each serving a particular function, the only issue being where these areas are located. This belief found its most extreme expression in *phrenology* – the doctrine first articulated in the eighteenth century by Gall and Spurzheim, which holds that the mind is composed of a finite number of mental faculties all located in some particular area of the brain and detectable by feeling the bumps on the head. Phrenology was very much the fashion in Britain and the United States in the early part of the nineteenth century, before becoming discredited by the total absence of supporting evidence.

Scientifically acceptable findings gradually began to emerge in the course of the twentieth century, coming from studies of both humans and animals. The former involved detailed investigations of patients with brain injury, of which a tragically large number became available as a result of the two World Wars. By describing the correspondence between structural damage and functional disability and by tracing the subsequent course of that disability an attempt was made to determine the extent to which recovery is possible as a result of non-damaged areas taking over the functions of damaged areas. Of particular significance in this respect were studies of children with brain damage, in that they introduced a developmental dimension to the notion of plasticity. Comparing patients who had suffered damage at various ages, it was first concluded that plasticity is directly related to age: the younger the child the greater the chances of compensation by other areas (Goodman, 1991). Some writers went so far as to conclude from this that the brain is initially a complete blank, with no area predisposed to serve any specific function. However, such an extreme expression of the equipotentiality view of the brain has turned out to be as unacceptable as its opposite, the belief that each area is destined for one particular purpose only and cannot take over any other function. As later studies have shown, age and plasticity do vary, but in a complex manner that requires consideration of other influences too.

Studies of human patients perforce rely on 'experiments of nature'; animal investigations can generally introduce a greater degree of precision – though in the case of brain functioning sometimes with the use of ethically questionable practices. Among the procedures employed are the following:

- Surgically disconnecting a specific area of the brain from its usual sensory input.
- 'Rewiring' sensory input so that it projects to another area.
- Transplanting a piece of cortex to a new location in the brain.
- Removing certain cortical pieces either unilaterally or bilaterally at various specified areas.

These and other experimental procedures (see Johnson, 1997) have yielded a considerable amount of information. However, it must be borne in mind that most of the studies have involved rodents or cats and not primates, and generalization across species, especially from rats to humans, needs to be done with great caution.

The concept of plasticity has in recent years attracted a considerable upsurge of **CURRENT** interest, resulting from the availability of new techniques for investigating its **STATUS** nature and developmental course. As to animal studies, findings obtained so far indicate that cortical reorganization is possible in the various species investigated, though constraints such as age set some limit on the extent to which this occurs (see Johnson, Munakata & Gilmore, 2002, for details). Some degree of plasticity is thus an inherent characteristic of the brain in these species.

As far as human beings are concerned, the following findings suggest a similar conclusion:

- Language functions normally depend on certain areas in the left cortical hemisphere. If these are damaged in childhood (but not thereafter) areas in the right hemisphere can substitute for them.
- However, the same degree of plasticity is not found with respect to other behaviour systems, such as visuo-spatial processing which is largely mediated by the right hemisphere. Damage in that part of the brain will not so easily be compensated for by the other hemisphere taking over.
- Variations exist even among subsystems: for example semantic and grammatical aspects of language processing are mediated by different neural pathways and as a result the constraints on plasticity differ for the two.
- Considerable reorganization occurs in the brain in cases of sensory deprivation such as caused by deafness. When deafness is present from early on enhanced activity in certain parts of the visual cortex occurs: other intact sensory systems, that is, are affected by the absence of auditory stimulation. This is not found, however, among those who become deaf later in life.
- Among users of manual sign language the right hemisphere becomes activated rather than the left as is the case for spoken language. The nature of language input thus affects the neural organization of the brain. Here too the effect is confined to those who acquire sign language in early childhood.
- In blind individuals the visual areas of the cortex become active during tactile tasks such as reading Braille; these areas, it appears, do not lie 'empty' but come to serve touch. Among sighted individuals tactile activity does not produce this effect.
- Amputation of a limb such as the arm also does not result in the corresponding cortical area becoming inactive. Instead, the area becomes responsive to stimulation of the face which would normally go exclusively to a part of the cortex adjacent to that which serves the arm. This is found even when amputation takes place in adulthood.

These and other examples (see Neville and Bavelier, 2002; Stiles, Bates, Thal, Tranner & Reilly, 2002) indicate that brain plasticity is a real phenomenon in human beings, in that reorganization of structure and function can take place under certain circumstances. The view that each area of the cortex is destined to serve only one particular purpose is clearly wrong: some transfer from one area to another is possible. The view at the other extreme, however, that the brain represents an empty region at the start of life and is thus infinitely malleable, is obviously also wrong: the fact that in nearly all human beings the same areas serve the same functions is an indication that some degree of predetermination does occur.

Thus, according to the present state of knowledge (and a great deal concerning plasticity still remains to be established) the main task is to investigate the precise conditions under which reorganization is possible. One such condition is clearly age. By and large (and there are many exceptions), the younger the individual the greater the degree of brain plasticity tends to be. As the brain grows, a 'restriction of fate' (as Johnson, 1999, has referred to it) takes place, resulting from the interaction of preset characteristics and experience. Experience brings work for the brain to do, giving rise to a range of neural changes, especially in synaptic organization (see Kolb & Wishaw, 1998), which account for the increasing differentiation of the brain into specialized areas and consequent decrease of plasticity. However, the extent to which this decrease occurs with age remains controversial. Charles Nelson (2000), for example, has argued strongly that given suitable experience the brain can remain remarkably plastic through much of the life-span, with particular reference to such cognitive systems as learning and memory. The other main condition for affecting plasticity is behaviour system: language and cognition can on the whole remain flexible for much longer than, say, sensory systems and spatial processing. The reasons for these differences remain uncertain.

Further reading

Johnson, M.H. (1999). Cortical plasticity in normal and abnormal cognitive development: evidence and working hypotheses. *Development and Psychopathology, 11*, 419–437. Reviews the evidence on plasticity in the human cortex, indicating an increasing restriction over age and the role that experience plays in this process.

Nelson, C.A. (2000). Neural plasticity and human development: the role of early experience in sculpting memory systems. *Developmental Science, 3*, 115–136. Sets out to demonstrate that plasticity is not confined to the young brain but can also be found in maturity.

See also **critical (sensitive) periods**

GENE–ENVIRONMENT EFFECTS
and: **GENE-ENVIRONMENT CORRELATION**
GENE-ENVIRONMENT INTERACTION

MEANING Gene–environment effects is the comprehensive term given to –

all aspects of the interrelationship among genetic and environmental influences on behaviour and development.

The concept thus signifies progress made in going beyond the crude dichotomy of nature *or* nurture and instead is part of the effort to analyse how hereditary and environmental forces *jointly* direct the developmental course of individuals along certain pathways.

A distinction is made between two main kinds of such effects. GENE–ENVIRONMENT CORRELATION refers to –

> *the extent to which the kind of experiences people have are related to their particular genetic make-up.*

Such correlations may be brought about in several distinct ways (see below), but all involve the tendency for individuals to live in environments that are compatible with their inherited propensities – academically intelligent children, for example, are likely to live in homes with many books, aggressive children watch more violent TV programmes and artistically gifted children tend to choose friends of similar inclination. Environment and natural inclination are thus often closely associated.

GENE–ENVIRONMENT INTERACTION refers to the fact that –

> *environments have effects on individuals that differ according to each person's genetic make-up.*

This concept draws attention to the differences among people in their genetically determined susceptibility to particular environmental influences – emotionally vulnerable children, for example, are more affected by family stress than emotionally robust children, just as babies who are unable to metabolize the amino acid phenylalanine found in milk are in danger of becoming mentally retarded whereas all other babies are not so affected.

Discussions about the nature–nurture issue are of long standing and were carried on in past centuries mainly by philosophers. It was not until the latter half of the nineteenth century that two men ensured that the subject became a matter of scientific investigation: Gregor Mendel, a monk working in his monastery garden on the inheritance of pea plants, whose paper published in 1866 laid down the basic rules of inheritance and who hypothesised the existence of genes (though he called them 'elements') long before they were actually discovered; and Francis Galton, who was inspired by the writings of his cousin, Charles Darwin, to investigate the hereditary mechanisms underlying evolution and who was the first to suggest the use of family, twin and adoption studies for this purpose in an 1869 book.

ORIGINS

With the discovery in the course of the twentieth century of genes as the basic units of heredity the nature–nurture issue was reformulated in terms of genes and environment, and when taken up by psychologists led to the advent of the science of *behavioural genetics*, the aim of which is to investigate the genetic *and* environmental factors that create behavioural differences among individuals (Plomin, DeFries, McClearn & McGuffin, 2001). Psychological studies of these factors have concerned themselves successively with three questions, each in due course replacing its predecessor as outdated:

1 Which of the two, genes or environment, is responsible for the development of behavioural characteristics? This is a continuation of the age-old assumption that the two act separately as independent forces and that particular traits are explicable in terms of either one or the other – an assumption now known to be mistaken and thus abandoned.

2 How much of any given characteristic can be ascribed to genes and how much to the environment? Instead of asking whether it is one *or* the other the issue became one of apportioning their respective influence among the two. Behaviour geneticists have defended this as a legitimate question even though the two sets of influences are still treated as separate (Plomin, 1994), for in this way one can ascertain whether both do play a part in shaping the development of traits. A measure called *heritability*, developed for this purpose and expressed as a ratio, is widely used to denote the extent to which genetic rather than environmental influences account for the variations among individuals in the expression of a trait. Thus a ratio of .50 for, say, intelligence indicates that genes and environment are equally important in accounting for differences among people's intelligence; a ratio of 1.00 on the other hand would suggest that only genes play a part and not environmental influences. Heritability has all the attractions of a single index, but like so many other single indices used in psychology to denote complex phenomena (e.g. the IQ) it is highly controversial, especially so because it is not a 'pure' measure but can vary from sample to sample and from time to time. Furthermore, it has nothing to say about the processes whereby the two sets of influences interact to produce the behavioural outcome in individuals.

3 The third question addresses itself to the last point: *how* do genes and the environment combine to shape development? In a highly influential paper entitled 'Heredity, environment and the question How?', Anne Anastasi (1958) stressed the importance of investigating the *processes* whereby nature and nurture jointly operate, arguing that a more fruitful approach than attempting to answer the 'How much' question is to examine 'How' aspects. It is with this aim in mind that the concepts of gene–environment correlation and interaction were developed.

CURRENT STATUS The fact that both genes and environment are involved in virtually all aspects of psychological functioning is now generally accepted. Indeed, whatever reservations there may be about the heritability index the research using it has demonstrated this clearly. Findings have led to two main conclusions. First, there is a genetic component in virtually all psychological characteristics investigated, from general intelligence to amount of television viewing. The size of that component varies from trait to trait: cognitive chararacteristics such as intelligence, visuo-spatial abilities, literacy and dyslexia have on the whole been found to be more heritable than personality characteristics such as extraversion, neuroticism and conscientiousness. And in the second place, in every instance where genetic factors have been implicated they account for only part of individual variability: even in cases of psychopathology such as schizophrenia the heritability index does not go above 50 per cent the remainder being mainly due to environmental influences (Plomin et al., 2001). Thus neither genes nor environments operate in isolation: there can be no behaviour without genes or without environment. The two operate conjointly to affect development.

Research on the developmental interplay of genes and environment is still sparse, but has at least shown the usefulness of distinguishing between the different forms that the relationship takes. Considering gene–environment correlations first, that is to say the association between people's genetic make-up and the environment they tend to be exposed to, one can differentiate three different ways in which this is brought about (Scarr & McCartney, 1983):

- *Passive* correlation occurs because parents provide both heredity and experience for their children. For example, children who inherit a predisposition to high intelligence from their parents are also likely to live in homes with a lot of book-related activity in the home, reflecting the interests of their parents; as a result of the two intertwined influences of heredity and environment it is highly likely that superior achievement by the child in an intellectual activity like reading will be found.
- *Evocative* correlation results from children eliciting particular kinds of response from carers by virtue of their inborn characteristics. A child inclined by nature to be outgoing and sociable will elicit a lot more positive responses from other people than a quiet, solemn one, and while in the past sociability in children was automatically attributed to their treatment by others this approach draws attention to the possibility that the cause-effect sequence may also operate from child to type of treatment.
- *Active* correlation refers to instances where individuals themselves take the initiative in choosing what environments to attend to, actively seek or even create. This is an example of *niche picking* (see **developmental niche**), that is, where people themselves actively select those settings that are compatible with their genetic predisposition. Thus an aggressive, hyperactive child will seek the company of like-minded peers, in order to have the opportunity to engage in congenial activities and act out his or her genetic tendencies. Similarly, a musically gifted child will pursue whatever opportunities present themselves to engage in music-related interests. We create our experiences, that is, in part for genetic reasons.

The respective prominence of these three mechanisms tends to change with age: in the early years passive and evocative kinds are most salient, whereas in later childhood and especially in adolescence, when individuals increasingly make their own choices, the active kind will dominate.

Genotype–environment interaction, describing the varying susceptibility of individuals with different genetic propensities to particular environmental influences, has so far attracted only a limited number of research projects directly investigating this relationship. Most of these are in the psychopathology area: see, for example, the demonstration by O'Connor, Caspi, DeFries & Plomin. (2003) that adopted children at genetic risk for maladjustment (as indexed by their biological parents' psychopathology) are more likely to be adversely affected by an environmental stress such as the marital troubles of their adoptive parents than adopted children not at genetic risk. In other words, genetic vulnerability is accentuated by major adverse life experiences: the experiences alone do not fully account for the effect on children. Similarly stressful events have been shown to be more likely to produce depression in individuals who are at genetic risk for depression (Kendler et al., 1995); adopted children are at greater risk of developing antisocial behaviour when *both* biological parents and adoptive parents have a criminal record (Bohman, 1996); and studies of temperament (a characteristic usually regarded as primarily genetic in origin – see **temperament**) have repeatedly pointed to the interplay of this characteristic and environmental experience (Sanson, Hemphill & Smart, 2004). This is particularly well illustrated by Kochanska's work (e.g. 1997), which showed that the effectiveness of any specific parental disciplinary technique depends largely on the temperament of the child to whom it is applied: a gentle style of discipline facilitates conscience development in fearful preschoolers but has little effect on fearless children. The general conclusion is that developmental outcomes, customarily attributed in the past to environmental factors, may well be mediated in part by genetic factors.

While we are still ignorant about many aspects of the relationship of genes and environment, it does seem likely that a **dynamic systems** view is the most appropriate model to adopt in attempts to understand the nature of this relationship. Genetic and environmental influences, that is, interact in a bidirectional manner where neither the one nor the other drives the process and neither can therefore be said to take precedence as the cause of development. Rather, development needs to be seen as proceeding in an **epigenetic** manner, where the progressive interaction of certain genes and certain environments will inevitably give rise to the sequential emergence of new developmental structures and functions (Gottlieb, 1997).

Further reading

Bateson, P., & Martin, P. (1999). *Design for a life: how behaviour develops.* London: Jonathan Cape. Written for the general reader, the book argues that psychological development is like cooking, with genetic and environmental influences as ingredients which, like the ingredients of a soufflé, are impossible to distinguish in the final product.

Deater-Deckard, K., & Cahill, K. (2006). Nature and nurture in early childhood. In K. McCartney & D. Phillips (Eds.), *Blackwell handbook of early childhood development.* Oxford: Blackwell. Succinct overview of recent findings in the field of behavioural genetics, including sections on gene–environment correlation and interaction.

Plomin, R., DeFries, J.C., McClearn, G.E., & McGuffin, P. (2001). *Behavioral genetics* (4th ed.). New York: Worth. A chapter on the interplay of genotype and environment is included in this authoritative book.

See also **developmental niche; dynamic systems; epigenesis; temperament**

INDIVIDUALITY

4

FOUR

According to William Damon (1983), when thinking about the growth of children's personality it is useful to distinguish between two developmental trends: *socialization* and *individuation*. Socialization refers to all those processes whereby children become integrated into their community by learning about and adopting as their own the values and customs prevailing therein: how to maintain relationships with others, how to communicate comprehensibly, how to regulate emotions in an acceptable manner and so forth. But whereas socialization ensures that children become *like* other people, individuation is concerned with children being *different* from others in that it refers to the processes whereby children acquire an identity that is unique to them – an identity that distinguishes them from others and that ensures that they are seen as individuals in their own right.

The need to define oneself and so be able to answer the question 'Who am I?' is a life-long process but assumes major importance in childhood and adolescence. This is a complex, multifaceted undertaking, starting with the biological characteristics that make children distinctive from the beginning and proceeding to the establishment of a sense of self and the progressive acquisition of both a personal and a social identity. It encompasses not only the objective reality of the child's uniqueness as assessed by, say, a professional person but also the subjective feelings which each individual has regarding his or her uniqueness. The following concepts have been used to help our understanding of these developments:

TEMPERAMENT
and: **Goodness of fit**
THE SELF SYSTEM
and: **Self-awareness**
    Self-concept
    Self-esteem
SOCIAL IDENTITY
and: **Identity crisis**
    Ethnic identity
    Gender identity
VULNERABILITY–RESILIENCE
and: **Risk factors and protective factors**
INDIVIDUALISM–COLLECTIVISM

TEMPERAMENT
and: GOODNESS OF FIT

MEANING   Various different definitions of temperament have been advanced, but there is general agreement that the term refers to personal characteristics that are biologically based, are evident from birth onwards, are consistent across situations and have some degree of stability, and that it concerns general dispositions rather than discrete traits. As Thomas and Chess (1977) have put it:

> Temperament may best be viewed as a general term referring to the *how* of behaviour. It differs from ability, which is concerned with the *what* and *how well* of behaving, and from motivation, which accounts for the *why* a person is doing what he is doing. Temperament, by contrast, concerns the *way* in which an individual behaves.

Emotional vigour, activity level, responsiveness and behavioural inhibition – these are some of the characteristics that come under the umbrella of temperament. It may thus be defined as –

> *the set of inborn characteristics that distinguish one person from another in the behavioural style they manifest.*

ORIGINS   The idea of temperament as a quality inherent in human beings goes back over 2000 years to the Greek philosopher Galen, who put forward a four-fold classification of temperament types, each linked to a particular body fluid said to be predominant in any one individual. Thus someone with a predominance of blood is sanguine in temperament (warm and affectionate); black bile is associated with melancholia (depressed, prone to sadness); yellow bile leads to a choleric temperament (irritable, prone to aggression); and phlegm characterizes phlegmatic (slow to respond, unexcitable) individuals.

Despite continued interest in individual variability, it was not until mid-twentieth century that systematic, large-scale efforts to investigate temperament empirically were made. The first of these was the highly productive and influential New York Longitudinal Study, carried out by Thomas and Chess and their colleagues (e.g. 1963, 1977). Based on a sample of 138 individuals who were followed up from birth to adulthood, a massive amount of data was gathered periodically by a variety of means from parents, teachers and the children themselves. Their findings convinced Thomas and Chess that whatever developmental changes in behaviour they observed over this period occurred against a background of continuity (see **developmental continuity**), which could best be expressed in terms of a number of temperamental dimensions that first manifested themselves in infancy as *primary reaction patterns* (as Thomas and Chess referred to them). Nine such dimensions were identified, largely by inductive content analysis of parental reports, namely activity level, regularity, approach–withdrawal, adaptability, response threshold, intensity, mood quality, distractibility and attention span. From these dimensions Thomas and Chess derived a further three-way typology, namely *easy* children (adaptable, positive in mood and regular in their behaviour), *difficult* children (intense and often negative in mood, resistant to change and unpredictable) and *slow-to-warm up* children (showing a mixture of the characteristics of the other two groups). Of these, the *difficult* category attracted most interest, and though eventually found to be too value-laden and dependent on parental reaction, a considerable amount of research was stimulated thereby in order to investigate the social and clinical implications of having children who, especially in infancy, provide their caretakers with problems of management (Sanson, Hemphill & Smart, 2004).

Other attempts to investigate the structure of temperament and isolate its component dimensions followed that by Thomas and Chess, but using rather more sophisticated methods like factor analysis for this purpose in order to avoid weaknesses such as overlap between dimensions which characterized the New York study. Various proposals have resulted from these efforts (for review see Rothbart & Bates, 1998), but though there is a certain amount of overlap between these no general consensus has as yet emerged as to the number, nature or naming of temperament dimensions.

Temperament continues to be seen as a focus for considerable research into the biological precursors of individual variability. Among the main topics currently being pursued are the following (for further details see Molfese & Molfese, 2000; Rothbart & Bates, 1998):

CURRENT STATUS

- *The composition of temperament.* As we have just seen, much uncertainty remains about the dimensions that describe the concept. There are indications that among the various proposals that have been put forward three basic dimensions tend to recur, though under a variety of names: reactivity (referring to such aspects as negative mood, irritability, inflexibility), self-regulation (emotional and attentional control, persistence, non-distractibility), and approach/withdrawal (the general tendency to respond positively or negatively to novel situations and people). No one would contend, however, that this is a final list, and it may well be that quite new dimensions will be identified as different behavioural items are fed into factor analyses.
- *Measurement.* How best to assess temperament is still a matter of debate. Of the two main ways used, parental report (or self-report at later ages) and observation (in real-life situations or in the laboratory), each has its advocates; however, in view of the general recognition that each has both advantages and disadvantages a strong case has been made for investigators wherever possible to use a combination of the two.

- *Heritability*. Research on the behavioural genetics of temperament carried out so far has indicated moderate to substantial heritability indices. However, as pointed out under **gene–environment effects**, the major challenge now is to find out by what means genetic and environmental influences interact to shape behavioural outcome, and this applies as much to temperamental characteristics as to any other psychological aspects. There is certainly no indication that any dimension of temperament is fixed for good by heredity: the highest heritability estimates reported are in the region of .60 and many are considerably lower, leaving plenty of room for life experience to help determine outcome.

- *Stability*. The last point has implications for the question of stability over age. As pointed out under **developmental continuity**, absolute stability of any trait is rarely found; the varying effects of experience on biological structures ensures this. Most studies of temperamental stability have come up with fairly modest correlations over time of .2 to 4; while these indicate a continuing influence of forces present from early on they also point out once again the need to investigate the processes whereby different environments can steer initially similar individuals into different directions (see **developmental trajectories**).

- *The relationship of early temperament to later personality characteristics*. Temperament itself, at least as manifested in infancy, may not be wholly stable over age, but does it nevertheless predict the kind of personality that is found in later childhood and adulthood? In other words, is there continuity of underlying structures despite change in overt manifestation? There have been various claims to this effect (e.g. by Caspi, 2000); specifically, there are hints that certain temperamental dimensions found in the preschool years show continuity with the Big Five factors (extraversion, agreeableness, conscientiousness, neuroticisms and openness to experience) that are said to constitute the basic framework of adult personality (Caspi, 1998). At present, however, these cannot be regarded as anything more than hints, as there is still insufficient evidence available to arrive at firmer conclusions.

There is one other topic which deserves special mention because, for one thing, it has a bearing on several of the others listed above and, for another it is likely to attract major research interest in the near future. This may best be described as the study of *temperament in context* (see Wachs & Kohnstamm, 2001), which starts from the basic premise that any biological bias acts within the framework of certain particular environments, and that treating temperament as a context-free concept therefore does scant justice to its real nature. This was a point already stressed by Thomas and Chess (1977) when they put forward the concept of **GOODNESS OF FIT**, which denotes –

the degree to which an individual's temperamental characteristics match the characteristics of the environment in which the individual lives.

The particular environment Thomas and Chess had in mind were the child's caretakers and their demands, expectations and attitudes when interacting with the child. 'Good fit' exists, for example, when a child with poor emotional control is cared for by tolerant yet firm parents; 'poor fit' when the same child has parents who are impatient, rigid disciplinarians. In the former case optimal development is the likely outcome; in the latter distorted development and maladaptive functioning may well be the result. **Context**, as we saw when describing this concept, is a highly complex phenomenon taking many different forms. Nevertheless, the goodness of fit notion can be applied also to other aspects of the environment such as its physical characteristics: a highly active child brought up in overcrowded surroundings is more likely to suffer than a less active child. And similarly it has been used in relation to different cultures and the value they attach to particular personality characteristics: the shy, quiet child will find greater acceptance in many Far Eastern countries, which foster such qualities in their children, than in the United States where a more outgoing, extraverted style is regarded as 'right' (Chen, Hastings, Rubin, Chen, Cen & Stewart, 1998).

The goodness of fit concept has been criticized for being vague and difficult to operationalize for research purposes (Campos, Barrett, Lamb, Goldsmith & Stenberg, 1983). More often than not it is used to explain findings post hoc rather than as a means of initiating research. It does, however, have considerable intuitive appeal, and serves to emphasize that temperament is not meaningful without reference to the particular environment in which individuals' development takes place. Increasing attempts are now being made to spell out the different forms which the relationship between temperament and context can take (e.g. see Wachs & Kohnstamm, 2001), based on the firm conviction that measures of temperament–context interaction are more likely to predict outcome variables such as psychosocial adjustment than temperament alone (Bates & McFadyen-Ketchum, 2000). And such an approach may also account, at least in part, for lack of stability in temperamental characteristics: if changes in the rearing environment take place there may well follow some change in the manifestation of temperament.

Further reading

Martin, J.N., & Fox, N.A. (2006). Temperament. In K. McCartney & D. Phillips (Eds.), *Blackwell handbook of early childhood development*. Oxford: Blackwell. For those who want a relatively brief overview of research in this area.

Rothbart, M.K., & Bates, J.E. (1998). Temperament. In W. Damon (Ed.), Handbook of child psychology, vol. 3 (N. Eisenberg, (Ed.). New York: Wiley. A highly authoritative, careful account of the current state of knowledge about this topic.

Sanson, A., Hemphill, S.A., & Smart, D. (2004). Connections between temperament and social development: a review. *Social Development, 13,* 142–170. Looks at the links between the various dimensions of temperament and particular aspects of psychopathology and social development, with special reference to contextual influences.

See also **context; developmental continuity; gene–environment interaction**

THE SELF SYSTEM
and: **SELF-AWARENESS**
     SELF-CONCEPT
     SELF-ESTEEM

MEANING The idea of the self is both very familiar and very elusive. It is familiar because each one of us has lived with our own private version of it since infancy, is almost constantly aware of it throughout daily life, and indeed regards it as the very essence of our individual identity. And yet it is elusive because it is in many respects a slippery concept: it is not easy to define, describe and investigate, and it is no wonder therefore that it has meant so many different things to different people. As Levin (1992) has pointed out, the self has been viewed as a soul, an underlying substrate, an activity, an explanatory hypothesis, a cognitive structure, a verbal activity, an experience, a process and a normative attainment. Moreover, some people regard it as a mere fiction, arguing that the self as some kind of substantive entity simply does not exist (Metzinger, 2003).

Despite such disagreement, or probably even because of it, a very considerable body of psychological research has come into being aimed at studying the nature, functions and developmental course of the self. There can be no doubt that people hold enormous amounts of information about themselves, and the particular ways in which this information is arranged by each individual and the kind of categories which these arrangements give rise to are clearly in need of investigation. There is, however, one lesson above all that we have learned from this research, namely that the self is by no means a simple, unitary concept but a highly complex organization of multiple constructs – interrelated, yet expressing a variety of different functions. It is therefore appropriate to refer to a *self system* rather than a *self*, and define it as –

> *the multifaceted theory that all individuals construct in the course of development as to who they are and how they fit into society, based on a sense of continuing identity at the core of one's awareness.*

Such a theory enables the individual to adopt a particular stance from which to view the world – a source of reference which mediates experience and organizes behaviour, which determines how we construe reality and what experiences to seek out, and which provides us with a sense of permanence because, whatever changes take place during the life course in the nature of this construction, we know that there is a core that has persistence in time.

From Socrates and St Augustine onwards, philosophers and theologians have speculated about the nature of the self (for a historical account of self theories see Levin, 1992). However, the first real step towards scientific analysis was taken by William James (1890). James in several respects anticipated ideas investigated a century later; above all, he proposed a distinction between two aspects of the self which he regarded as essential if we are to understand this concept, namely the 'I' and the 'Me':

ORIGINS

- The *I-self* is the subjective self, the self-as-knower, that part which thinks and feels, which organizes and interprets experiences in a purely subjective manner and which is aware of one's own distinctiveness and personal continuity over time.
- The *Me-Self* is the objective self, the self-as-known, that is the object of our perception when we contemplate ourselves and which thus expresses the way we define ourselves in terms of personal qualities and as a member of particular categories such as age, gender and ethnicity.

The distinction has remained fundamental to all subsequent efforts to analyse the self system, conceptually and empirically, even though various different terms are now usually employed for the two aspects, such as self-awareness for the 'I' and self-concept for the 'Me'. And James has also been proved right when he warned that the I-self would be much more difficult to investigate: certainly the bulk of research has concerned itself with Me-features, successfully developing measures whereby we can externalize the ways in which individuals construe and evaluate themselves.

James himself had a lot more to say about the *Me* than the *I*. The *Me*, he proposed, has three constituents, namely a spiritual, a social and a material *Me*, arranged in that order in a hierarchy of levels. He was thus one of the first to put forward a multifaceted, multi-level model; he was also one of the first, in discussing the social *Me*, to suggest that at least parts of the self have their origin in the child's interpersonal relationships. This theme was taken up and given prominence by a group of writers collectively known as *symbolic interactionists* – interactionists, because they believed the self to be a social construction formed in the course of the child's encounters with other people; symbolic, because they considered linguistic exchanges to be the most influential channel whereby this occurs. Baldwin (1895), Cooley (1902) and G.H. Mead (1934) each put forward his version of the origins and development of this constructive process, and though their accounts differ they all stressed the role of children's social experience in the formation of each individual's self. Cooley's notion of the *looking-glass-self* illustrates this most clearly: we come to view ourselves as others view us; in the course of growing up children will gradually internalize the opinions of other people, especially those closest to them; and the final product is therefore what we believe others think of us. The process is not in fact as mechanical as the metaphor suggests, for Cooley stressed the active nature of the child's efforts to incorporate the views of others in any existing self structure; nevertheless, he believed that without social experience there would be no self.

The social origins of the self is a theme also taken up by psychoanalysts such as Winnicott (1958), who believed that the major developmental task for infants in the early months of life is to differentiate themselves from the mother and establish a sense of their own identity. How successful the differentiation process is depends very much on the quality of the relationship with the mother: on the one hand she must learn when not to over-involve herself with her infant, as otherwise the child will not acquire the 'capacity for aloneness' that Winnicott regarded as central to the emergence of a stable self; on the other hand she must also not be under-involved because then she cannot provide the 'holding environment' that an infant requires to become organized as a person. The mother's sensitivity, moreover, may have long-term implications, for the pattern of the primary relationship as perceived by the infant will be internalized and not only lay the foundations for the quality of later relationships but also determine the kind of self-image the child takes away from these early encounters.

The last point has been taken up by attachment theorists and developed into a much more refined and far-reaching account. According to Bowlby (1969/1982), children, in the course of relating to their caregivers, form mental representations (**internal working models**, as he called them) of their early relationships, of the persons with whom they are formed and of themselves in tandem. The inner representation of the self thus emerges out of that first relationship though remaining open to some extent to the effects of further experience. Bowlby, like Winnicott, regarded the quality of the relationship as crucial to the course of self-development: mothers sensitive to their child's needs are likely to have secure children who will develop a positive self-image; insensitive, rejecting and ambivalent mothers will have insecure children with a negative self-image. Subsequent empirical work has by and large confirmed this view, but quite apart from the detailed information it has provided concerning the development of primary social ties, attachment theory has also played an important part in continuing to draw attention to the social origins of the self, with particular reference to its basis in early relationships.

CURRENT STATUS   Since the days of William James, an enormous amount of information has been gathered about the self system. Yet most of it is about specific aspects of the system rather than about the system as a whole. Despite some valiant efforts to model the self, its nature as an entity remains elusive.

Turning first to studies of specific aspects, the self has been cut up in different ways by different writers. Neisser (1988), for example, suggested that there are five sorts of selves that can usefully be distinguished, namely an ecological, an inter-personal, a remembered, a private and a conceptual self, each specifying a different set of information people have of themselves and thus defining a distinctive point of view from which to consider the self as a whole. However, the majority of empirical studies have singled out three aspects for investigation: self-awareness, self-concept and self-esteem.

SELF-AWARENESS refers to –

> *the realization by children that they are each a distinct being – an entity separate from all others and possessing an identity of their own.*

Such an awareness is, of course, fundamental to a sense of self and is the first part of the system to emerge. Different writers have given somewhat varying accounts of this process (e.g. Lewis, 1994; Pipp, 1993; Stern, 1985); on the whole, however, there is agreement that the development of self-awareness is a gradual process taking place over the first two years, that it involves a number of components that emerge at varying times during this period, and that the essentials of self-awareness can be said to be in place when children are capable of visual self-recognition and start using personal pronouns like 'I', 'my' and 'mine'.

The **SELF-CONCEPT** (also known as the *self-image* or as *self-representation*) refers to –

> *the specific mental representation individuals build up of themselves, in order to provide an answer to the question 'Who am I?'.*

A lot of empirical information is now available as to the nature of children's self-representations and the developmental trends evident in this respect, based on various instruments used to elicit the way children think of themselves (Harter, 1998). A number of such trends are apparent, such as the change from a focus on physical and activity-based characteristics ('I have got blue eyes and I like running') to a concern with psychological characteristics ('I am rather shy'). In addition, however, there have also been attempts to explain the processes whereby self-representations come into being and develop with age. Some of these have stressed interpersonal experiences as vital formative influences (e.g. Tomasello, 1993), while others are concerned primarily with underlying cognitive mechanisms (e.g. Markus, 1980), with special attention recently paid to the role of *autobiographical memory* in providing the child with data about past experiences. These, being personal and often of considerable emotional significance to the child, become incorporated in the individual's self-concept, are reinforced when they are shared (often repeatedly) with parents and others (Nelson, 1993b), and provide the child with a sense of continuity when the past is linked to the present and used to anticipate future events (Moore and Lemmon, 2001).

SELF-ESTEEM (also referred to as *self-worth*) is sometimes, confusingly, mixed up with self-concept. But whereas the latter is concerned with the way in which individuals *describe* themselves, self-esteem refers to the way they *evaluate* themselves, and may thus be defined as –

> the value that individuals attach to their personal qualities,
> answering the question 'How good am I?' and thus relating to
> the worthiness and competence an individual experiences with
> respect to his or her personal attributes.

According to William James (1890), such feelings are a function of the discrepancy between the *real* self and the *ideal* self – between what one has achieved and what one would like to achieve. This approach has remained basic to all subsequent thinking about self-esteem (though according to Higgins, 1991, we should also add an *ought* self, referring to the attributes we feel we ought to possess). Following the Jamesian formulation, self-esteem is therefore not so much an absolute quality but a ratio: an individual, for example, who has no aspiration to excel at mathematics will not think badly of himself if he achieves little at any mathematical task. Self-esteem in general has been linked to mental health: medium to high levels are associated with satisfaction and happiness; low levels with depression, anxiety and maladjustment (Harter, 1998).

A number of self-report instruments have been constructed to measure self-esteem, of which Susan Harter's (1999) scales are probably the most used. These distinguish different domains in which to assess individuals' beliefs about themselves, such as (in the case of young children) scholastic competence, athletic competence, social acceptance, physical appearance and behavioural conduct. Self-esteem is thus seen as made up of a number of different componets, yet Harter found it useful also to add a global self-worth scale, which asks how much individuals like themselves as people. As individuals get older more domains are added: for adolescents, for example, close friendship, romantic appeal and job competence are also taken into account. Other scales, for example that by Marsh and his colleagues (1998), are based on different ideas as to how self-esteem is constituted; as a consequence they refer to different domains in which this concept is assessed.

Turning to attempts to understand the self system as a whole, a variety of theoretical models have been put forward to account for its structure (see Marsh & Hattie, 1996, for a review of many of these). All are based on the assumption that (a) the self-system is multidimensional, (b) that the constituent dimensions are not separate factors but are interrelated and (c) that they are arranged in a hierarchy of several levels. Particularly influential is a model proposed by Marsh and his colleagues (e.g. 1990, 1998); however, different models have also been put forward – differing, that is, in the number of levels, the number of dimensions at each level, the identity and naming of both levels and dimensions, and in how they relate to each other and in particular in how they are integrated into a global self. Thus, while models are becoming increasingly sophisticated and well constructed, there is still no consensus how the self system as a whole should be conceived.

Clearly a lot more work is required to bring light to this area. According to Hattie and Marsh (1996), future research should give priority to five directions:

- Clarify how lower-order components of the self-hierarchy are linked to higher-order ones.
- Investigate how the conceptions people have of their selves affect their lives and how enhancement of their self-esteem can improve the quality of life.
- Examine the effects of social and cultural influences on the self system, including those related to gender.
- Sort out the confusion of terminology resulting from the profusion of 'self' terms currently in use.
- Sift through the very large number of instruments available for assessing the various aspects of the self in order to establish their efficacy.

Further reading

Bracken, B.A. (Ed.) (1996). *Handbook of self-concept.* New York: Wiley. Contains chapters by some of the best-known contributors to research on the self, covering a wide range of topics.

Harter, S. (1999). *The construction of the self: a developmental perspective.* New York: Guilford Press. A wide-ranging, detailed examination of all aspects of self-development, including clinical and practical implications.

See also **domain specificity; context; social identity; internal working models**

SOCIAL IDENTITY

and: IDENTITY CRISIS
GENDER IDENTITY
ETHNIC IDENTITY

MEANING There are two aspects to the concept of *identity* that can usefully be distinguished: personal and social. Personal identity refers to individuals' subjective feelings about the combination of personality characteristics which distinguishes them from others, providing them with a sense of uniqueness; it is also sometimes known as ego identity or self-identity and is used by some as equivalent to the **self-concept**. But while personal identity is concerned solely with individuals' *distinctiveness* from others, social identity refers, on the one hand, to the ways in which they are the *same* as some people by virtue of belonging to certain social groupings (ethnic, national, religious, occupational etc.) and, on the other hand, to the characteristics that *distinguish* them from all those who are members of different groupings. The concept thus covers simultaneously two core human motives: the need to belong and the need to be unique.

Social identity may thus be defined as –

> *an individual's sense of belongingness to particular social groups and a feeling of distinctiveness in comparison with members of other groups.*

Belongingness, it should be emphasized, refers to a psychological feeling and not to mere formal assignment to a social group. Membership of particular groups provides individuals with a sense of 'we'; its importance lies in the fact that it helps them in establishing a place in society – as male or female, black or white, English or Scottish and so forth. However, it should also be borne in mind that the groups from which people get their sense of social identity are not just the large-scale, mostly permanent categories to which the major share of attention has been given by writers, such as gender, ethnicity, religion, nationality and class, but also small-scale, local, maybe temporary groups as seen, for example, in gangs, athletic clubs, political societies and supporters of football teams. These too can elicit fierce loyalties and in-group/out-group feelings and so become very much a part of an individual's social identity. They may do so for only a limited period of time, but social identity is by no means a *state*, that is, an entity that inevitably remains the same once established, but should rather be thought of as a *process*, a dynamic development that retains its capacity for change in response to new circumstances. Even identities derived from such built-in characteristics as gender and race can assume new meaning in the light of, for example, changes in social attitudes or in how individuals themselves decide to construe such categories.

The idea of individual identity and the importance attached to it have always been closely associated with the nature of society prevailing at the time. Thus in medieval times, when individuals' social position was rigidly determined by birth and their status was more or less permanently fixed in society's pecking order as lord or serf, nobleman or labourer, the concept had little significance and aroused scant interest. Only much later, when society became more fluid with the rise of a middle class that could gain wealth and recognition by sheer effort, when individuals were confronted with choices and opportunities but when also, by the same token, they had to cope with far greater uncertainty as to their future life course, did the notion of identity assume meaning and eventually the status of a scientific concept (see Baumeister, 1986, for a historical account).

ORIGINS

Much of the credit for the current interest must go to Erik Erikson (1950, 1968), whose clinical orientation as a psychoanalyst led him to investigate such diverse problems as combat crises in World War II veterans, the emotional difficulties of disturbed children as revealed in their play, and the struggles of adolescents to find their place in society. The core theme, he believed, in all these individuals concerns their identity – its loss, or a failure to gain it in the first place, or a feeling of bewilderment as to how to consolidate it as a life achievement. Erikson regarded identity as a feeling of inner wholeness, as an unconscious striving for 'ego synthesis' and as 'a subjective sense of an invigorating sameness and continuity'. The quest for identity he believed to be the principal developmental task confronting every individual throughout the life-span – a quest that assumes a different form at each of the various developmental stages the individual passes through.

There are, according to Erikson, eight such stages – the 'eight ages of man' (see **developmental stages**), and of these the fifth, that corresponding to adolescence, presents the most severe challenge to young people in their attempt to establish an individual identity. It is then that they are likely to experience an **IDENTITY CRISIS** – Erikson's most notable concept among those he passed on through his writings. The term denotes –

> *a period of confusion and low self-esteem that occurs as a normative event during adolescence.*

It is a crisis because the post-puberty individual is simultaneously confronted by a changed body image, by the new pressures of sexuality and by the need to make crucial choices among different educational and occupational possibilities and among alternative belief systems, all giving rise to considerable emotional upheaval and making this a time of conflict and uncertainty. Resolution of these conflicts is required if the individual is to proceed to the next stage, that of early adulthood, and face the relevant task awaiting there, whereas failure to resolve them means continuing bewilderment as to the individual's role in life, setting the stage for a range of psychosocial problems in later years. Subsequent work has challenged Erikson's assertion that identity crisis is a universal phenomenon; in some societies, such as the Pygmies of the Kalahari Desert, adolescence is simply not recognized as a separate stage, in that children are regarded as adults as soon as they reach puberty and do not experience the storm and stress regarded in the West as a necessary accompaniment of this period of life. In general, however, Erikson's writings are widely acknowledged as having provided a most valuable developmental orientation to our attempts to understand the nature of identity, and have also inspired a considerable number of empirical research studies to fill in the details in his theoretical account (e.g. Bosma, Graafsma, Grotevant & deLevita, 1994; Marcia, 1999).

While Erikson did not differentiate between personal and social identity, the other major relevant theory in this area quite specifically focused on social identity – not surprisingly as its origins lay in social rather than developmental psychology. *Social identity theory*, as spelled out by Henri Tajfel and his colleagues (e.g. Tajfel, 1978; Tajfel & Turner, 1979), and its subsequent extension by John Turner's *self-categorization theory* (Turner, Hogg, Oakes, Reicher & Wetherall, 1987), is primarily concerned with intergroup relationships; however, Tajfel was also very much aware of the fact that groups are able to furnish individuals with a sense of identity, and the theory thus sets out to explain the implications that group membership has for identity formation. The following propositions provide a framework for the theory:

- Human beings have a natural tendency to categorize the information they obtain from their environment; this enables them to order and make predictable their experiences.
- This applies not only to the inanimate world but also to other people; these are categorized primarily as similar to or different from oneself (in-group or out-group respectively).
- A substantial portion of individuals' sense of identity is derived from their membership of particular groups. As people are generally motivated to evaluate themselves positively they will also evaluate their in-groups positively.
- This is achieved partly through comparison with groups to which the individual does *not* belong (out-groups); these are evaluated negatively or at least less positively than the in-group. The perceived difference between in- and out-groups is frequently exaggerated; this may result in stereotyping, discrimination and even overt conflict.
- Group membership gives individuals a sense of belonging; the positive social identity that they thus obtain contributes to feelings of worthiness and well-being which individuals will strive to maintain.

Social identity theory thus suggests that a close link exists between individuals' group membership and their social identity, and indicates the mechanisms whereby that link becomes established. The writings of Tajfel and his colleagues do not approach this from a developmental point of view; however, among the numerous studies that have been stimulated by the theory (see Capozza & Brown, 2000), there is now an increasing number that have examined these processes also in children (see Bennett & Sani, 2004).

Recent attempts to spell out the nature of social identity have largely taken place by examining its manifestation in specific domains such as, in particular, gender and ethnicity. As to the former, a large body of work has focused on gender differentiation generally (see Archer & Lloyd, 2002; Ruble & Martin, 1998), with gender identity development being one of the main themes investigated. **GENDER IDENTITY** refers to –

CURRENT STATUS

> *the knowledge that each individual belongs to one sex and not the other and that certain physical and behavioural attributes distinguish the two sexes.*

The ability to identify oneself and others as male or female is already present by 1½ to 2 years of age, by which time children can correctly label themselves as a boy or a girl; the ability to identify others emerges soon after. Thus gender identity appears to be the earliest form of social categorization children can make, probably because there are only two categories to distinguish and because it is so prominent in parents' differential behaviour to their children. According to Kohlberg (1966), however, in a seminal paper analysing the development of gender identity, the ability correctly to label males and females is, on its own, not a sufficient index that children have grasped this concept. In addition, they must also understand that an individual's gender remains stable throughout life – an insight they acquire around 3–4 years of age; and furthermore they need to realize that it is a consistent attribute, in that an individual's masculinity or femininity remains constant despite changes in clothes, hairstyle or other irrelevant characteristics, and this does not generally appear until 5 or 6 years. There are thus three aspects to gender identity, concerned respectively with *labelling, stability* and *consistency* – a distinction that has become apparent by adopting a developmental approach and thereby discerning the different ages of emergence. There are doubts whether (as Kohlberg believed) these differences can be explained by means of Piagetian stages of cognitive development – whether, for example, children cannot achieve gender consistency until they are capable of operational thinking. What is widely agreed, however, is that the acquisition of gender identity is not an automatic development proceeding in passive children but that, on the contrary, it involves children's active attempts to understand and interpret both their own and others' gender, gradually constructing this concept over a number of years and thus eventually incorporating it as one of the main filters of social cognition.

ETHNIC IDENTITY may be described as –

> *an awareness of being a member of a specific ethnic group combined with a sense of belonging to that group.*

In an ethnically homogenous society such a concept is virtually meaningless, in that it requires comparison with other ethnic groups to become real to individuals. The extent to which it assumes such reality is very much dependent on prevailing attitudes in society: where there are tensions between different ethnic groups, and especially where minority groups feel discriminated against by the majority, people's identity is highlighted and becomes a prominent feature in their lives. Synagogue attendance among Jews, for example, increased sharply in pre-World War II Germany as the distinction between Aryans and non-Aryans became ever more publicised and Nazi persecution of the latter ever more severe. However, conflicts based on ethnicity occur not only *between* but also *within* individuals, as seen especially among recent immigrants who may be torn between wanting to preserve their original cultural customs and adopting those of their new homeland (e.g. Farver, Bhadha & Narang, 2002).

Ethnic identity, like gender identity, is made up of different components. Among those that have been distinguished are *salience* (that is, the extent to which ethnicity is regarded as an important part of individuals' self-concept), *centrality* (the extent to which individuals customarily define themselves in terms of their ethnicity), *ideology* (the beliefs, opinions and attitudes which individuals hold concerning the actions of members of their ethic group) and *regard* (positive or negative feelings towards one's ethnicity). For the sake of empirical study assessment instruments have been developed to measure these various aspects, for example the Multidimensional Inventory of Black Identity (Sellers, Shelton, Cooke, Chavours, Rowley & Smith, 1998). The lists produced, however, are of an a priori nature and derived from adolescents or adults; tracing the development of children's ethnic identity over age has produced a rather different set. The developmental phases pinpointed vary slightly from one writer to another; the following is derived from a number of proposals (see Nesdale, 2004; Ruble, Alavasez, Bachman, Cameron, Fuligni, Coll & Rhee, 2004):

1 *Undiffferentiated.* In the first 2 years or so children show little awareness of the perceptual cues that distinguish members of different ethnic groups; even when they do by, for example, differentially attending to photos of black and white faces, they are unlikely to do so consistently.

2 *Ethnic awareness*, being the ability to distinguish people on the basis of their ethnicity, is evident from about 3 years and is mostly well in place by age 4. This is usually assessed by asking children to label pictures or dolls that differ in such cues as skin colour, though here as with other aspects of identity the precise age of achievement depends very much on the particular method used for assessment.

3 *Ethnic identification* refers to children's understanding that they belong to a particular ethnic group and that others belong to particular groups too. That is, they can talk and think about themselves as members of that group and thus show at least a dawning of a sense of 'we', though whether the development of self-identification coincides with or precedes that of other-identification remains uncertain. The age of attainment is thought to be about a year or more later than that for ethnic awareness, though there is considerable variability in this respect from one study to another.

4 *Ethnic preference* for one's own group, at least as shown by white children in North America and Europe, first appears around age 4 and increases in strength from then to age 7. Minority children, on the other hand, are less certain in their preference, sometimes showing a 'white bias' and not settling for their own group until several years later.

5 *Ethnic constancy* involves the knowledge that ethnicity is not changeable and that it is a consistent characteristic that is not influenced by changes in appearance or manner. As with gender, it is thought by some to require the cognitive ability to think in operational terms and appreciate the immutability of entities despite contextual changes. It appears after age 5 and has been achieved by most children by age 7.

Empirical studies have examined both the antecedent influences on ethnic identity development such as parental and peer pressures (e.g. Aboud & Doyle, 1996) and its consequences for such aspects as self-concept, psychosocial adjustment and academic attainment (e.g. Chavous, Bernat, Schmeelk-Cone, Caldwell, Kohn-Wood & Zimmerman, 2003). Few attempts, however, have been made to combine the various domains included under social identity in one overall conceptual scheme and examine the developmental sequences and processes that may be common to gender, ethnic, national and other forms of social identity (though see Ruble et al., 2004). In general, however, the focus has swung away from descriptive studies, such as those aiming to trace the succession of phases characterizing the development of social identity, to investigations of the meaning which children of different ages attach to membership of social groups, that is, how they think about and understand social identity and how eventually they internalize it as part of the self.

Further reading

Bennett, M., & Sani, F. (Eds.) (2004). *The development of the social self*. Hove: Psychology Press. A useful, up-to-date account of work on social identity as inspired by the social identity theory, including chapters on gender and ethnic identity formation.

Kroger, J. (Ed.) (1993). *Discussions on ego identity*. Hillsdale, NJ: Erlbaum. Provides an account by various contributors of theoretical and empirical developments inspired by Erikson's theory of identity.

See also **individualism–collectivism; self-concept**

VULNERABILITY–RESILIENCE
and: RISK FACTORS and PROTECTIVE FACTORS

MEANING Among the very many characteristics that distinguish people some have received rather more attention than others. One of the more prominent is the extent to which individuals are susceptible to adversity and stress – an important topic because of its link to the development of psychopathology. As has become very apparent, children experiencing abuse, deprivation, neglect and other misfortunes vary greatly in their response: while many become maladjusted there are others who survive apparently unscathed. A continuum from vulnerability to resilience describes these individual differences in susceptibility.

Vulnerability and resilience may respectively be defined as –

> *the susceptibility to develop malfunctioning following exposure to stressful life events, as opposed to the capacity to maintain competent functioning following stress.*

The two terms are regarded by most writers as representing the opposite ends of the same continuum, so that individuals can be ranged at all points between the extremes. Initially, vulnerability–resilience was regarded as referring to a fixed attribute of individuals – a permanent, stable characteristic in the sense that, say, intelligence used to be thought of. There is now considerable doubt about this view: while in any one situation and at any one age individuals do vary greatly in their susceptibility to stress there are also variations within individuals over time and situation, making it more appropriate to think of that characteristic as a dynamic state that tends to fluctuate (though within limits) according to ongoing circumstances (Cummings, Davies & Campbell, 2000).

Vulnerability and resilience are closely linked to another pair of concepts, namely **RISK FACTORS** and **PROTECTIVE FACTORS.** These refer respectively to –

conditions that increase the probability of some undesirable outcome or, on the contrary, conditions that buffer individuals against undesirable outcomes.

They draw attention to the fact that a child's reaction to stress takes place in the context of a wide range of other influences: some, such as the child's success in dealing with previous stress encounters (a protective factor) stemming from past history, while others, such as a disorganized family situation (a risk factor), refer to ongoing circumstances. Risk research has its roots in epidemiology and the efforts made to explain variations in mortality and morbidity; when applied to psychopathology it similarly aims to find the factors that, on the one hand, bring about or aggravate maladjustment and, on the other, prevent or ameliorate it. The extent to which children are able to withstand adversity, that is, does not just depend on the nature and severity of that experience but will also be affected by the various risk and protective factors to which they are or have been exposed and the balance between these two sets (Masten, Best & Garmezy, 1990).

ORIGINS

In popular opinion children have always been regarded as vulnerable, at any rate in comparison with adults, and therefore in need of extra care and protection. Reports on the effects of abuse, deprivation, neglect and other adversities tended therefore to concentrate on ill-effects, and it is only comparatively recently that proper appreciation has been given to the fact that there are not only victims but also survivors, that is to say that some children do not show signs of consequent pathology and it is therefore necessary to pay attention to the nature of resilience as well as to that of vulnerability (see Clarke & Clarke, 2003, for a review).

One of the earliest systematic examinations of resilience was by Lois Murphy and her colleagues (Murphy & Moriarty, 1976). They preferred the term *coping* to designate children's successful adaptation to stress, but widened its scope to refer also to the capacity to deal with opportunities and challenges, all of which they considered to result from the operation of a number of mechanisms including biological homeostasis and past success in dealing with challenging tasks. However, of special significance to our knowledge of this topic was the account by Emmy Werner and Ruth Smith (1982) of a highly ambitious research project, in which all children born in one year on the Hawaiian island of Kauai were followed up from birth to adulthood in order to investigate the roots of resilience in children born and reared under conditions of high risk, brought about by such conditions as poverty, pre- and peri-natal complications, parental mental illness or alcoholism and disruption of the family unit. Many of these children developed a range of behaviour problems; what was also notable, however, was the further finding that a large proportion (about one-third) of those faced with the same adversities remained unscathed and developed into competent adults who 'worked well, played well, loved well and expected well'. In attempting to investigate what distinguished these individuals and enabled them to escape their early adversity, Werner and Smith listed a range of factors, including an easy temperament that elicited positive attention from others, a smaller family unit with wider spaces between siblings, the establishment of close bonds with parents, greater access to emotional support outside the family, more close friends and the availability of opportunities at major life transitions to improve their educational and social condition (Werner, 1993). When a chain of protective factors such as these was experienced a positive outcome in adult life was likely, in that they minimized the effect of previously encountered risk.

As a result of further studies such as Werner and Smith's, a considerable number of risk and protective factors have been identified. They take a wide variety of forms, but can be grouped under three headings (Rutter, 1987b), namely:

- *Personality features*, such as temperament, educational success and self-confidence.
- *Family characteristics*, for example, cohesion, discord, poverty, parental problems and attachment bonds.
- *Availability of external support systems*, provided by relatives, schools and peers, which encourage a child's coping efforts.

However, merely identifying such factors is not sufficient; we also need to understand how they bring about their effects – a task to which more recent work has turned.

CURRENT STATUS The lively interest presently shown in the area of developmental psychopathology has in its turn stimulated considerable work in the area of risk research and children's susceptibility to adversity. Three phases can be discerned in this work:

1 Initially the principal aim was to establish links between various risk conditions (e.g. low birth weight, parental divorce, poverty) and undesirable outcomes in children. Interest lay primarily in the strength of the statistical association between 'cause' and 'effect', with little note taken of individual variability or the processes that bring it about. A largely mechanistic conception thus prevailed, with children seen as passive recipients pulled and pushed by external forces.

2 Subsequently, the need to refine both the precipitating risk conditions and the outcome came to be recognized if one wants to move towards understanding *how* the two are linked. Parental divorce, for example, is a global descriptor that refers to a variety of more specific conditions such as marital conflict, father absence and reduced financial resources, any one of which may be more potent in individual cases than the others. Similarly on the outcome side: global categories like maladjustment need breaking down into more specific symptom classifications such as *internalizing* and *externalizing* disorders; justice is thereby done to the fact that exposure to risk results not only in different degrees of pathology but also in different kinds of pathology in different individuals. Refinements such as these have resulted, first, in greater predictive power from risk to outcome, and secondly in a start on understanding the processes that account for individual variability.

3 The third and currently prevailing phase involves a shift from the mechanistic view of a direct association between adversity and negative outcome to a more dynamic model, whereby the precise **developmental trajectories** are traced for individual children that lead from risk conditions to pathology or adjustment. This means a consideration of all the surrounding circumstances and ensuing processes that may play a part in bringing about particular results: *moderating* influences such as genetic vulnerability, temperament and social support that are able to change the relationship between adversity and outcome; and *mediating* influences that have a direct causal role in bringing about the end result: for example, poverty as such does not bring about a child's maladjustment, but when poverty leads to a change in the parent–child relationship because of its effect on the parent's mental state it is that change which impacts on the child and mediates the consequences of poverty.

Current work has gone beyond merely listing risk and protective factors but has begun to gain some insight into how they exert their influence. Thus it has become clear that risk factors rarely operate singly but mostly occur in combination – low socio-economic groups, for example, are not only characterized by poverty but may also experience inadequate nutrition, lack of pre- and postnatal facilities, poor mental and physical health, overcrowding, addiction problems, lack of educational opportunities and other physical and psychosocial factors that are less likely to occur among more advantaged groups. What is more, there is a linear relationship between number of risk factors experienced in early childhood and subsequent maladjustment: irrespective of the identity of the risk factors their sheer number can predict the severity of behaviour problems in adolescence (Appleyard, Egelund, van Dulmer

& Sroufje, 2005). In addition, it has been shown that an individual's resilience or vulnerability is not solely a matter of risk and protective factors of environmental origins but that genetic influences also play a part in interaction with the environmental factors (Kim-Cohen, Moffitt, Caspi & Taylor, 2004).

It is generally agreed that vulnerability–resilience remains a useful way of describing people's susceptibility to stressful events. However, it is no longer seen as a generalized disposition – one that holds for all situations and circumstances. Rather, it is recognized that individuals can be both vulnerable and resilient, depending on the context in which they are placed. It is also no longer seen as having the stability over time that a fixed trait would have: individuals can change as a result of previous encounters with stressful events. Success in dealing with these can breed self-confidence leading to greater resilience, just as failure may increase vulnerability. Statements about individuals' vulnerability–resilience ought therefore to be context- and time-specific, and caution must be exercised in assigning people to some particular point on the continuum as though that is their 'score' for life. Some degree of stability can often be found; for example, infants with a 'difficult' **temperament** are generally more likely to become vulnerable children. Nevertheless, prediction from one time point to another or from one set of circumstances to a different one is generally hazardous.

This gives weight to the proposal that vulnerability–resilience should not be regarded as a static trait but as a dynamic state that can manifest itself in a different form at different times according to ongoing circumstances. To quote Cummings, Davies and Campbell (2000):

> Resilience refers to psychological processes that operate in opposition to processes of vulnerability to adversity ... It is the balance between processes of resilience and vulnerability in contexts of development that determine whether psychopathology or normal development is the outcome at any given point in time.

The aim of those fostering mental health is therefore to ensure that resilience processes (or protective forces) come to outweigh vulnerability processes (or risk factors) in the lives of individual children.

Further reading

Cummings, E.M., Davies, P.T., & Campbell, S.B. (2000). *Developmental psychopathology and family processes.* New York: Guilford Press. Chapter 5 is specifically concerned with risk and protective factors and gives a useful overview of the most recent thinking and work in this area.

Glantz, M.D., & Johnson, J.L. (Eds.) (1999). *Resilience and development.* New York: Kluwer. Includes many valuable contributions concerning conceptual, definitional and measurement issues, and also the implications of resilience for intervention efforts.

Masten, A.S., & Gewirtz, A.H. (2006). Vulnerability and resilience in early child development. In K. McCartney & D. Phillips (Eds.), *Blackwell handbook of early childhood development.* Oxford: Blackwell. Presents the latest thinking and research on the nature of vulnerability and resilience and the implications of this work for intervention and prevention.

See also **developmental continuity; developmental trajectories; temperament**

INDIVIDUALISM–COLLECTIVISM

As a corrective to the idea that individuality, to which this whole section is **MEANING** devoted, has a significance that is universal and corresponds everywhere to views held in the West, it is important to stress the culture-dependent nature of this concept. Individualism–collectivism serves this purpose; it is derived from an analysis of the values and practices found in many different countries throughout the world and constitutes a –

> *bipolar dimension along which societies can be arranged according to the extent to which people give priority to personal goals as opposed to those of their social group.*

For descriptive purposes the two extremes of the dimension are generally used as anchors; thus, to quote Hofstede's (1991) characterization:

> *Individualism* pertains to societies in which the ties between individuals are loose: everyone is expected to look after himself or herself and his or her immediate family. *Collectivism* as its opposite pertains to societies in which people from birth onwards are integrated into strong, cohesive ingroups, which throughout people's lifetime continue to protect them in exchange for unquestioning loyalty.

In individualistic societies people are mainly motivated by their own preferences, needs and rights; individuals are seen as autonomous and oriented towards personal goals, and the values stressed by the culture are generally those of self-assertion, self-expression and self-actualization. Children are accordingly brought up to become independent, assertive and achievement-orientated. In collectivistic societies, on the other hand, the emphasis is on individuals' connectedness to other members of the in-group; they are expected to subordinate their own interests to those of the group as a whole and their social behaviour is largely a consequence of the norms, duties and obligations imposed on them. Children will therefore be raised in ways that foster the cultural values of cooperation rather than competition and of reliance on others rather than autonomy (Markus & Kitayama, 1991). In short, in one set of societies the idea of the individual predominates; in the other set that idea is of secondary consideration.

Countries in which individualistic characteristics prevail are largely in North America and Western Europe; collectivistic characteristics typify mainly those in the Far East and also some in Africa and Latin America. The most striking contrast is usually found between the United States on the one hand and China, Japan and Korea on the other.

ORIGINS   Anthropologists have for long drawn attention to the fact that cultures differ in the value they attach to the individual as opposed to the group (whether family, village or tribe) – something especially evident in Margaret Mead's book *Cooperation and competition among primitive peoples* (1967). However, it was not until Geert Hofstede (1980), in a detailed analysis of 40 national cultures (added to and updated in 2001), put forward individualism–collectivism as one the main dimensions along which cultures can be ranged that psychologists began to appreciate the potential of this concept for understanding human behaviour. A considerable amount of research came into being as a result, much of it by cross-cultural psychologists of whom Harry Triandis and his colleagues (e.g. 1990, 1995) in particular helped to bring further elaboration to this way of viewing the individual–society relationship.

Hofstede's proposal, it should be stressed, refers to a sociological, not a psychological dimension. It characterizes different societies and is not a description of different personalities – a point often misunderstood but subsequently emphasized again by Hofstede (e.g. 1994). Individualism–collectivism is a single bipolar dimension that subsumes a varied set of national, cultural differences and is correlated with a range of other measures characterizing countries such as national wealth, indices of modernity, press freedom and even frequency of traffic deaths. Hofstede did not rule out the possibility, even likelihood, that at the level of the individual the values expressed by the dimension would assume a different form – that a multidimensional model, for example, would be more useful than a unidimensional one, and that correlations between variables at the cultural level may well be different from those of the same set of variables at the individual level. This is one of the points with which much of the research that followed the original publication of Hofstede's ideas has been concerned.

CURRENT STATUS   The concept of individualism–connectivism is of continuing interest and is still stimulating a considerable body of research, mainly by cross-cultural psychologists. There is also, however, rather more caution in its usage, ranging from doubts as to whether it is necessary at all (see Kagitcibasi, 1994, for a discussion) to a variety of proposals for further refinement. These concern in the main the following issues:

- *Polar opposites or a mixture?* Although originally formulated as a continuous dimension, individualism–collectivism has frequently been discussed as though referring to two distinct categories to which cultures are allocated on an either–or basis. It has become evident, however, that this is not justified: designating a culture as one or the other merely indicates a *predominance* of that pattern, for all cultures are found to display signs of both individualism and collectivism. For example, when Wang and Tamis-LeMonda (2003) compared parental child rearing values in Taiwan with those in the United States they found that a clear dichotomy did not do justice to their data, in that parents used a variety of strategies depending on the situation in which they found themselves with their children. Individualism and collectivism, that is, are not mutually exclusive but may co-exist.

- *Does the dimension require further differentiation?* Initially, individualism–collectivism was used as a unidimensional concept, but it has become increasingly apparent that further distinctions need to be introduced to do justice to the within-group differences that exist among individualistic cultures and among collectivistic cultures. Take two countries such as the United States and Sweden: both are highly individualistic societies, yet in the former competition and personal status are emphasized while in the latter equality is stressed. Accordingly, Triandis (1995) introduced a *vertical–horizontal* scheme as an additional categorization. Whereas individualism and collectivism respectively designate *independence* and *interdependence*, vertical and horizontal refer to *difference* and *sameness*, that is, whether a society accepts the principle of a social hierarchy where people belong to different ranks or whether all individuals are regarded as equal in status with the same rights and privileges. It is thus possible to construct four categories: individualistic–vertical (independent and different, e.g. the United States), individualistic–horizontal (independent and same, e.g. Sweden), collectivistic–vertical (interdependent and different, e.g. India) and collectivistic–horizontal (interdependent and same, e.g. Israeli kibbutzim). This four-fold distinction has been found in some studies to be meaningfully related to various external constructs (e.g. Soh and Leong, 2002); if confirmed, it represents a refinement of the individualism–collectivism concept that may well give rise to further refinements.

- *Same or different levels of analysis?* In his original formulation Hofstede (1980) firmly anchored individualism–collectivism to the cultural level, and denied that one can automatically generalize the concept to the individual level. As he put it, '[Cultures] are wholes, and their internal logic cannot be understood in the terms used for the personality dynamics of individuals.' Cultures, that is, are more than the mere sums of the characteristics of their individual members but possess properties of their own. Nevertheless, the caution is sometimes overlooked, as though the two levels of analysis are identical. To counteract this tendency, Triandis, Leung, Villareal & Clark (1985) proposed the use of a different pair of terms to designate the beliefs of individuals in the primacy of personal independence or of social interdependence, namely *idiocentrism and allocentrism*. The rationale for the distinction between the two sets of concepts is confirmed by the finding that the two present a different structural pattern: whereas at the cultural level individualism–collectivism are arranged along a single bipolar dimension, at the individual level idocentrism and allocentrism represent two independent dimensions. Someone scoring high on idiocentrism, that is, will not necessarily score low on allocentrism (as well as vice versa), in that they may endorse both sets of values without contradiction (Rhee, Uleman & Lee, 1996).

The cultural and the individual levels are nevertheless functionally interrelated, though in a complex manner that has generated much research. Of most relevance here are the links of individualism and collectivism with adults' socialization practices, as they help to shape the psychological characteristics of children growing up in the different types of culture. For example:

- Various studies have shown that Japanese mothers approach the rearing of children in a very different way from mothers in the West (e.g. Shimizu & LeVine, 2001). Whereas Western mothers see their task as helping the child to proceed from dependence to independence, the traditional Japanese mother considers childhood to proceed in the opposite direction, from independence to dependence. In Japan, that is, the newborn baby is viewed as a separate, autonomous being, whom the mother must socialize into becoming dependent on other members of the group. To accomplish this she maintains physical closeness to an extent rarely seen in the West, by sleeping with her child for the first few years, remaining near throughout each day and generally encouraging dependence through a high degree of indulgence.
- In a comparison of American, Japanese and Chinese nurseries Tobin, Wu and Davidson (1989) found marked differences in orientation. 'Groupism' was the key distinguishing feature of the Asian nurseries: nearly all activities were carried out in groups; play, for instance, was seen as an opportunity for children to learn to do things with others and not, as in America, as something for individual expression and development. Teachers thus set out with different aims which reflected the values of their particular culture and inculcated these in the children in their care.
- Harkness and Super (1992) analysed the way in which mothers in an isolated rural community in Kenya described their children and compared their descriptions with those of American mothers. The latter tended to concentrate on their children's cognitive abilities and used words like 'intelligent',

'smart' and 'imaginative', but also made frequent references to their independence and self-reliance ('confident', 'able to play by himself', 'defiant'). The Kenyan mothers, on the other hand, paid most attention to their children's obedience and helpfulness by using words like 'respectful', 'honest', 'trustworthy' and 'good-hearted' – all characteristics reflecting the importance attached to fitting in with the group and contributing to common needs. Considering that these mothers lived in a poor, materially deprived part of Africa where individuals cannot achieve much on their own and cooperation with others is essential for survival, one can readily understand that it is interdependence and not independence, cooperation and not competition, that is valued most and that is therefore expressed in socialization techniques.

There is no doubt that individualism-collectivism, as originally conceived, is too simple a formulation to do justice to the many varied phenomena it purports to encompass. Nevertheless, it has served as a useful starting point for much research into cultural differences and their associated psychological differences, and most of all it has demonstrated that individuality is an essentially relative idea which is emphasized and defined in various ways depending on the values of each culture.

Further reading

Kim, U., Triandis, H.C., Kagitcibasi, C., Choi, S-C., & Yoon, C. (Eds.) (1994). *Individualism and collectivism: theory, method and application.* Thousand Oaks, CA: Sage. A collection of individual views which continues to provide one of the best summaries of this topic.

Markus, H.R., & Kitayama, S. (1991). Culture and the self: implications for cognition, emotion and motivation. *Psychological Review, 98,* 224–253. Stresses the importance of viewing psychological characteristics in the context of specific cultures.

See also **context; social identity**

5
FIVE
COGNITIVE DEVELOPMENT

Cognition refers to knowing, and cognitive development to the acquisition of knowledge in childhood. Included here are such processes as perception, remembering, classifying, understanding, reasoning, thinking, problem solving, conceptualizing, classifying and planning – in short, all those expressions of human intelligence that we use to adapt to and make sense of the world. These are all *mental* functions, that is, internal and therefore not directly observable, with some aspects wholly outside consciousness. Instead, psychologists infer their characteristics from the actions they give rise to, usually under controlled experimental conditions, though increasingly new neuroimaging techniques are also used to throw light on the processes 'inside' the mind.

Three theoretical orientations have dominated thinking about cognitive development, namely those associated with Piaget, Vygotsky and information processing approaches. For the most part each of these has developed in isolation from the others, with its own theoretical assumptions, its own methodology and its own terminology. Thus many of the concepts used in this area stem from one or the other of the three orientations, yet these different approaches are by no means wholly incompatible and attempts have been made at cross-fertilization, mainly between Piagetian and information processing ideas.

As with all other aspects of development, the principal issues to be settled concerning cognitive development are description and explanation: what is the nature of children's cognitive functions at various ages and what accounts for change across development? The following concepts are some of those that have been employed to think about these questions:

COGNITIVE ARCHITECTURE
and: **Multistore models**
    Central conceptual structures
FUNCTIONAL INVARIANTS
and: **Equilibration**
    Assimilation
    Accommodation
SYMBOLIC REPRESENTATION
and: **Dual representation**
COGNITIVE STRATEGIES
and: **Mediational, production and utilization deficiencies**
    Metacognition
THEORY THEORY
and: **Folk theories**

COGNITIVE ARCHITECTURE
and: **MULTISTORE MODELS**
CENTRAL CONCEPTUAL STRUCTURES

Under the influence of information processing theories there have been various **MEANING**
attempts to liken the mind to a computer. The comparison, while forced in certain
respects, does hold in others. For example, just as computers are described in terms
of hardware and software, that is their structural organization and their operating
programs respectively, so one can describe the human cognitive system in terms of
its structures and its processes. Here we are concerned with the former; the other
concepts in this section refer to the latter.

By cognitive architecture we mean –

> *the innate structural characteristics of the brain that*
> *constitute the foundations required for human information*
> *processing.*

The structures, that is, are the building blocks of the cognitive system, and just like
an architect so the psychologist needs both to specify the characteristics of the various component blocks and to set out the nature of the total organization of which
they form a part. Not everyone agrees that such structures are inevitably innate, and
even when that assumption is made there is disagreement as to whether they
remain fixed or are open to subsequent change. Moreover, in the absence of the necessary evidence the link with the brain remains for the most part conjectural.
Nevertheless, to most people the assumption seems justified that evolution has
equipped us with the basic means whereby we acquire knowledge and that these
means reflect the way in which the brain is organized at birth. Babies, that is, are
provided with preprogrammed mechanisms which enable them to be attuned to,
inter alia, the sight of human faces, to perceive speech in adult-like ways and to
learn language with comparative ease, as well as to acquire certain categories of
knowledge such as causality, space and number. These mechanisms are usually
referred to now as *modules* and are just some of the structures that have been mentioned as forming part of the individual's inherent cognitive architecture (see
modularity).

As we shall see below, there have been various attempts to put together a model
that can represent the architectural make-up of the cognitive system. These have
taken different forms and are based on different assumptions about the nature of
the mind; all are agreed, however, that the inborn structural components of the system serve two functions, an *enabling* and a *limiting* one. Enabling is seen in the
speed with which certain competencies appear early in life, in that the state of
biological preparedness avoids the need for a lengthy period of learning. By the

same token, however, structural characteristics also limit what infants become aware of in the outer world, in that differential susceptibility protects them from stimulation that is not directly relevant to their well-being and, having no survival value, will thus not be accepted by their perceptual apparatus.

ORIGINS Since at least the time of Aristotle, philosophers have debated the make-up of the mind. Aristotle himself saw the mind as composed of *faculties*, that is, various powers such as sensation, imagination, memory, practical reason and creative reason, from which all mental functions were said to be derived. The faculty view lasted an astonishingly long time, each writer happily putting forward his own list, convinced that a distinct mental process was associated with each item on that list. Phrenology, the nineteenth-century belief that each mental power corresponds to a specific region of the brain and makes itself evident on the surface of the head (see **brain plasticity**), was one further assertion by the faculty movement before a more empirical attitude began to make itself felt and replaced the often somewhat unbridled speculation of the faculty proponents.

First, however, Immanuel Kant, writing in the course of the eighteenth century, put forward a scheme that departed radically from faculty lists and that in some respects has turned out to be remarkably prescient. Pondering the origins of knowledge, Kant concluded that what we know about the world cannot simply be a direct reflection of data coming to the mind through the senses, as philosophers such as John Locke believed; if that were the case we would be overwhelmed. Rather, the mind is structured all along so that it imposes order on sense data, and does so by means of certain *categories of pure understanding*, namely very general abstract ideas referring to concepts such as time, space and causation which are an inherent part of the mental apparatus and serve to organize and make coherent our experience. We are so constructed, that is, that every event is, for example, automatically perceived as having a cause, of occurring in a certain space and as lasting for a specific time period, and in this way the mind actively shapes our experience to conform to what it can understand. The architecture of cognition, to put it in present-day terms, is thus composed of a finite number of innately determined domains into which we fit our perceptions – an idea that has in recent times been revived, though with empirical backing.

The explicit notion of cognitive architecture itself did not surface until mid-twentieth century, in particular in the writings of Newell (1973; Newell & Simon, 1972) and other information processing theorists. The human mind, according to this view, can be regarded as a symbol-manipulating system which passes information sequentially through the cognitive system in order to subject it to various operations such as inspection, sorting, storing and transforming. To depict these sequences flow diagrams are customarily employed, which show the various mental stores where each step is performed, together with the connections between them. The total pattern of stores can then be said to constitute a model of cognitive architecture. Atkinson and Shiffrin

(1968) provided one early but highly influential example of such a model, though in more recent work this has become greatly more detailed and elaborated.

Among the various models proposed to depict cognitive architecture the information processing paradigm remains the most productive. This has been put forward in a number of versions, but all are based on the belief that it is necessary to postulate a **MULTISTORE MODEL**, which refers to –

> *the hypothetical mechanisms in the brain deemed to be implicated in the sequential manipulation of incoming information.*

Following on from Atkinson and Shiffrin's original proposal (1968), such a structure may best be thought of as made up of three basic parts (see Schneider & Pressley, 1997 for further details):

1 *The sensory register*, the function of which is to log external stimulation when it is first received through the sense organs and hold it for just a fraction of a second in perceptually intact form.

2 *The short-term store*, which has a limited capacity, in that it can normally hold only a few items at a time and for only a brief period (about 15–30 seconds).

3 *The long-term store*, which receives information kept initially alive in the short-term store and can retain it for periods of months or years.

What is most striking about work stemming from information processing ideas is that systems like memory have been shown not to be unitary in nature; indeed even the above tripartite structure considered a few decades ago to characterize memory turns out to be an over-simplification. Rather, memory is made up of a variety of systems serving different modalities of stimulation, different stages of information processing and the various operations performed in the course of processing – all linked and cooperating, but each nevertheless having an identity of its own. Thus the short-term store has been found to be made up of three components, namely a *visuo-spatial* store which holds material received through the visual system, a *phonological* store confined to auditory information and a *central executive*. The function of the last is to control the flow of information through the short-term store and evaluate it, to combine it with information from the long-term store and to apply various special procedures such as rehearsal whereby the retention period in the short-term store can be considerably prolonged. Similarly, it has been established that a distinction needs to be made between different long-term structures such as those serving *declarative* and *non-declarative* (or *procedural*) *memory* respectively. The former refers to our knowledge of facts and events and, being accessible to consciousness, is also referred to as *explicit* memory; the latter concerns our knowledge of procedures (skills like tying shoe-laces, for example) and is *implicit* in character in that it does not necessarily require awareness. The evidence for the multifaceted nature of the system comes mainly from experimental studies; however, investigations of brain-damaged patients, neuropsychological findings and the use of neuroimaging techniques have shown that different aspects have different anatomical loci and are served by different neurological networks (C. Nelson, 1997). They thus support the conclusion that there are many separable memory systems, each with its own functions, and that the underlying cognitive architecture is greatly more complex and specialized than was thought at one time (Gathercole, 1998).

A rather different account of cognitive architecture to that presented by information processing theories is that stemming from *connectionism*. This theory views information as stored in the form of a pattern of connectivity among neural units and not as the depositing of symbols in a long-term store; memory therefore is a matter of the activation of a configuration of neurons that had on previous occasions functioned together (see **connectionist networks**). Thus the basic building blocks in the brain hypothesized to be involved in dealing with information are very much simpler and smaller-scale than the various stores described by information processing theorists; they are individual networks (loosely based on neural networks), each comprising a group of very elementary units connected together in a particular configuration. While all connectionist networks share the same fundamental make-up of units and connections, they may differ greatly among themselves in the pattern of connectivity, and learning about cognitive architecture thus becomes largely a matter of understanding how the different patterns operate. In general, while connectionist networks are only models they nevertheless have considerable plausibility in the light of what we now know about brain functioning (Thomas & Karmiloff-Smith, 2002).

One further way of conceptualizing cognitive architecture takes us back to Kant's proposal, mentioned above, that the mind at birth is equipped with certain *categories of pure understanding*. This notion has resurfaced in more recent times, variously named core concepts, fundamental categories of thought or (the term we shall use following Case, 1998) **CENTRAL CONCEPTUAL STRUCTURES**. This term refers to

> *certain concepts essential to our understanding of the world such as time, space, number and causality, which are part of the individual's inherent cognitive structure and which lay the foundation for more sophisticated kinds of understanding emerging in the course of subsequent development.*

Insofar as these structures are said to exist in the young baby, in however nascent a form, they provide an 'instinctive' understanding of the properties of the world – a 'leg-up' mechanism enabling young children to obtain a ready hold on complex notions such as causality, which do not therefore have to be taught. The totality of such modules provides a framework (a set of *knowledge networks*, as Case, 1998, has put it) that defines the architecture of the cognitive system (see **domain specificity** and **modularity**).

Each of the main conceptual structures put forward as an example has attracted a considerable body of research aimed at tracing its developmental course from early infancy on (see Haith & Benson, 1998, for details). It has, for example, been claimed that infants aged 5 months show evidence of possessing 'true numerical concepts', suggesting that they are 'innately endowed with arithmetical abilities' (Wynn, 1992). This conclusion has repeatedly been challenged; rather more convincing are the findings from studies on causality, which indicate that from about mid-first year on infants expect events to occur in causal sequences and that they must therefore have an elementary 'understanding' of causality based, according to Leslie (1988), on a causality module capable of automatically detecting the occurrence of causal events. While this claim has also proved controversial there is little doubt that young infants do show surprise or upset when violations are experimentally arranged of expected cause–effect sequences, and that they do appear capable quite early on of treating causal and non-causal events in a different manner.

The three approaches to the problem of delineating the architecture of the cognitive system, involving respectively information processing, connectionism and core conceptual structures, represent distinct theoretical traditions. They all agree, however, that the complexity of the system is such that it needs to be broken down into a much greater number of separate components than was thought at one time, each representing a domain specific mechanism based on its own neural foundation but all also at the beck and call of certain central coordinating mechanisms, the nature of which still requires to be ascertained.

Further reading

Gathercole, S. (1998). The development of memory. *Journal of Child Psychology and Psychiatry, 39*, 3–28. A masterly summary of cognitive research, as seen from an information processing viewpoint.

Haith, M.M., & Benson, J.B. (1998). Infant cognition. In W. Damon (Ed.), *Handbook of child psychology*, vol. 2 (D. Kuhn & R.S. Siegler, Eds.). New York: Wiley. A critical but constructive review of what has been learned about the earliest development of central conceptual structures.

See also **brain plasticity; connectionist networks; domain specificity; modularity; theory theory**

FUNCTIONAL INVARIANTS
and: EQUILIBRATION
ASSIMILATION
ACCOMMODATION

MEANING Piagetian theory has provided us with a considerable number of concepts, some of which have gained wide acceptance outside the confines of the theory itself while others remain very much Piaget's own creatures. Those described here were regarded by him as fundamental to his account of cognitive development; they represent Piaget's answer to the question 'Why does development occur?' and are thus the processes whereby he attempted to provide an explanation of the reasons for change.

Functional invariants is Piaget's generic term for –

> *mechanisms of development that operate in unchanging form throughout the life-span.*

Equilibration, assimilation and accommodation are three such mechanisms; they are part of the child's innate endowment and operate in basically unchanging (*invariant*) form at all stages of an individual's life from birth onwards. Their joint function is to ensure that the individual remains adapted to environmental demands, whatever changes may be occurring within the individual and in the nature of the environment.

Of the three mechanisms **EQUILIBRATION** was regarded by Piaget as the most central to his efforts to explain how cognitive development occurs. It is in many respects a nebulous and difficult concept, but may be defined as –

> *the unceasing process whereby individuals throughout life attempt to integrate their diverse experiences into unified, stable wholes in order to avoid the tension that would result from conflicting mental elements.*

This, according to Piaget, is the mechanism that provides the ultimate power behind development. In the words of the subtitle of one of his publications, it is 'the central problem of intellectual development' (Piaget, 1985). Any sense of disequilibrium, brought about whenever individuals become aware that their present level of understanding does not match the information they receive from the environment, is unpleasant, produces tension and therefore motivates them to change their cognitive structures and progress to a new, more advanced level. Yet the equilibrium thus achieved may in turn be only a temporary state; once the child becomes dissatisfied with the adequacy of the new level of understanding there will be a repetition of the sequence: (1) equilibrium at a lower level, (2) disequilibrium resulting from awareness of the short-comings of existing understanding, (3) new equilibrium at a higher level seen as more adequate. In this way progressively more complex and sophisticated mental structures are created, with equilibration providing the driving force for this progression.

Equilibration encompasses the two further processes of **ASSIMILATION** and **ACCOMMODATION**. Assimilation is –

> *the transformation of incoming information so that it fits existing ways of understanding, even though that information may thereby be distorted to some degree.*

Accommodation is –

> *the adaptation of existing ways of understanding to new information.*

The two processes are complementary, take place simultaneously and can therefore only be conceptually separated. For example, infants come into the world with a particular way of sucking that is finely adapted to obtaining milk from a nipple. When their mouth comes into contact with a different object they will attempt to *assimilate* it to their present sucking structure (or *scheme*, as Piaget referred to it), but if it does not fit will gradually *accommodate* the scheme so that sucking becomes more flexible and adapted to a variety of objects. They thus progress to a more advanced level of functioning, going through the sequence of (1) equilibrium at the innate level of functioning to (2) disequilibrium as they discover the short-comings of this level, to (3) a new equilibrium when the original scheme becomes more adaptable.

ORIGINS

The concepts described above represent the most basic building blocks in Piaget's theory of cognitive development. The theory as a whole is an extraordinarily wide-ranging and ambitious one, and one of its admirable features is that it sets out to form a three-way linkage between biology, philosophy and psychology.

Piaget started off as a biologist, and his biological orientation remained with him throughout his career. It is therefore no wonder that he saw cognitive development primarily in terms of adaptation – a notion commonly used by biological scientists and considered by Piaget as equally applicable to psychological as well as physiological functions. Thus cognition (or intelligence, as he always referred to it) is a form of biological adaptation to environmental challenge, and due to the joint operation of assimilation and accommodation this comes to take a progressively more complex form throughout the course of development. Equilibration too was regarded by him as a general biological tendency – one that denotes all aspects of self-regulation and that lies at the heart of all types of developmental processes.

However, even as an adolescent Piaget also developed an interest in epistemology – that branch of philosophy concerned with the nature of knowledge. What is knowledge? How is it acquired? Why does it take the form it does in human beings? Piaget became convinced that the answers to such questions can be obtained not just by speculation but by applying the scientific methods employed in biology, and he therefore decided that he needed to specialize in 'biological philosophy'. Yet this in turn led him to psychology, for, in order to formulate a biologically oriented theory of the nature of knowledge, the psychological study of children's thinking appeared the most appropriate means, on the basis that to understand something one must investigate how it grows. Piaget therefore set himself the task of studying the formation and growth of knowledge in childhood, in order to accumulate a body of observations that would enable him to construct a general theory of cognitive development.

CURRENT STATUS   Piaget's theory in general has become extremely influential, yet ironically the concepts that he regarded as fundamental to that theory have turned out to be highly controversial and the least accepted parts of that theory. Take the following comment:

> For 40 years now we have had assimilation and accommodation, the mysterious and shadowy forces of equilibration, the Batman and Robin of developmental process. What are they? How do they do their thing? Why is it after all this time we know no more about them than when they first sprang on the scene? What we need is a way to get beyond vague verbal statements of the nature of the developmental process. (Klahr, 1982)

Most criticism has been directed at Piaget's conception of equilibration. Bruner (1959), for instance, has dismissed this concept as 'surplus baggage'; in similar vein Bryant (1990) has criticized it for being pitched in such general terms as to be quite untestable and referred to it as a *deus ex machina* because of the absence of empirical evidence supporting it. Flavell, Miller and Miller (1993) also doubt whether the equilibration model is capable of explaining every aspect of cognitive advance even if such a process can be said to occur. While many other Piagetian concepts have found general acceptance, very few developmental psychologists have adopted equilibration as an explanatory device or, for that matter, made use of any of the concepts included under functional invariants.

Yet of late there have been signs that this generally negative attitude is lifting. This is largely because of the striking similarity of equilibration with concepts such as **epigenesis** and **self-organization** which have more recently become of considerable interest (Boden, 1994). All of these address themselves to the same problem, namely how one can explain the emergence of new structures in the course of development when neither maturation nor learning can account for them. Chapman (1992), for example, has described equilibration as an 'embryonic theory of self-organizing systems', and though the details of Piaget's account are in many respects very different from current formulations, marked parallels do exist between them. Piaget's conception of equilibration was by no means a static one but went through repeated modifications and refinements, including the differentiation of several kinds of equilibration (1985). Admittedly it remained throughout excessively abstract – too much so ever to become testable. But as Smith (2002) has pointed out, testability is not the only criterion of the worth of a theory; its ability to highlight important problems to be solved is another, even if it cannot itself provide a solution. Insofar as the concept of equilibration drew attention to the apparently spontaneous acquisition of new mental structures as an essential problem for investigation it can at least claim to be one of the first efforts to address one of the most important features of cognitive development.

Further reading

Beilin, H., & Pufall, P. (Eds.) (1992). *Piaget's theory: prospects and possibilities.* Hillsdale, NJ: Erlbaum. Contains a lot of thought-provoking chapters, but that by Michael Chapman is especially relevant here.

Boden, M.A. (1994). *Piaget* (2nd ed.) London: Fontana. A short but wise book reviewing Piaget's theory as a whole, with special attention in the Introduction to the relationship of Piagetian ideas to contemporary theories.

Flavell, J.H. (1963). *The developmental psychology of Jean Piaget*. Princeton, NJ: Van Nostrand. This is the book that originally introduced Piaget's theory to English-speaking readers, and remains an important source.

See also **constructivism; epigenesis; self-organization**

SYMBOLIC REPRESENTATION
and: DUAL REPRESENTATION

The capacity for mental representation has been referred to as the hallmark of cognition and (though rather more controversially) as a uniquely human attribute. Yet, as any perusal of essays on the subject will show (e.g. Sigel, 1999), different authors have attached different meanings to the term and provided different definitions.

MEANING

Overall, one can distinguish two groups: those that see representation in a broad sense as equivalent to stored information and thus equate representation with knowledge (e.g. Mandler, 1998), and those who see it in a more narrow sense as referring to the use of symbols to denote aspects of experience. We shall focus here on the latter, for the capacity for symbolic representation is widely regarded as lying at the core of cognitive development – Piaget in particular saw age changes in the nature of representation as the principal characteristic differentiating the various stages of development outlined by him (see **developmental stages**).

At its most basic, a symbolic representation is –

something that an individual intends to stand for something else.

When, for example, a child pretends a banana is a telephone the banana stands for the telephone, the former being a *symbol* that denotes the latter, which is the *referent*. Some symbols can be wholly idiosyncratic: the child can choose a spoon, a piece of wood or his own hand instead of the banana; what matters is the meaning the child attaches to the pretend object. Other symbols, however, take a conventional form, in particular the most important form of representation, namely words. It is true that words too have an arbitrary relationship to their referent: the word 'banana' does not by means of its sound characteristics as such evoke the real thing; however, it is part of the accepted language system in the English-speaking community and must therefore be used if the child is to share meaning with other people. It is true that some types of symbols such as pictures, maps and models, do show a systematic relationship to the referent, though even here there is no necessity for the reproduction to be a faithful one (consider a Picasso picture of a face, or a Henry Moore sculpture of a person). But while there are many different types of symbols, all bear the common characteristic that they are used to denote something other than themselves, and as such can be internalized to become private tools of thought and an economical way of storing experience, as well as serving for communicative purposes and as a means of conjuring up the past and anticipating the future.

ORIGINS Philosophers through the ages have pondered the problem of mental representations and their relationship to reality. For psychologists this only became an issue when behaviourism, with its refusal to acknowledge anything mental and unobservable, fell out of fashion and a combination of Piagetian and information processing ideas ushered in the 'cognitive revolution' in the mid-twentieth century.

Piaget's view of representational development was a clear-cut one, with his assertion that children are initially incapable of forming representations, that these only appear in the middle of the second year when the child has grown out of sensorimotor ways of relating to the environment, and that subsequently and throughout childhood they undergo periodic transformation, becoming more abstract, complex and flexible before assuming mature form in late adolescence. The most interesting and provocative part of his proposal was the first part, that infants know the world only in terms of the direct actions they perform upon objects, that knowledge is confined to such actions and that mental representations, when they do appear, are in essence internalized actions. Thus initially infants make no use of images, symbols, memories or any other internal devices, and to back up his belief Piaget referred principally to two phenomena, namely *object permanence* and *deferred imitation*.

- *Object permanence* is Piaget's term for the child's understanding that objects are independent entities that continue to exist even when the individual is not perceptually aware of them. According to Piaget, infants initially see the world entirely in terms of fleeting sensory impressions; they live in the here-and-now and show no orientation to anything that is not in their direct perceptual field. When shown an attractive toy they will reach for it, but if the adult covers it with a cloth just before they can grasp it they stop reaching, turn their attention elsewhere and behave as though the object has ceased to exist ('out of sight, out of mind'). Only older infants, from about 9 months on, will continue their attempts to obtain the toy – evidence according to Piaget that an idea of the toy remained in their minds despite its perceptual absence. This is the beginning of object permanence; however, there are still limitations to this insight, such as seen when a delay is introduced between hiding the toy and the opportunity to retrieve it. It is only around the age of 18 months that Piaget considered children capable of mentally representing the absent toy in a properly mature manner.
- *Deferred imitation* refers to copying someone's behaviour that was seen some significant time before. To achieve this the individual must have formed a mental representation of the action and stored it, in order to retrieve it after an interval and be able to repeat it. Again, Piaget observed this to occur first around the middle of the second year, though here too he found an earlier form already evident from the last quarter of the first year, but one that involves immediate imitation and thus misses out on the crucial criterion of a time delay.

Thus from around 18 months onwards (sensori-motor stage 6) children become capable of mentally encoding their experience – a point when, according to Piaget, the *semiotic* (or symbolic function) emerges and, among other things, enables words to be used as symbols. Children then progress from wholly overt to covert functioning: they no longer need to act directly on objects but can begin to manipulate them in symbolic form. There is, however, a basic continuity between the two forms of functioning, in that Piaget saw representations as an internalized, abbreviated form of the actions they had previously performed overtly. Mental representations, that is, are the products of activity (Piaget, 1951).

Information processing theories also regard representations as playing an important role (Klahr and MacWhinney, 1998), in that they see them as an internal code standing for stimuli from the environment. Thus input received through the senses is transformed into symbolic representations as the first step in the passage through the cognitive system. The representations are organized into symbol systems according to the form they take – visual images, auditory sensations, words and so forth, which are then passed on for storage, analysis, combination, retrieval and other purposes. By and large, however, information processing accounts have paid more attention to the structures and the processes involved in the handling of information at each step of its passage (see **cognitive architecture**) than to the nature of representations and how this may change in the course of development. A notable exception to this neglect is Case (1992), though as a 'neo-Piagetian', dedicated to bringing Piaget's theory up to date by introducing information processing concepts into it, his account of representational change over age is not substantially different from Piaget's. Thus children in the first developmental stage form representations that are composed solely of sensory input; in the next stage representations include concrete internal images, and subsequently these become more abstract, more complex, more interrelated and more systematized.

CURRENT STATUS   The very lively research on representations carried out in recent times has focused mainly on charting their developmental course in the earliest years of childhood. One of the main lines of enquiry concerns Piaget's assertion that the first year and a half is a representation-free period – an assertion based to a large extent on his observations of object permanence and delayed imitation.

- *Object permanence.* The timetable Piaget gave for the emergence of this achievement was based on one type of test, namely the hide-and-retrieve task. Subsequent research, by using other ways of testing which make fewer demands on infants and are more in keeping with their abilities, have found evidence of object permanence abilities at much younger ages than those given by Piaget. This is most clearly shown by the work of Baillargeon (1987; Baillargeon & De Vos, 1991). By using an experimental paradigm that examined infants' visual reactions to events that violate the rules of object permanence she found that infants as young as 3½ months already show 'surprise' when such violations occur, suggesting that they understand that hidden objects still exist. Thus, by employing a task that assessed competence from simple looking behaviour rather than from more complex motor behaviour it could be concluded that quite young infants have considerable knowledge of object properties, including their continuity over time. As Spelke (1991), on the basis of similar findings, has argued, the idea of permanently existing objects appears not to be constructed gradually over the first 1½ years; instead, such knowledge derives from 'universal, early developing capacities to represent and reason about the physical world' (see **central conceptual structures**).

- *Deferred imitation.* Here too more recent research has found evidence of abilities appearing much earlier than Piaget's stated ages. According to Meltzoff and Moore (1994), 6-week-old infants are capable of imitating a gesture such as an adult sticking out a tongue, even when seen on the previous day. While there are no systematic longitudinal investigations it does seem from a comparison of results obtained by various investigators that this ability increases quite rapidly with age: for example, Carver and Bauer (1999) observed imitation in 9-month-old infants after a 5-week interval. Thus infants from quite early on are already able to store a memory representation of something perceived on an earlier occasion and retrieve it subsequently (Meltzoff, 2004, gives further details).

These observations give credence to Mandler's (1998) argument that representations should not be equated with adult-like symbolic (usually verbal) forms but that the possibility of *sub-symbolic* representations should also be considered.

The fact that children have qualitatively distinct kinds of representations at different ages is indicated by various lines of research. Take work by Judy DeLoache and her collaborators (2002; DeLoache & Smith, 1999), focusing on developments in the third year of life, with specific reference to children's understanding of models as symbols. In their basic experimental paradigm children watched while a miniature toy dog was hidden in a scale model of a real room. The children were then asked to find a large stuffed dog in the comparable location of the full-sized room. To succeed the child has to use the model as a representation of the real room – a challenge that most of the 2½-year-olds could not meet whereas 3-year-olds did manage to solve the problem.

DeLoache explained these findings as indicating the development of **DUAL REPRESENTATION** in the second half of the third year. This concept refers to –

> *the ability mentally to represent a symbolic object both as an entity in its own right and as something that stands for something else.*

Thus a child, confronted by the model of a room, needs to see this both as the concrete object which it is and as a symbol of the real room, and should be able to switch easily from one to the other. At 2½ years children, according to DeLoache, can respond to only one of these; by 3 they have acquired *representational insight*, that is, the ability to think abstractly about the relationship between the concrete object and its referent. Such knowledge is at first somewhat tentative and implicit; in subsequent years it becomes increasingly conscious and thus a surer guide to the use of symbols in solving problems.

At present there is no generally accepted overall scheme for describing the precise sequence in which representational abilities emerge in the early years. However, one plausible proposal has been put forward by Perner (1991), involving a three-stage progression:

1 *Primary representation* (from the first to the second year): children during this period become capable of forming mental models of the world but these merely depict, photo-like, the aspects they represent. Representations are therefore stimulus-bound.

2 *Secondary representation* (from the second year to 4 years): children can now form new models of the world by decoupling their representations from reality and re-arranging at will the information obtained through the senses. This means that children can form multiple models of the same thing: in their pretend play, for example, a banana, a stick and a cardboard tube can all equally well serve as a telephone.

3 *Metarepresentation* (4 years on): children realize that inner representations are just mental creations and therefore not exact copies of the world. They can therefore think about another person's representations; in other words, they can represent representations.

It is thus not a matter of having or not having representational ability. Distinctions need to be made between lower- and higher-order types: at first children have the ability to represent aspects of the world to themselves; subsequently they become capable of representing the representations.

Further reading

Mandler, J. (1998). *Representation*. In W. Damon (Ed.), *Handbook of child psychology,* vol. 2 (D. Kuhn & R.S. Siegler, Eds.). New York: Wiley. Deals exclusively with representations in infancy, but written by one of the most perceptive authors in this area and full of thought-provoking ideas.

Sigel, I.E. (Ed.) (1999). *Development of mental representations: theories and applications.* Mahwah, NJ: Erlbaum. Covers a wide range of approaches to the topic, with chapters by Sigel, Martinez and DeLoache particularly relevant to the above material.

See also **cognitive architecture; cognitive strategies; internal working models**

COGNITIVE STRATEGIES
and: **MEDIATIONAL, PRODUCTION and UTILIZATION DEFICIENCIES**

MEANING How children develop and select appropriate cognitive strategies to enable them to acquire knowledge has been a very active topic of research for several decades.

By strategies we mean –

> *mental operations that are consciously and deliberately employed to achieve some specified goal.*

There is no complete consensus regarding all parts of such a definition; in particular, some writers argue that strategies are not necessarily conscious processes but can be carried out automatically and therefore out of awareness. Nevertheless, all agree that at the core of strategies lies their goal-directed nature, in that they are usually deliberately instigated in the service of some specific task (Bjorklund & Harnishfeger, 1990).

One can find strategies in most aspects of cognitive behaviour; however, the majority of studies have investigated the role they play in memory and it is therefore from that field that we shall draw most of our material.

Strategies form an essential part of the information processing apparatus, and especially so at the input (or encoding) and the output (or retrieval) ends. One can see them, for example, when a child is attempting to commit to memory a list of items and uses rehearsal as an aid before being tested, thus furthering the encoding process; or when, in order to retrieve required material, the child resorts to a range of tricks acquired for the purpose of bringing information from the long-term memory store back to consciousness. For the most part children discover useful strategies quite spontaneously, but they can also benefit from being explicitly taught to use them – if, that is, the child is developmentally ready to acquire them.

Most of the research in this area has concerned itself with the developmental progression in children's use of strategies, for the concept draws attention to the important problem of how children acquire deliberate and conscious control over their cognitive processes. It is clear that there are definite limitations in this respect in the preschool years, and to understand these three further concepts have been put forward, namely **MEDIATIONAL, PRODUCTION** and **UTILIZATION DEFICIENCIES.**

Mediational deficiency describes –

> *the inability to benefit from a strategy even if it is imposed.*

Production deficiency is –

> *the inability to use a strategy spontaneously even though the child can be instructed in its use.*

Utilization deficiency refers to –

> *the child's failure to benefit from a strategy despite being able to produce it spontaneously.*

As outlined below, these three types of deficiency have provided a focus for a large number of investigations, aimed at understanding children's cognitive development in the years up to adolescence (for detailed review, see Bjorklund & Douglas, 1997).

ORIGINS Research on strategies began in the 1960s – another of the many consequences of the onset of the 'cognitive revolution'. To a large extent this was due to the efforts of John Flavell, whose pioneering study (Flavell, Beach & Chinsky, 1966) first drew attention to the phenomenon of rehearsal as a strategy for memorizing material. By using an observer trained in lip reading it was shown that most 10-year-old children, in the interval between being shown a set of pictures and having to recall them, spontaneously repeated the names of the pictures to themselves over and over, whereas very few 5-year-olds did so. The older children's much greater recall success was accordingly attributed to their use of rehearsal as a memory strategy.

Following this study much work went into trying to identify other strategies. These are some of the main ones described:

- *Organization*: rearrangement of randomly presented items into conceptually meaningful categories.
- *Elaboration*: constructing a link between otherwise unrelated items by, for example, making up a sentence that includes all of them.
- *Selective attention*: allocating attention specifically to those items that need to be recalled subsequently.
- *Retrieval techniques*: finding ways of making items more memorable and easier to recall by, for example, breaking up a complex name into easier components.

Much of the motivation for undertaking this work came initially from the hope of finding ways of enhancing children's memory and overcoming their cognitive limitations, thereby making them more effective learners. A wave of training studies followed, designed to instruct children in the use of strategies; however, it soon became evident that even then, especially in younger children, there are age-related constraints in benefiting from such techniques – constraints which came to be expressed in terms of the various deficiencies mentioned above. Strategy development, it was concluded, goes through a number of stages:

1 An initial period, spanning much of the preschool years, when *mediational deficiency* prevents children from using any strategy.

2 A period characterized by *production deficiency*, as a result of which children can only use strategies when these are made available but cannot produce them spontaneously.

3 A further period when children are able to call up strategies spontaneously but due to *utilization deficiency* cannot apply them to improve their performance.

4 Finally, children overcome even this deficiency and are able to function at a fully mature level.

Thus strategy development was seen as proceeding in an orderly, linear fashion – a view, however, on which more recent work has thrown some doubt.

Research on cognitive strategies, especially as applied to memory, is continuing, but as a result of recent findings a number of changes have taken place in how we think about the way in which children acquire strategies. For one thing, the notion that children are totally lacking in strategic ability in the early years is seen as misleading. They may not be able to produce the more sophisticated, mainly verbally based techniques usually associated with this concept, but even 2-year-olds have been shown to use simple retrieval cues when told to remember the location of an object under a pillow (DeLoache, Cassidy & Brown, 1985). What is more, verbal techniques such as rehearsal can also be found much earlier than the age of 5 or 6 usually given if the task is simplified and is carried out in a familiar context rather than in a laboratory situation (Wellman, 1988).

CURRENT STATUS

For another thing, the focus of previous writers on one strategy at a time has also been found to be misleading. As Siegler (1996) has pointed out with his *strategy-choice model*, children have a number of strategies available at any one time which compete with one another and may be used successively or even simultaneously on any one task, the choice depending on the nature of the task and the child's cognitive abilities. The concept of **metacognition** (see below) has been used by some writers in this connection; that is, the idea that children become increasingly adept at thinking about and regulating their own thought processes and that they can therefore intentionally select from their arsenal of strategies whatever is most appropriate. Metacogniton is thus seen as a higher-order process that controls the use of specific strategic processes. There is, however, some debate as to whether this is a correct interpretation, for the direct relationship between metacognitive and strategic abilities is by no means a strong one and varies considerably as a function of age and task variables (Holland Joyner & Kurtz-Costes, 1997).

Perhaps most telling are the findings from a number of more recent longitudinal studies (e.g. Sodian & Schneider, 1999), which have come to supplement the exclusively used cross-sectional work of the past. When individual children are followed up over a number of years, considerable unevenness of development is found: children who employ a particular strategy at one age appear to have lost it at a later age, only to resume its use subsequently. Moreover, great variation has been found in the age when children first discover a strategy; in addition, quite a lot of children jump suddenly from chance level of use to near-perfection. Gradual, steady increases appear to be the exception: the previously held view of an orderly, step-wise progression is thus in need of revision.

Further reading

Bjorklund, D.F. (Ed.) (1990). *Children's strategies: contemporary views of cognitive development*. Hillsdale, NJ: Erlbaum. Provides a useful idea of the variety of approaches to the study of strategies and their role in a range of different fields such as attention, reading and mathematics.

Bjorklund, D.F., & Douglas, R.N. (1997). The development of memory strategies. In N. Cowan & C. Hulme (Eds.), *The development of memory in childhood. Hove: Psychology Press*. Though specifically concerned with memory, this chapter gives a helpful overview of work on strategy development generally.

Siegler, R.S. (1996). *Emerging minds: the process of change in children's thinking*. New York: Oxford University Press. A detailed account of the author's theory of strategy development and the empirical data on which it is based.

See also **developmental stages; metacognition**

METACOGNITION

MEANING Human beings are not only able to think; they also have the unique ability to think about thinking. They can stand apart from their own thought processes, as it were, and contemplate, monitor and evaluate them, and as a consequence change their behaviour if they consider this to be appropriate. This ability is generally labelled as metacognition, a term that may be defined as –

knowledge of one's own cognitive abilities and processes,

or, at its simplest, as *thinking about thinking*.

Such an ability plays an important role in many types of cognition, hence the use of terms like metamemory, metacommunication, meta-attention and metareasoning. In each case individuals show that they are aware of knowing what they know and what they do not know, what they are able to learn and how best to learn it, and also how to differentiate between such distinct mental processes as attending, remembering and reasoning and what can be done to foster each of these activities.

Various schemes have been put forward for classifying the different activities that are subsumed under the general heading of metacognition, but the most common distinguishes between two components, namely metacognitive knowledge and metacognitive monitoring and regulation (Flavell & Wellman, 1977):

- *Metacognitive knowledge* refers to the fund of knowledge children have about the way cognitive processes such as thinking, remembering and reasoning operate both in themselves and in other people. At a very young age, for example, they learn that thinking is essentially a private activity, that by its means they can conjure up the past, and that they need to make certain specific efforts to ensure that they will remember particular experiences. In due course such knowledge becomes increasingly sophisticated and can be deliberately and consciously drawn on in order to foster activities such as studying and problem solving that children are engaged in.
- *Metacognitive monitoring and regulation* is a mostly subconscious process, which enables children to keep an eye on and evaluate their own cognitive activities and change them if necessary. Preschool children will, for example, correct their own speech while talking to someone; they thus show that they were automatically monitoring the language they were using, that they were comparing it against some standard and that any failure in this respect is brought to consciousness and can be dealt with. The regulatory component is also seen in children's selection of **cognitive strategies** for tasks such as committing something to memory – implementing the strategy, monitoring that it is appropriate for the job required and modifying it if need be.

Effective metacognitive processes are regarded as one of the more important acquisitions of childhood, on the assumption that they are the key to effective cognition. They are lacking in very young children; not surprisingly, they are slow to develop, appearing mostly between the ages of 5 and 10 but not reaching maturity until late adolescence.

ORIGINS

Metacognition is a relatively new concept, in that it was first introduced in 1971 by John Flavell in a paper discussing the development of memory. Such development, he concluded, proceeds at two levels. On one level, the child acquires various skills and abilities that facilitate memory and other cognitive activities; on the other, the child develops an awareness of the self as an actor who can deliberately engage in cognitive processes such as the storing and retrieving of information and who, in the course of development, shows an increasing awareness of and knowledge about the memory system – 'a kind of meta-memory perhaps', as Flavell (1971) put it.

The notion of such a second level rapidly spread from the study of memory to other cognitive areas, and in the years following Flavell's 1971 paper metacognition became the focus of lively theoretical discussion and empirical research. A more elaborate analysis of the concept appeared in Flavell and Wellman's 1977 contribution, though again mainly with reference to memory. Here the authors draw attention to three areas in which metacognitive knowledge plays a part, namely persons, tasks and strategies:

- The *person* category includes the knowledge children acquire about themselves and others as cognitive processors. It is seen in such statements as 'I have a poor memory for dates' or 'My friend Jim studies best while listening to music, but I prefer quiet'. In the preschool period such knowledge is still inadequate; this is seen, for example, in children's tendency grossly to overestimate their mental capacities. Asked how many pictures out of 10 displayed on a card they thought they could remember, preschoolers mostly predicted that they would recall all of them. Only after age 9 did children show a more realistic appreciation of their ability (Flavell, Friedrichs & Hoyt, 1970).
- The *task* category contains all those characteristics of a task that children must take into account when tackling it. They must know, for example, that a short list of items is easier to memorize than a long one, or that a list of rationally ordered items can be memorized more easily than a list of random items. Such knowledge may well help a child to select what to study and decide how to study it.
- *The strategy* category concerns the child's awareness of the various possible techniques that can be used to accomplish a given cognitive end. Thus children must learn which strategies are within their scope, how to employ them and what benefit they may bring. This has been discussed in greater detail above under **cognitive strategies.**

Reviewing the work done on metacognition in the 1970s, Brown, Bransford, Ferrara & Campione (1983) discovered that a considerable amount of relevant findings had already become available, especially with respect to developmental trends. However, Brown et al. also voiced disquiet and uncertainty as to what metacognition ('this fashionable but complex concept') in fact refers to, fearing that the various phenomena covered by it may be too diverse to justify a single family name. In particular they wondered whether the two components, knowledge and regulation, although closely related are nevertheless so distinct that the use of the term metacognition as a unitary entity gives rise to confusion and may represent an obstacle to scientific research. They acknowledged that metacognitive processes are central to children's learning, but raise the possibility that the concept be used to cover only the knowledge and not the regulation component.

It is interesting to note that much of recent research is on one *or* the other component, knowledge *or* regulation, even though most writers continue to use metacognition as a term to cover both. While they may acknowledge that in certain respects the two are fundamentally different and that the definition of the concept is complicated by referring to both, there is also the general feeling that they apply to the same general area of 'meta-behaviour' and that (as Brown et al., 1983) conceded, there is an incestuous relationship between them. For the time being at any rate metacognition continues to refer to knowledge *and* regulation.

CURRENT STATUS

A major issue for research has been, and still is, how to assess metacognition in children, especially with respect to the knowledge component (for a detailed discussion see Holland Joyner & Kurtz-Costes, 1997). Insofar as this is not a process one can observe, techniques rely mostly on interviewing children or on giving them questionnaires. This raises the problem of all self-report tools: it assumes that the relevant material is available in consciousness and that it can be verbalized – both doubtful conjectures. It also restricts the techniques to an age range where a certain degree of verbal facility can be taken for granted, thereby excluding the earlier years which in certain respects are of special interest. The use of pictures and filmed material as aids are being tried; in the meantime standardized batteries of items for the use with older children have been constructed, with established reliability and validity.

Much of the research on metacognition has concerned itself with tracing developmental trends. There are still many gaps in our knowledge, but certain facts have been established. For example, it is apparent that by the age of 4 or 5 children know that thinking is an internal activity, that it has content and that it is unique to humans. However, they greatly underestimate the amount of mental activity people engage in, in that they believe that someone sitting still, even if reading, has nothing going on inside their head. By age 7 or 8, however, children are aware that there is such a thing as a stream of consciousness and that there never is an 'empty mind' (Flavell, Green & Flavell, 1995).

The major issue still outstanding concerns the relationship between metacognition and performance: does knowledge and understanding of, say, memory processes improve memorizing ability in children? If so, teaching metacognitive skills should help, and various trials have accordingly been conducted with a view to training children in acquiring the appropriate insight. However, these have produced mixed results; where a relationship has been found between understanding and performance, it is mostly not a strong one. The problem is that much depends on age, task, assessment techniques and setting, and it seems that the most positive results are found only when a long list of conditions are met (Siegler, 1998).

Further reading

Flavell, J.H., Green, F.L., & Flavell, E.R. (1995). Young children's knowledge about thinking. *Monographs of the Society for Research in Childhood*, 60, no. 1, Serial no. 243. A series of studies, showing how children's ideas about thinking can be investigated.

Holland Joyner, M., & Kurtz-Costes, B. (1997). Metamemory development. In N. Cowan, (Ed.), *The development of memory in childhood*. Hove: Psychology Press. A good overview of the issues raised by metacognitive research, although primarily focused on metamemory.

See also **cognitive strategies; theory of mind**

THEORY THEORY
and: FOLK THEORIES

MEANING In keeping with the general belief that young children have considerably greater cognitive capacity than was ascribed to them just a few decades ago, the recently formulated theory theory view expresses –

> *the proposition that the development of understanding is best regarded as the formulation of a succession of naïve theories which enable children from the early years onwards to interpret their experience.*

Or, to put it more informally, *theory theory is the theory that children have theories about the world.*

The use of the term *theory* requires comment, particularly in the light of two further proposals by theory theory adherents: first, that even young infants 'have' theories and that the mechanisms for constructing them must therefore be innate, and second that these theories share many of the characteristics of those formulated by scientists (see Gopnik & Meltzoff, 1997, and Gopnik & Wellman, 1994 for details). A theory is often thought of as a highly sophisticated, carefully constructed and explicit set of propositions; however, as is now generally agreed, all of us have various sets of beliefs that we use all the time to explain aspects of experience that are important to us – beliefs which may be implicit rather than conscious and in certain respects erroneous, but which are nevertheless equivalent to primitive theories.

According to Gopnik and Meltzoff (1997), to characterize such theories as scientific is more than a mere metaphor. The theories may not be explicit but they are abstract, have internal coherence and constitute propositions that go beyond empirical data and so enable individuals to make sense of these data and to predict future events. Even young children are capable of evaluating a theory in the light of counter-evidence and of changing it accordingly. Initially children tend to ignore such evidence; in due course, however, they will feel impelled to reorganize their knowledge and incorporate the new evidence in a new theory. Thus (to quote Gopnik and Meltzoff), 'the processes of cognitive development of children are similar, indeed perhaps identical with, the processes of cognitive development of scientists'.

ORIGINS

Theory theory is a relatively new proposition, first formulated by Alison Gopnik and her colleagues (e.g. Gopnik, 1988; Gopnik & Wellman, 1992). It began as an attempt to fill the void (as seen by many developmental psychologists) resulting from the criticisms of Piagetian theory, and has rapidly become an influential new conception of children's cognitive development.

In certain respects theory theory builds on Piaget's views: both formulations, for example, see children as actively involved in constructing their own cognitive progress, and both give similar accounts of change from one way of understanding to another, namely that a period of uncertainty or disequilibrium takes place when the old view is found to be inadequate, resulting in the child trying out new solutions in order to regain balance by adopting a new way of interpreting experience (see **equilibration**). There are, however, some basic differences, namely:

- Piaget believed that mental structures and thought processes have their origin in the child's primitive sensori-motor actions and begin to manifest themselves only gradually in the course of the second year; theory theorists consider that such structures are innate and need only some experience and the development of skills to become overtly evident.
- Piaget believed that even after the first two years and the end of the sensori-motor period children's cognition remains action bound for several years yet; theory theorists on the other hand regard the belief systems of even very young children as considerably more abstract in nature and complex in form.
- According to Piaget all developmental change occurs in a domain general fashion; most theory theorists hold to a domain specific view: children's **theory of mind,** for example, develops quite independently from their understanding of objects in the physics domain (see **domain specificity**).

The theory theory view was also formulated as a reaction to **modularity**, as expressed by Fodor (1983) and others. Both approaches consider that the child's understanding starts with innate 'knowledge'; Fodor, however, believed that the modules which represent the mechanisms underlying this knowledge are tightly specified to process information in only certain ways and cannot subsequently be changed by experience. There is, for example, a theory of mind module, which will be triggered by certain specific kinds of experience once the module comes 'on stream', but when it does the interpretations of human behaviour it gives rise to are mandatory in that they are innately specified and cannot be modified. According to theory theorists, however, experience does not merely act as a trigger for innate mechanisms but plays an essential part in revising and reorganizing understanding in the light of counter-evidence. As they argue, initial beliefs are often quite erroneous and it seems unlikely they would be built into the mind once and for all as the modularity theorists would have it. Thus, theory theorists hold what has been termed a *starting state* position, which emphasizes that what is innate is very general in nature and provides only a start to development, whereas modularity adherents believe in a *final state* position in that they consider the innate equipment to specify for good the nature of the child's understanding.

CURRENT STATUS

The theory theory approach has attracted a great deal of attention and is currently one of the most influential views of cognitive development. Much of the research it refers to comes under the general heading of **FOLK THEORIES** (see Wellman & Gelman, 1998, for a detailed discussion).

Folk theories (also known as naïve, common sense, everyday and lay theories) may be described as –

> *the sets of beliefs that people spontaneously develop concerning various everyday domains of experience.*

The three core domains to which most attention has been given are naïve theories pertaining to physical, biological and psychological phenomena. These are central to survival and everyday living, are assumed to be based on innate, neurological mechanisms, and are believed to play a role in also shaping the more sophisticated theories that scientists construct to explain the world in more formal terms. Folk theories concerning physics address themselves to such phenomena as causation, gravity and the solidity and movement of objects. Those in the biological domain include the understanding of animate–inanimate differences and such processes as illness, birth and death. As to naïve psychology, the focus is on the understanding of mental phenomena and how they function – i.e. the topic of **theory of mind** which has attracted by far the most attention of all folk theories.

There are other possible content areas (morality, for instance, has been suggested), but with respect to all of them theory theorists mostly believe them to be domain specific (see **domain specificity**). For each realm, that is, people form distinct theories; what happens in one regarding the form and rate of its developmental course need have no implications for any other.

Theory theory has not been without its critics. Most of all, questions have been raised about the use of the term 'theory' – is it justified to refer to infants' and young children's understanding in this way, and especially so when these theories are said to be similar to those of scientists? A number of writers have objected to the idea that anything so abstract and complex can already be found in the early months of life: to explain a young baby's imitation of another person's tongue protrusion, for example, one does not need to hypothesize anything so complex as a theory behind the action. Moreover, even when children show evidence of being able to formulate some general belief system, a number of developmental psychologists such as Paul Harris (1994) argue against likening the pattern of their cognitive development to the construction and revision of theories as found in science. Children's belief systems are radically different in that they are not rationally constructed as internally consistent sets of statements, not formally tested and compared with other possible explanations, and rarely consciously inspected and sceptically mulled over. This position is thus very much opposed to the view expressed by Gopnik, Meltzoff and Kuhl (1999) and their assertion that 'Children and scientists ... both seem to operate in very similar, even identical ways'. This, Harris believes, is simply based on a false analogy.

There are other concerns, such as the uncertainty as to how to identify specific domains and determine their boundaries (see **domain specificity**), and the problem of justifying the claim that theories are in some (not defined) way derived from innate mechanisms. In general, however, the thesis underlying theory theory, that even very young infants are cognitively capable of far more than was formerly attributed to them, and that this includes being able to organize their experience in quite sophisticated ways, is now mostly accepted. Thus theory theory has become an important part of the move towards abandoning the view of infants as mindless creatures, capable of only primitive sensori-motor responses, in that it recognizes instead that even quite young children may possess precocious understanding of a kind Piaget was not prepared to acknowledge.

Further reading

Gopnik, A., & Meltzoff, A.N. (1997). *Words, thoughts and theories.* Cambridge, MA: MIT Press. The most detailed and authoritative statement available of the theory theory position.

Gopnik, A., & Wellman, H.M. (1994). The theory theory. In L.A. Hirschfeld & S.A. Gelman (Eds.), *Mapping the mind: domain specificity in cognition and culture*. Cambridge: Cambridge University Press. A more succinct account of theory theory than that in the above book.

Gopnik, A., Meltzoff, A., & Kuhl, P. (1999). *How babies think*. London: Weidenfeld & Nicolson (in USA: *The scientist in the crib*. New York: William Morrow). A delightfully written, popular account of recent findings in the cognitive development field, including those on theory theory.

See also **domain specificity; theory of mind**

SOCIAL COGNITION

6

SIX

We use the term *social cognition* to refer to our knowledge of people – not only of other people but also of ourselves. Or, to put it another way, it refers to the study of how people make sense of others and of themselves. It is an area at the intersection of cognition and social behaviour, and has emerged as a subject for investigation in its own right only relatively recently. Nevertheless, it is already a very lively research field, and especially so since the 1980s due to the enormous interest generated by one particular topic, namely theory of mind research.

The very fact that we refer to *social* cognition indicates that we think of cognitive behaviour towards people as different in certain fundamental respects from cognitive behaviour towards objects. It is certainly well established that infants arrive in the world already well attuned to human faces and voices, and that whatever other kinds of pre-tuning one can find in their perception of the material world the evolutionary importance of a special orientation towards the human world is clearly apparent. According to a considerable number of studies examining infants' behaviour towards people and objects this differentiation increases: children not only act differently to these two features in their environment but also expect them to act differently. And once children are able clearly to express their awareness of others' mental qualities – their motives, points of view, feelings and beliefs – and appreciate that other humans are able to behave as independent agents in a way objects cannot do, the two-fold classification is firmly established, justifying the study of social aspects as a separate endeavour.

Let us note that there is one other sense in which the term social cognition is also used, namely to denote the effect the social context has on cognition. According to Mary Gauvain (2001): 'Social experience is an essential component of cognitive development', and similarly: 'The long-held approach of dividing the intellectual from the social ... parts of growth has kept us from understanding key components of cognitive development.' Also known as the socio-cultural approach to cognition, its most influential proponent has been Lev Vygotsky; whereas Piagetian and information processing theories tended to study children in isolation, Vygotsky brought a social perspective to the study of cognitive development. The first set of concepts below emphasizes this orientation; the remainder examine social cognition in the other sense mentioned above. The following will be described:

ZONE OF PROXIMAL DEVELOPMENT
and: **Cultural tools**
    Scaffolding
    Guided participation
EGOCENTRISM
and: **Centration**
THEORY OF MIND
and: **Appearance–reality distinction**
ATTRIBUTION
SCRIPTS
and: **Schemas**
EMOTIONAL COMPETENCE
and: **Emotional regulation**
    Social referencing
    Emotional display rules

ZONE OF PROXIMAL DEVELOPMENT
and: CULTURAL TOOLS
SCAFFOLDING
GUIDED PARTICIPATION

Although Vygotsky devoted only limited space to the zone of proximal (i.e. next) **MEANING**
development in his description of socio-cognitive theory, this concept has become
the best-known part of his account. The ZPD (as it is always referred to) expresses
Vygotsky's belief that children's cognitive development occurs essentially as a
result of interacting with more knowledgeable and competent others, who are willing to provide guidance and support in problem solving situations and will sensitively adjust their help in such a way that the child is challenged to participate in
activities just beyond his or her current level of understanding. The ZPD is thus –

> *the region between what children already know and what they are
> capable of learning under guidance.*

It is in this region that children are most receptive to new learning; it is there that
any new intellectual skill is first of all performed jointly with a competent adult
before it is in due course taken over by the child and internalized. It is the region
where children are not quite capable of managing on their own but where the
adult can stretch their abilities by suitably pacing demands so that the child can
gradually assume responsibility for performing the task in a solo capacity.

The ZPD is an expression of the basic proposition that Vygotsky set out to convey,
namely that cognitive development is not a process that occurs spontaneously nor
can it merely be explained by the child's interaction with the physical environment.
It occurs because children are embedded in a social context, surrounded by people
of greater expertise willing to share their knowledge with the child. Cognitive development can thus be seen as a progression from *intermental* to *intramental*, from joint
regulation to self-regulation. The adult acts as tutor, the child as apprentice, but the
interaction of the two is of a dynamic, mutually adjustive nature, for the child is no
mere passive participant but an active partner in the learning process, albeit a junior
one. Cognition is socially created, and the ZPD is a means of bringing this about.

According to Vygotsky, the ZPD has one further use, namely in the assessment
of intelligence. Vygotsky was convinced that children's potential is best demonstrated when working with a more competent person than when working on their
own. Such an assertion goes, of course, directly counter to the generally accepted
view, as seen in psychometric and other assessment procedures, that children's true
capacities can only be revealed by tests administered to them in isolation. However,
Vygotsky argued that children's ability to profit from help can tell us more about
their eventual capacities than their efforts at unsupported problem solving. As he

put it, it is in the ZPD that the 'buds of development' are to be found rather than the 'fruits', and it is the former that he considered to be of greater diagnostic value with respect to an individual's future progress.

ORIGINS   Although Vygotsky became aware of Piaget's writings, he did not formulate his ideas in direct opposition to them – as an effort, that is, to correct the latter's view of children as lone learners. Rather, Vygotsky (1896–1934) was very much a child of his time and place – a Russian steeped in Marxian theory who saw human nature as a socio-cultural product and childhood as the time when the accumulated wisdom of previous generations is handed on to the new generation.

The ZPD was conceived by him as the primary setting in which such handing on is accomplished; the significance of these encounters, therefore, extends beyond the cognitive benefits derived by individual children: they also play an essential role in bringing the child in contact with the culture, the continuity of which is thereby ensured. To explain this process Vygotsky used the concept of **CULTURAL TOOLS**, these being –

> *the psychological and technological devices perfected in the course of each society's history for the purpose of supporting and extending our understanding of the world.*

Psychological tools include language, writing, counting systems and scientific theories; among technological tools are books, clocks, calendars, calculators and computers. All these serve to channel our thinking in particular culturally valued directions: clocks and calendars, for example, ensure that we organize our ideas in a time dimension, the importance of which we set out to convey to children from an early age.

However, by far the most important cultural tool is language, for it is the pre-eminent means of passing on society's experience. Children first encounter language as an integral part of their social exchanges with their caretakers, who sensitively (though usually quite unconsciously) adapt both the complexity and the content of their speech to the child's ability to comprehend, thus facilitating the eventual acquisition of language in children themselves (see **motherese**). Language thus begins in a social setting and, according to Vygotsky, is also initially used solely for social purposes, that is, to influence the behaviour of others. Eventually its function becomes extended: private speech (or what Piaget called egocentric speech) appears, whereby children talk to themselves in order to regulate their own behaviour, to be replaced subsequently by internal speech which forms the beginning of thought. Thus, what was in the first place behaviour that took place between child and others is transformed in the course of development to an internalized activity: the intermental becomes the intramental; an essentially social function evolves into the principal tool for cognitive functioning.

Vygotsky did not produce any fully fledged theory, nor did he leave behind a coherent body of research, and it was not until many years after his early death that his two major books, *Thought and language* (1962) and *Mind in society* (1978), were translated into English and began to attract international attention. Even in his own country his work was neglected when his writings were suppressed during the Stalinist purges – an ironic fate to overcome a convinced Marxist who firmly believed that human behaviour is moulded by social organization and that the historical forces shaping our society need to be taken into account if we are to understand how children's development takes place. Indeed his aim was not merely to throw light on the nature of individual development; he was also convinced that by understanding the processes responsible for children becoming adults one can help to create a better socialist society. His vision was thus much wider than that of any other child psychologist: it extended beyond psychology to history, sociology, politics, economics, education and linguistics, all of which he regarded as relevant to the study of individual development. No wonder his theory is variously characterized as socio-cultural, socio-historical and socio-cognitive.

In the past few decades Vygotsky's writings have attracted enormous attention, and most of all serious consideration has been given to his belief that we need to think of the child-in-context as the basic unit rather than the child-in-isolation (see **context**). He is also responsible for stimulating a considerable amount of research on topics such as the analysis of parent–child joint problem solving (e.g. Wood, Bruner & Ross, 1976), peer tutoring (e.g. Foot & Howe, 1998), the role of private (egocentric) speech (e.g. Bivens & Berk, 1990) and cross-cultural comparisons of socialization and training practices (e.g. Rogoff, Mistry, Goncu & Mosier, 1993). The notion of the ZPD in particular has been the starting point for a lot of further work.

CURRENT STATUS

However, Vygotsky's conception of the ZPD has also been seriously criticized. Much of this has been directed at the following features:

- *Vagueness regarding processes.* The ZPD has been condemned for using a unidimensional concept to represent a multifaceted phenomenon (Paris & Cross, 1988). It does not specify the many and diverse processes that socially supported learning involves, nor does it provide a guide to the variations in zones that one can expect across different domains, settings and teachers.
- *The failure to consider developmental aspects.* Vygotsky conceived of a prototype child, who functions in the ZPD in the same way at the age of 2 as at the age of 12. The roles of adult and child remain fixed; the appearance of new motives, needs and abilities are neglected, as are children's changing definitions of what constitutes their social context.
- *The disregard of children's individuality.* Although Vygotsky stressed the active part played by the child in the ZPD, he paid more attention to the adult's contribution. At any one age children differ in what they bring to a social interchange, but Vygotsky had nothing to say about individual differences in such aspects as learning style, motivation and emotional regulation, nor about the various relationship qualities that distinguish different adult–child dyads.
- *Vagueness concerning the precise means whereby learning is produced.* Just what are the processes taking place between child and partner that result in children taking over responsibility for more and more parts of the task and inernalizing them as skills of their own? Vygotsky did not go into detail; it has been left to others to pursue this line of enquiry.

One attempt to provide an answer to this last question is built around the concept of **SCAFFOLDING**, first put forward by Wood, Bruner and Ross (1976). Scaffolding is –

> *the process whereby a more expert partner offers help to a child in problem solving by adjusting both the amount and kind of help to the child's level of performance.*

In order to determine precisely what adults actually do in a joint task in order to help children become independent problem solvers, Wood and his colleagues observed the teaching techniques adopted by mothers when their 3- to 4-year-old children were confronted by a construction task that they could not initially cope with on their own. They observed a great range of actions employed by the mothers to keep the children on task and simplify the problem to an appropriate degree, but their use appeared to follow two rules: first, when a child is struggling the tutor should immediately offer more help; second, when the child is succeeding the tutor should give less help and fade into the background. By offering support that is always contingent on what the child is achieving, the child is given considerable autonomy and yet also has the opportunity at every step of relying on assistance, this diminishing as the child increasingly takes over responsibility for completing the task. A scaffold is thus put in place, but used in a far more flexible manner than this metaphor might suggest, in that the two contingency rules mean that the adult's behaviour is constantly modified in the light of what the child is achieving, thus leading the child step by step to eventual success.

Such a notion of scaffolding certainly expresses the essence of what Vygotsky had in mind for the ZPD, and has been used in a large number of studies investigating a range of problem solving tasks. Yet this concept too is not without its critics (e.g. Stone, 1993), mainly because it pays insufficient attention to the communicative processes taking place in the adult–child interaction; also because it does not allow for the fact that the effectiveness of adults' actions is dependent on the particular relationship they have with the child. Another approach, that based on the concept of **GUIDED PARTICIPATION**, has attempted to correct these deficiencies.

Guided participation is a term proposed by Barbara Rogoff (1990, 2003) as one of the mechanisms employed to advance a socio-cultural view of human development. Children, that is, become immersed in the practices of their particular culture from the moment of birth onwards; everything they experience transmits to them the accumulated beliefs and values of their society, and the main setting in which this occurs is in the child's exchanges with its caretakers, teachers and other concerned adults. Thus, as Rogoff (1998) put it, 'Cognitive development occurs as new generations collaborate with older generations in varying forms of interpersonal engagement and institutional practices.' Guided participation may therefore be defined as –

> *the process by which children develop through their involvement in the practices of their community.*

By its use Rogoff wanted to emphasize that adult and child play essentially complementary roles in the latter's development, namely guidance by the adult and participation by the child. On the one hand the adult acts as guide to the culturally valued practices the child is expected to adopt – a role that can be played in many ways, some didactic as in structured teaching situations (which Vygotsky mainly concentrated on), others informal as when the child is given the opportunity to observe and join an adult in performing some activity. On the other hand the child acts as apprentice – not merely as passive bystander, that is, but as an active contributor to the activity that is the joint focus of the partner's attention. Thus guided participation is not some particular method of support for learning, nor does it depend on some conscious, previously formulated goal. A lot of joint teaching-learning is of an informal nature, and Rogoff uses a wealth of observations from different cultures to illustrate its role in enabling children to participate in the activities of their society and to advance from their present to a more advanced level of understanding.

The general theme conveyed by Vygotsky, Rogoff and other socio-cultural theorists, as signalled by the concepts they employ such as the ZPD and guided participation, is that cognitive growth can only be understood if we acknowledge the social origins of mental processes and recognize that cognitive functions, especially in the early years, extend beyond the skin. This is in marked contrast to the customary individualistic assumption of psychologists – an assumption difficult to abandon despite the lipservice now paid to the importance of context, but well illustrated by the complete failure to take up Vygotsky's suggestion that intellectual assessment should take into account children's performance in joint sessions. Vygotsky was convinced that thinking is not just something that goes on inside an individual's head but is an activity that can be shared – indeed of necessity has to be shared in the early stages of development. As Rowe and Wertsch (2002) have put it, 'Study of the "I" is thus abandoned in favour of study of the social, cultural and historically situated ways by which "we" create "I's".'

Further reading

Faulkner, D., Littleton, K., & Woodhead, M. (Eds.) (1998). *Learning relationships in the classroom*. London: Routledge. Written mainly from an educational point of view, this collection contains a lot of material relevant to the concepts described above.

Fernyhough, C. (1997). Vygotsky's sociocultural approach: theoretical issues and implications for current research. In S. Hala (Ed.), *The development of social cognition*. Hove: Psychology Press. A concise account of the main themes in Vygotsky's theory.

Rogoff, B. (2003). *The cultural nature of human development*. Oxford: Oxford University Press. Gives a very detailed description not only of Rogoff's theoretical position but also of the research and thinking by other socio-cultural writers.

See also **constructivism; context; social constructivism**

EGOCENTRISM
and: **CENTRATION**

MEANING As used by Piaget in his account of children's cognitive characteristics, egocentrism refers to –

> *the tendency for children to perceive the world solely from their own perspective and to be unaware that other people may have different perspectives.*

There are many illustrations of this tendency in the behaviour of young children. A particularly vivid one is provided by listening to 3- or 4-year-old children's telephone conversation with another person (see Warren & Tate, 1992): their talk is littered with references to things in their immediate environment ('do you like my new dress?') or to their recent experiences ('the two of us went to that shop this morning') without realizing that the other person cannot see the dress or share in the child's prior knowledge of who 'the two' are or what shop they visited. A non-egocentric person will describe and identify such things in order to establish a common knowledge basis with the conversational partner; young children take for granted that such knowledge already exists.

It should be stressed that egocentrism need not denote a deliberate attribution of one's own point of view to another; rather, in young children it takes the form of not realizing that that they have points of view, or that others do, or that these may differ. It is for this reason that they automatically assume that their particular perspective is shared by everyone else – an indication, as Piaget put it, of a failure to differentiate subjective from objective aspects of experience.

Piaget also believed that egocentrism is a manifestation of a very general cognitive state prevalent among young children, which he referred to as **CENTRATION**. This is –

> *the tendency to focus on only one particular feature of an object or situation at a time, to the exclusion of all other potentially relevant features.*

This is seen, for example, in conservation tasks: young children witnessing the transfer of liquid from a tall, slim container to a short but wide one will maintain that there is less liquid now in the latter than there was in the former, because they centre their attention on only one dimension, namely height and do not make allowance for the change in width that is also taking place. Conservation only becomes possible when the child becomes able flexibly to switch attention from one dimension to the other and simultaneously take both into account – a process referred to by Piaget as *decentring*. And just as children cannot free themselves of whatever feature of an object is the most striking one (height in this example) and attend to others as well, so they remain centred on their particular point of view and cannot also consider those of other people. Centration has not yet given way to decentration.

Egocentrism is a key concept in Piagetian theory, with implications for many aspects of behaviour (Piaget, 1929). For instance:

ORIGINS

- *Perceptual egocentrism* refers to the assumption that others see a particular object or scene in the same way as the child does. This is illustrated by what has become the best known of Piaget's examples, the three-mountain task. A child is seated in front of a model of three mountains of different size and shape, shown photographs of the model taken from each side and asked which one corresponds to the way they see it – something preschoolers can usually do quite easily. A doll is then placed at one of the other sides and the child is asked which photo corresponds to the doll's viewpoint. Most young children will then again point to the photo corresponding to their *own* viewpoint.
- *Communicative egocentrism* is illustrated by the above example of children's talk on the telephone. It is also seen in young children's conversations with each other: each child talks about his or her own interest, does not follow on to anything the partner says and so helps to produce what Piaget called a *monologue conversation*. As Piaget (1955) put it, the child 'feels no desire to influence his hearers nor to tell them anything: not unlike a certain type of drawing room conversation where everyone talks about himself and no one listens'.
- *Peer play* at early ages tends to take the form of parallel play rather than joint play. As with verbal interaction, children find it easier to pursue their own activities and have not yet developed the ability to link their individual contribution to those of others in order to bring about a cooperative product – a conversation in the one case, a game in the other.
- *Moral understanding* is also affected, because in the early years children believe that moral rules depend solely on the authority of their own parents, whose edicts and prohibitions are absolute and must be rigidly adhered to, irrespective of the particular circumstances in which actions occur. It is only later in development that children can take into account such circumstances too and realize that rules can be modified by these, and it is also only later on, mainly in the context of interacting with peers, that they learn that rules depend on mutual negotiation and reciprocity (Piaget, 1932) (see **moral conduct rules**).

There are other phenomena which Piaget interpreted as an expression of egocentrism: *animism*, for example, which is the tendency of young children to attribute consciousness to inanimate objects, and *realism*, the belief that psychological

131

phenomena such as thoughts and dreams have a physical existence. Thus egocentrism, Piaget asserted, is a fundamental characteristic of children's cognition in the first 6 years or so, which they only grow out of when they become aware that others may not share their particular perspective – something most likely to occur when playing with other children and coming up against the need to resolve differences of opinion and goals ('the shock of thought coming into contact with that of others', as Piaget put it). Yet he also believed that traces of egocentrism can be found later on in development: in adolescence, for example, when young people are convinced that their particular grandiose schemes for creating a better world are the right ones, irrespective of what adults may say.

CURRENT STATUS
There is general agreement now that egocentrism is a useful concept to characterize young children's approach to the world, and many aspects of Piaget's work in this area have received support from later research. This applies to a wide range of functions including, for example, problem solving, play, spatial orientation and communication – all indicate that there is a marked tendency early on for children to be centred on themselves and to have difficulty in adopting a more flexible perspective.

Yet in certain respects Piaget's views of egocentrism have also had to undergo some drastic revision. Criticism has for the most part taken two forms: first, findings show that children very much younger than age 6 or so do have some capacity for acting in a non-egocentric manner, and secondly it appears that egocentrism is not a unitary concept but shows every sign of **domain specificity**. Consider some of the results obtained by later research:

- Young children were given a hollow cube with a picture on the inside bottom surface, and asked first to look at it themselves and then to show it to an adult sitting opposite them. To do so meant children had to tilt the container towards the adult, thereby losing sight of it themselves. Children as young as 2 years were able to do so, thus demonstrating that they realised that the adult's perspective was different from their own (Lempers, Flavell & Flavell, 1977).
- Preschool children listened to short stories about various emotion-provoking events, and then were asked to indicate how the child in each story felt by choosing from pictures of a happy, sad, angry and afraid face. Even at age 3 children had some limited success in choosing the appropriate face, and by age 4 they had become quite proficient in recognizing how someone else might feel in a given situation. The children, that is, were able to empathize with the feelings of another individual whose perspective they could take (Borke, 1971).
- Four-year-olds were paired in turn with an adult, a peer and a 2-year-old and their spontaneous talk with each partner recorded. Linguistic analysis showed that the children quite automatically adapted their speech style to the developmental status of the other individual: with 2-year-olds, for example, the children used shorter sentences, fewer complex constructions and more attention-getting devices than with older partners (Shatz & Gelman, 1973) (see **motherese**).

- In a highly influential critique of Piaget's work, Margaret Donaldson (1978) has argued that tests such as the three-mountain task are too complex and demanding for young children. A more meaningful task can produce different results. When, for example, children were shown a model composed of intersecting walls in which a naughty boy doll was trying to hide from a policeman doll, childen as young as 3½ were able to disregard what they themselves were able to see looking down at the model and consider only the point of view of the figures behind the walls.

These and many other studies have contributed to the general belief that Piaget exaggerated the extent of egocentrism in young children and grossly overestimated the age when it wanes. Moreover, the work on **theory of mind** has shown that quite young children can already recognize and empathize with other people's emotions and realize that others can know things the child does not know. Piaget correctly identified a developmental trend, but his account of its time course has had to be modified. In addition, it has become apparent that egocentrism needs to be regarded as a domain specific concept and not as a global entity: intercorrelations of different manifestations are generally low, and some aspects give way to perspective-taking abilities considerably earlier than others. Across-the-board changes, as proposed by Piaget, do not take place; each domain runs its own course (see **domain specificity**).

One further consideration: egocentrism is usually considered in negative terms, as a characteristic that imposes constraints on an individual's behaviour in both interpersonal and problem solving situations. Bjorklund (1997), however, has put forward the provocative idea that there may be some adaptive advantages to being egocentric in the early years. Young children, he argues, have so much to learn about the world that they ought to be self-centred and not distracted by how others think and feel, for then their learning is likely to be more efficient. As research has demonstrated, anything that individuals can relate to themselves is more meaningful and therefore more likely to be remembered, and this applies especially to young children. Thus, seen from an evolutionary point of view, egocentrism is beneficial rather than detrimental (see **evolution**).

Further reading

Cox, M.V. (1991). *The child's point of view* (2nd ed.). Hemel Hempstead: Harvester Wheatsheaf. Reviews what has been found out about children's awareness of other people's points of view in areas such as visual perspective, drawing and conversational role-taking, and also refers to theory of mind research.

Donaldson, M. (1978). *Children's minds*. London: Fontana. A highly influential review and critique of Piagetian theory, including his work on egocentrism.

See also **developmental stages; domain specificity; symbolic representation**

THEORY OF MIND
and: APPEARANCE-REALITY DISTINCTION

MEANING Adults construe other people not just as physical beings but also in terms of their internal mental states – their emotions, desires, beliefs, thoughts and intentions, which they regard as the forces that bring about and guide all overt action. In short, adults make use of a *theory of mind* (ToM, as it is customarily referred to). The origins and nature of such a theory in children has been the focus of an enormous research effort in the past two decades or so, resulting in an impressive body of literature (for general reviews see Further Reading below).

Broadly defined, a theory of mind is –

> *people's intuitive understanding of their own and others' mental states.*

The terms *mind reading* and *mentalizing* are also sometimes used in this connection.

Two points need to be made here. First, the term *theory* is said to be justified because mental states are based on inferences, in that they are not directly observable but are deduced from their overt manifestations. The theories are, of course, intuitive rather than strictly scientific – naïve or **folk theories** that are constructed informally, usually out of the individual's awareness, but that nevertheless serve as intellectual devices for explaining and predicting overt phenomena (Gopnik & Wellman, 1992). In the second place, there has been some disagreement in the past as to what should be included under *mental states* that is relevant to ToM. On the one hand, broad definitions of ToM like that given above encompass all internal states that characterize the human mind; on the other hand a more narrow definition recognizes only the states that mark the attainment of a mature, adult-like ToM (usually somewhere around the age of 4), refusing to admit states such as desire, emotion and perception, which develop earlier, and concentrating instead on children's ability to understand more complex states, among which belief has attracted most research attention.

To a large extent this disagreement is artificial, depending on where one wants to draw the line on the developmental course. More to the point, there is widespread recognition that somewhere around the age of 4 children take a major step forward in their understanding of people by developing a *representational* concept of the mind. Children, that is, begin to comprehend that mental contents is not just a *copy* of reality but an *interpretation* of reality, that the mind is not just a perceptual tool but is also capable of forming its own representations of experience, and that knowledge of people's mental world is a surer way of predicting their behaviour than the real world they inhabit. Two conclusions follow: children now realize that different people may represent the same thing differently, and any one individual may have representations that are inaccurate and that give rise to false beliefs about the world.

The assessment of children's understanding of false belief has become somewhat of a litmus test for the attainment of a mature ToM. There are various versions of the test, but the most commonly used is the *unexpected transfer task*, involving a story about a child watching an object such as a piece of chocolate being hidden in a box. This is also witnessed by another person, who then leaves the room. In his absence the chocolate is transferred to a different container. The crucial question is then put to the child: when the person returns, where will he look for the chocolate? As repeatedly found by numerous studies (Wellman, Cross & Watson, 2001), 3-year-olds will opt for the new container on the basis of their own knowledge; 4-year-olds, however, will choose the previous one because they can appreciate that a person can hold a false belief. Younger children, that is, assume that a person's beliefs are a true copy of reality and cannot therefore comprehend that others may hold different beliefs about a particular event; at the older age they understand that people act on the basis of whatever information is represented in their minds, and as that information is sometimes misleading people are capable of acting on the basis of false beliefs. They thus show that they have made the crucial transition to comprehending that mental contents is distinct from real world contents and that both need to be taken into account in understanding behaviour. Whether the false belief test does serve as the litmus test it has been claimed to be is, however, becoming increasingly controversial. Thus Bloom and German (2000) have pointed out that there is more to passing false belief tests than ToM; moreover, there is more to ToM than false belief. In consequence, they are in favour of abandoning the test altogether.

Nevertheless, the evidence for a transition in children's understanding of the mind around the age of 4 is overwhelming. There are indications that this step is part of a more general developmental trend, as shown by the close theoretical and empirical relationship with the growth of children's ability to understand the **APPEARANCE–REALITY DISTINCTION** (Flavell, 1993). This concept refers to –

> *the realization that things may be different from what they appear to be,*

that is, the knowledge that looks can be deceiving. As Flavell, Green and Flavell (1986) have shown in a series of experiments, 3-year-old children are as yet unable to make that distinction. A sponge made to look like a rock *is* a rock as long as the child examines it visually; when the child then feels it, it *is* a sponge. Similarly with a glass of milk: the milk is described as white by the child when first seen, but when a red filter is then wrapped round the glass the milk is 'really and truly red'. As Flavell (1988) has put it, these children 'do not clearly understand that even though something may be only one way out there in the world, it can be more than one way up here in our heads, in our mental representations of it'. By age 4, however, children do know that one and the same object can give rise to two different representations, that is to say, that the object is, in some sense, both a rock *and* a sponge. They are able to consider two apparently contradictory impressions at the same time and realize that one is for real and the other only apparent. Thus findings about the emergence of the appearance–reality distinction give rise to the same conclusion as those from the studies of ToM: both indicate that for the young child there is only one reality, namely that given by immediate perception, whereas the older child knows that perceptions give rise to mental representations and that some of these may be inaccurate. The understanding of false beliefs and of the appearance–reality distinction both appear within the same age range of 3 to 5 years; in individual children they develop concurrently; and both herald the same profound achievement, namely the emergence of a *representational conception of the mind*.

ORIGINS   Research on theory of mind issues arose in the first place as part of the fascination with mental states in the post-behaviourism era in the second half of the twentieth century. In a remarkably short time it burgeoned into a sizeable body of findings, and there is no sign that this interest is in any way diminishing.

The concept of ToM can be said to have been officially launched in 1978 by Premack and Woodruff, in a paper speculating whether chimpanzees possess anything like a theory of mind. The ideas advanced in this paper, and in the comments on it by various authors following it, were taken up by Wimmer and Perner (1983) by means of a procedure they devised for checking children's understanding of false belief, namely the now classic *unexpected-transfer task* outlined above. In the following years other versions of this task were also proposed – all, however, designed to answer one question, namely at what age children begin to comprehend false beliefs, this being taken as the ultimate criterion for a ToM. As shown by Wellman, Cross and Watson (2001), it is now generally agreed in the literature that false belief understanding emerges between ages 3 and 5 and that the results are real and not due to artefacts from overly difficult tasks.

Nevertheless, there has been concern about the almost exclusive focus in the past on this particular development, giving rise to the impression that it emerges *de novo* and represents the only criterion for assessing children's understanding of mental states. Yet when Bartsch and Wellman (1995) recorded young children's spontaneous conversations about people they found that from soon after age 2 children already talk about mental states, especially desires, using words like *want, wish* and *like*. Only in the fourth year words such as *think, know* and *wonder* appeared, revealing an awareness of people's beliefs and thoughts. Such extensions downward along the age range from 4 years, as well as research tracing later changes, have given rise to a more complete picture of ToM development which may be summarized as follows (see Hala & Carpendale, 1997, for a fuller description):

- Already in infancy *rich precursors*, as they have come to be known, are present which indicate that children have some rudimentary knowledge of mental phenomena and the way they differ from physical phenomena. The 1-year-old, for example, who uses pointing in order to share an interest in some object with someone else shows awareness that the other person has an attentional focus distinct from the child's, and that it is necessary to redirect this focus in order to bring about sharing.
- After 2 years of age children begin to show an understanding of non-representational states such as desire. This is demonstrated not only by their spontaneous use of desire words but also by their response to open-ended stories about characters expressing various kinds of desire. Thus around age 2½ and 3 children know that particular kinds of action result from specific desire states, and appear therefore to have acquired what Wellman (1990) called a *desire theory of mind*.
- It is not until age 4, however, that children acquire a *belief-desire theory of mind*, as indicated by their solving of false-belief tasks. They now understand the mind to be an essentially representative device, and can therefore make allowance for the fact that a person's belief may differ from what is happening in the real world and may also differ from the child's own belief.
- ToM developments continue in subsequent years, though the little research that has been done on this age range does not clarify whether these are merely quantitative in nature, that is to say that theories become more accurate, or whether they involve qualitatively new skills grafted on to the existing ones.

There can be no doubt that the concept of ToM has become firmly established and will be the basis of yet further theoretical and empirical investigation. Now that the outline of development is widely agreed, attention has switched to other issues, of which two are noteworthy.

CURRENT STATUS

One concerns the effects of social experience on the development of ToM skills. There are considerable individual differences among children in the age when they reach such milestones as false-belief understanding – are these explicable by the extent and nature of their interactions with other people? There is growing evidence that social experience does play a part (for review see Hughes & Leekam, 2004). For example, both cultural and socio-economic differences have been found to be associated with the age when false-belief understanding emerges. Parenting style and attachment have also been singled out, both reflecting the quality of the child's emotional relationship with the parent. And according to several studies family size appears to play some part: the larger the family the greater the rate of ToM development – an effect found mainly in younger siblings and ascribed to the opportunity of picking up ToM skills in play with older, more mature siblings.

A crucial aspect of children's social experience appears to be the language to which they are exposed. As Dunn and her colleagues have shown in a series of studies (e.g. Dunn, Brown, Slomkowski, Tesla & Youngblade, 1991), in families where there is more talk about feelings, emotions and other mental states children are more likely to be advanced in their understanding of both their own and others' desires and beliefs. Such conversational exchanges draw children's attention to the existence and nature of inner states; what is more, they do not just learn verbal labels for different states, but also have the opportunity of finding out that the same event can provoke quite different mental states in others to those they themselves experience. And the fact that some deaf children are late in acquiring false-belief competence (Peterson & Siegal, 1995) confirms that access to conversational exchanges plays an important part in ToM development.

The other issue which has attracted a lot of attention is the role mind reading abilities play in children with autism. Autism is characterized by severe impairment in social interaction and communication, and it is therefore highly pertinent that these children also fail in tasks such as false-belief designed to assess their ToM understanding, even though they show no other signs of cognitive deficiencies. Such children, according to Baron-Cohen (1995), suffer from *mindblindness*: an innate condition said to result from a specific deficit in the brain, evident already early on in an infant's failure to develop such precursors as pointing for communicative purposes. There is some disagreement as to whether mindblindness indeed forms the core of this disorder; what is beyond dispute is that autistic children fail in a considerable range of tasks linked to false-belief abilities, including the understanding of intention, deception, complex emotions, jokes and pretence (as in pretend play). ToM deficiency does seem to account for many of the problems that these children have in their everyday social behaviour.

While much has been learned at a descriptive level about the nature of ToM development, considerable uncertainty remains regarding the mechanisms responsible for this development. Three theoretical perspectives can be distinguished:

- *The theory-theory* viewpoint (spelled out in detail by Gopnik & Wellman, 1992) maintains that children undergo a series of changes in their theories of the mind, each new theory replacing a previous one with a more sophisticated and accurate version and each stemming from a profound conceptual change. At least two such changes occur in the first 5 years: the first when the child acquires a *desire theory of mind* around age 2, the second when that is replaced by a *belief-desire theory* at age 4. The theories should be seen as a set of hypotheses which, as with scientific theories, children test in the light of evidence from their everyday life (see **theory theory**). Social experience is thus assigned a major formative role in ToM development.
- *Innate module theory* (see Leslie, 1994) puts the main onus for ToM developments on inborn factors, with the proposal that we all come into the world with a processing mechanism specifically geared to understanding mental states. This mechanism is viewed as a domain specific module in the brain – the theory-of-mind mechanism (ToMM) – which operates primarily through maturation, while the role of social experience is confined to merely triggering its functioning but not as determining its nature. The workings of ToMM

are evident from early on, but are initially constrained by the child's slowly developing information processing capacity which imposes limits on cognition generally, and it is this, not hypothesis testing, which accounts for developmental progress in understanding the mind.

- *Simulation theory* (Harris, 1992) maintains that children become able to understand other people's minds because they have direct access to their own minds and, by means of a process of analogy, can simulate what they would feel or think in a given situation. In other words, they put themselves in the other person's shoes and, by assuming the role of that person, can understand what is going on in their mind. To resort to anything more complex like a theory as a means of explanation is thus not necessary; we already know about mental states from our own personal experience. Development of that knowledge is simply a matter of increasingly accurate simulation.

The debate about which of these theories is most useful is at present unresolved and will no doubt continue for some time. Each has its advantages and its disadvantages (see Hala & Carpendale, 1997, for a detailed discussion); insofar as the debate has generated additional research it must be regarded as all for the good and in time may well result in a further, more encompassing theory.

Further reading

Astington, J.W. (1994). *The child's discovery of the mind*. London: Fontana. A beautifully written, popular account of work on theory of mind that remains one of the best introductions to this topic.

Hala, S., & Carpendale, J. (1997). All in the mind: children's understanding of mental life. In S. Hala, (Ed.), *The development of social cognition*. Hove: Psychology Press. A chapter-length account of some of the main issues in theory of mind research and theorizing.

Mitchell, P. (1997). *Introduction to theory of mind*. London: Arnold. A comprehensive account, that includes detailed summaries of work on autism and on the evolutionary origins of theory of mind.

See also **domain specificity; egocentrism; modularity; symbolic representation; theory theory**

ATTRIBUTION

MEANING

It is a natural tendency for all of us to attribute causes to everything we see people do – to ask ourselves continually, almost automatically, what may have prompted someone to behave in some particular way. Why is a normally friendly colleague so ill-tempered today? Why is one child in the family so successful at school mathematics while another fails dismally? Why has a teenage girl suddenly become so very withdrawn? In each case we believe that the behaviour can be attributed to some specific cause or set of causes; moreover, by means of such attributions other people's actions become more meaningful and predictable to us. For that matter, the same process is applied to our own behaviour: here too we are convinced that our actions are usually the result of certain definite influences and motives, and gaining insight into these helps in understanding ourselves. No wonder the attribution tendency has been referred to as a basic and pervasive form of social cognition.

Attribution is thus the term given to –

> *the inferences people make about the causes of their own and others' behaviour.*

Inference is necessary because, unlike the overt behaviour we directly perceive, the cause is frequently a matter of assumption. We assume, for instance, that our ill-tempered colleague has quarrelled with a partner, basing this on our knowledge of previous relationship problems, and therefore as the most likely hypothesis to explain his behaviour. This explanation may, of course, turn out to be wrong; too much to drink at a late party the night before could turn out to be the true cause. In any case, we are not content simply to witness the ill-tempered behaviour: we immediately set about searching for the underlying reason to which the behaviour can be attributed.

The term *attribution* is sometimes used interchangeably with such other aspects of social cognition as person perceptions, expectations, beliefs and attitudes. However, the psychological literature on attribution has now developed to the point where the concept is given a very specific meaning and theoretical grounding. A number of theories (listed below) have been put forward to account for it, and though they differ in various ways all attempt to give a precise account of the manner in which we go about assigning causes to observed behaviour (see Fincham & Hewstone, 2001, for details). Thus the basic aim of attribution theories (also sometimes referred to as *social causal inference theories*), is to describe in detail the various processes involved in our attempts to explain and evaluate other people's as well as one's own actions, with particular reference to the kind of information that is selected for this purpose, the reasons for such selection and the way attributions are influenced by and influence social interaction. And as to developmental aspects, the questions raised concern the age when children become capable of making attributions, the nature of their attributions and the kind of changes that occur in the course of development (for an overview see Durkin, 1995).

ORIGINS The concept of attribution first surfaced among social psychologists investigating adults' interpersonal behaviour, and quickly became the focus of a great deal of theoretical discussion and empirical research. This has remained at a high level, whereas developmental psychologists not only came rather late to attribution theory but even now give the concept only passing acknowledgement. Indeed many developmental textbooks do not so much as mention it, despite its clear relevance to our attempts to understand the way in which children construe their social world.

The first person to use the term was Fritz Heider (1958) in his book *The psychology of interpersonal relationships*, where he put forward his version of attribution theory. This was based on the belief that the lay person acts like a naïve scientist in attempting to explain observable behaviour by unobservable causes (see **folk theories**). These causes can be divided into two basic classes: internal, that is, those within the individual such as ability, intention or effort, and external, that is, influences from the environment. A child's school failure, for example, may be attributed to lack of intelligence or to poor teaching. The first and principal task of the person making attributions is to decide to which class the cause of the observed action belongs, given the information available about the other person's behaviour and the context in which it occurs. The internal–external distinction has stimulated a considerable amount of research on adults' person perception and has also become a topic for discussion among those working with children.

Two other versions of attribution theory subsequently became prominent:

- The *correspondent inference* theory developed by Jones and his colleagues (e.g. Jones & Davis, 1965) proposes that the goal of attributions is to infer that observed behaviour and the intention that produced it correspond to some underlying disposition in the person. There are thus two sequential parts to the process: first, attribution of *intention*, that is, a decision needs to be made as to whether the act was deliberate or accidental; secondly, attribution of *disposition*, that is, determining just what kind of personal characteristic could have been responsible for producing the observed act. Specific proposals are put forward by the theory as to the particular cognitive processes which are involved in each of these two attributional steps.
- *Kelley's cube* model (Kelley, 1973) also sets out to provide a detailed analysis of the way in which people process information when explaining an observed item of behaviour, and proposes that this involves the integration of three types of data: *consensus*, the extent to which other people would behave in the same way in that situation; *consistency*, whether the behaviour is typical of the person's past behaviour; and *distinctiveness*, the extent to which the behaviour is peculiar to the particular situation in which it was observed. Each of these three factors can be judged to be high or low, leading to eight possible combinations as in a $2 \times 2 \times 2$ cube. For example, when consensus is low, consistency high and distinctiveness low, observers tend to attribute the behaviour to internal causes stemming from the actor's personal characteristics; when consensus is high, consistency low and distinctiveness high it is attributed to external, situational causes. Thus different combinations of the three factors give rise to different explanations of the behaviour, and to arrive at these the observer needs to carry

out a multi-variable mental computation analogous to that required for analyses of variance statistics – hence the term *Kelley's ANOVA model* is also used for this view of the attribution procedure.

Each of the three theories has given rise to a large number of social psychological research studies, yielding further insight into people's causal reasoning about human behaviour. The *actor–observer effect*, for example, describes the tendency of adults to cite situational influences when accounting for their own behaviour but dispositional influences when accounting for the behaviour of other people – something that has also been found in children as young as 4 years (Abramovitch & Freedman, 1981). Or to give another example: the principle of *discounting* is the tendency to consider a cause as less influential when several plausible causes are present than when it is the only possible cause. This involves an ability to evaluate several causes simultaneously and weigh up their respective influences – something difficult for younger children who have been found to use an additive rule instead, that is, to attribute equal weight to each possible cause (Fincham, 1983).

CURRENT STATUS Attribution is alive and well in social psychology, where it continues to generate an impressive amount of research on adults' interpersonal judgements. Much of this is guided by cognitive theorizing and concerned with processes outside consciousness; however, there has also been increasing interest in the way in which social contextual influences shape attributions and in intercultural differences. At the same time the theoretical positions initially advanced to account for attributional processes have come under more critical scrutiny; that by Jones and Davis (1965) in particular has failed to find support (for further details see Fincham & Hewstone, 2001).

As far as children's attributional abilities are concerned, the research efforts of various investigators have made it possible to categorize these in an orderly developmental progression (Flavell, Miller & Miller, 1993):

- The beginnings can be traced to the first awareness of *agency*, that is, the realization that human beings (unlike objects) can act of their own accord without any external cause – something that emerges already during the first year of life.
- From the second year onwards a more refined version of agency appears, namely *intentionality*. This refers to the child's understanding that an inner, mental state can lie behind the observed behaviour and that it is specifically this which brings about the act.
- In the preschool years children gradually develop more sophisticated kinds of causal reasoning. They become able to distinguish between intended and accidental acts; they no longer over-attribute intentionality by assuming that all actions are deliberate, even yawning and sneezing; and eventually they start trying to infer the precise intention and specific psychological cause responsible for a given action.

- There is a developmental trend in the kinds of perceived causes of behaviour which children single out, proceeding from a preference for external, situational attributions by preschoolers to internal, psychological attributions by school-aged children. However, according to a detailed review of the evidence by Miller and Aloise (1989) the trend is not as marked as it has often been portrayed, in that even quite young children do have some awareness of the psychological causes of behaviour (see **theory of mind**).
- Another developmental trend, namely in the types of psychological causes mentioned by children, is rather firmer. The causes referred to by preschoolers are mostly temporary mental states such as feelings or motives, and it is not until the school years that stable personality characteristics (traits, dispositions, etc.) are cited as the sources of certain kinds of actions. It is only then that causal reasoning about behaviour can be said to resemble that of adults.

As well as providing theoretical insights into the nature of social cognition, attribution has also been found to have some useful practical implications, especially in clinical and educational areas. To a large extent these have been based on a theory advanced by Weiner (1986), which links an individual's customary attributions (their *attributional style*) to their motivation and sense of being in control. For example, some forms of depression are thought to be largely due to the kind of attributions people make for life events, as summarized by the concept of *learned helplessness* (Seligman, 1975). This is the belief that the individual is not in charge of his or her own fate but is caught up by inescapable stress and insoluble problems. Similarly a school child, dogged by failure and attributing the cause to personal inadequacy, may also experience learned helplessness, with drastic effects on future performance and self-esteem. Weiner's model sets out a scheme for analysing the mental processes linking attribution, performance and emotional feeling, and has been used with both adults and children as a basis for developing treatment programmes, designed to train individuals to adopt a different, more positive attributional style (Dweck, 1975).

Further reading

Durkin, K. (1995). *Developmental social psychology*. Oxford: Blackwell. Includes a full account of research on children's attributions; particularly useful on practical implications.

Fincham, F., & Hewstone, M. (2001). Attribution theory and research: from basic to applied. In M. Hewstone & W. Stroebe (Eds.), *Introduction to social psychology* (3rd ed.). Oxford: Blackwell. A detailed account of the way in which work on attribution has developed from Heider to the present day.

See also **folk theories; parental belief systems; theory of mind**

SCRIPTS
and: SCHEMAS

MEANING   We think about the world not just in terms of static objects but also as series of ongoing events. Family meals, shopping at the local supermarket, visiting relatives, bedtime routines – these and many other events occur as regular sequences in everyday life, giving it a structure that is predictable and therefore reassuring. We store these in memory; their mental representations are known as *scripts*.

A script can formally be defined as –

> *a mental structure that organizes information about some frequently repeated everyday event in temporal sequence and in generalized form.*

Scripts tell us 'how things are supposed to happen'. It is therefore vital that children acquire them early on in life: being able to anticipate what will happen when, for example, they go to nursery school in the morning or pay a visit to granny or eat out in the local McDonald's gives them a sense of security. Scripts, that is, are mental models of regularly occurring experiences and are therefore useful as guides to behaviour whenever the appropriate situation arises. No wonder they have been referred to as 'the young child's most powerful tool for understanding the world' (Flavell, Miller & Miller, 1993).

The following characteristics are necessary ingredients of scripts (Nelson, 1986):

- Scripts are generalized representations. They do not refer to single occurrences of some event but are abstractions based on repeated encounters with that event.
- Scripts are temporally organized. They have a narrative structure, with a beginning, middle and end, and indicate that children are capable from an early age of storing experience in memory in sequential form.
- Scripts contain *slots* that need to be filled. Some of these are obligatory: the child's bath time script, for example, contains getting undressed as a necessary component; others are variable: the adult supervising the child at bath time may be mother or father or perhaps some other person.
- Scripts are hierarchically organized. They can be depicted as a tree structure, made up of a main goal (getting clean, in the example of the bath time script), subgoals (undressing, washing, etc.), certain specific actions constituting each subgoal, and outcome. The level of detail and concreteness increases the lower down the structure one examines a script. The extent to which children of different ages are sensitive to the hierarchical organization of their scripts and are able to report them at different levels is one of the main interests from a developmental point of view.

- Scripts are built around contents that is culturally determined. They contain themes (e.g. eating at a fast-food restaurant, shopping at supermarkets) that are specific to particular societies; they thus serve to emphasize certain practices and values that are regarded as important by parents and other socializing agents in that particular culture.

Scripts are derived from another, very widely used concept, namely **SCHEMAS**.   **ORIGINS**
A schema is –

> *a knowledge structure that has been acquired from prior experience.*

The term was first used by the neurologist Henry Head, specifically to denote the body image that people acquire of themselves. However, it was given most prominence by Frederick Bartlett (1932), who used it to account for his observation that people, when attempting to recall a story, tend to make errors that make the story more conventional. This is because every new experience is assimilated to an existing mental structure representing some aspect of previous experience, that is, a schema, which serves to facilitate, but sometimes also to distort, our perception and interpretation of new information in terms of existing knowledge and which thus influences the way we encode and store the information. This also explains why unfamiliar material is difficult to recall.

A schema, as so conceived, refers to all kinds of stored material. This also applies to Piaget's use of the term – he too saw it as a basic cognitive structure that individuals use to make sense of their experience. The first to use the term *script* as a special kind of schema, namely one for representing event sequences, were Schank and Abelson (1977) in their highly influential book *Scripts, plans, goals and understanding*. In it they proposed that scripts, like the more general notion of schemas, exist in order to guide the establishment of mental representations, but are distinctive with respect to three key components, namely (1) they contain actions that are appropriate to some specific spatial-temporal context, (2) they are organized around a goal and (3) they are temporally ordered. Scripts can thus be seen as a primary means of comprehending and re-creating real-life experiences in their temporal order in which they were encountered.

Schank and Abelson's account was not a developmental one, and it is primarily due to Katherine Nelson's initiative that the concept came also to be applied to children's cognition (Nelson, 1981; Nelson & Gruendel, 1979). Nelson asked two questions: first, do young children possess scripts, and secondly, if so, are they similar in structure and content as those of adults? The answer from her studies turned out to be affirmative to both questions: children as young as 3 are capable of recalling event sequences, and the nature of their accounts is basically much like that of adults. By asking preschool children to recount 'what happens' in such familiar events as eating at McDonald's or attending a friend's birthday party Nelson demonstrated that children can give a reasonably accurate verbal account of these experiences, that their recollections are coherent and show consistency over a period of time, and that they are structurally similar to those of adults by faithfully preserving the temporal order in which the various parts of each event took place. Scripts, Nelson concluded, are 'the basic building blocks of cognition' in that all kinds of information about the world is organized around them. What is more, they have social implications, insofar as they provide a means of sharing knowledge with others and learning from their accounts what variations there can be to familiar experiences.

CURRENT STATUS

The concept of scripts has been found to be a useful addition to the various types of memory store that have been identified (see **multistore models**). Among developmental psychologists it has stimulated a considerable number of investigations, designed to flesh out the concept and provide answers to a variety of questions concerning the nature of its developmental course.

One of these refers to the age when children first become capable of forming scripts. Initially this was thought to be around the age of 3, as it was then that children started to give sensible accounts of event experiences. However, this turned out to be a function of the verbal methods used for investigation: when Bauer and Mandler (1992) showed infants aged 11–20 months a series of simple actions (for example, putting a ball in a cup, placing another cup on top, shaking the cups) the children were able to imitate the sequence in the same order as they had witnessed. Even preverbal infants, it appears, store their experiences in script-like form.

This means that from very early on children are sensitive to the temporal arrangement of the components making up their event experiences, and have the equipment (presumably biological in nature) to detect and store these with impressive accuracy. What is perhaps even more impressive is the finding that quite young children can differentiate between types of temporal sequences, in particular those that describe causal relationships and those that are arbitrarily connected. To take an example of a cause–effect sequence, one must open a door before going through it: the former is a necessary precondition for the latter. On the other hand, going through the door and finding a broken window in the room does not express a cause–effect sequence but only a chance connection. According to various studies (e.g. Bauer & Mandler, 1990), young children are capable of recalling events with causal sequences more easily and at earlier ages than non-causally linked sequences – a finding that holds from at least the age of 16 months.

However, a great many studies have shown that up to the age of 5 or 6 scripts do undergo some significant developmental changes (summarized in Hudson, 1993). In particular:

- Scripts get longer, more detailed, more complex and more elaborate over age.
- Younger children's accounts refer only to actions carried out; older children also mention the goals and feelings of participants.

- At earlier ages scripts stick rigidly to one stereotyped sequence; subsequently children realize that there are not only obligatory components but also slots that can vary from one occurrence of the event to another (for example, where to sit and what food to ask for in the McDonald's script).
- As children get older they become more aware of the hierarchical organization of events, as demonstrated by their ability to report at different levels of detail. These may range from a focus on just certain core actions to providing accounts that include the components of these actions and also the optional slots making up the event.

One further question that has occupied research workers concerns the way in which scripts become established, with particular reference to the role played by the child's social context. Some earlier accounts gave the impression that this is to be explained entirely in terms of the child's own individual effort, whereas it is now generally accepted that scripts are jointly constructed with other people, especially with parents (Nelson, 1986) (see **social constructivism**). As observations of family interaction have shown, past events frequently form the topic of conversation between parents and children – according to one study as often as five to seven times an hour (Fivush, Haden & Reese, 1996). In the case of younger children this is usually a matter of parents reminding the child of previous experiences and encouraging him or her to reminisce about 'what happened next', whereas the older child is more likely to refer to these events quite spontaneously, thus stimulating the parents to join in and make the recollection a mutual one. In addition, parents' story telling is a particularly effective way of drawing attention to the sequential structure of scripts, for stories are usually firmly organized around a beginning ('Once upon a time …'), a middle and an end ('… and they lived happily ever after'), and so reinforce the child's evolving tendency to think about events in a time dimension.

Further reading

Hudson, J.A. (1993). Understanding events: the development of script knowledge. In M. Bennett (Ed.), *The child as psychologist*. Hemel Hempstead: Harvester Wheatsheaf. A useful summary of research and theory concerning the development of scripts.

Nelson, K. (1986). *Event knowledge: structure and function in development*. Hillsdale, NJ: Erlbaum. A collection of chapters written by Nelson and her collaborators, which remains one of the best accounts of children's representation of their everyday experience in the form of scripts and of the role that scripts play in cognitive development.

See also **multistore models; social constructivism; symbolic representation**

EMOTIONAL COMPETENCE
and: EMOTIONAL REGULATION
SOCIAL REFERENCING
EMOTIONAL DISPLAY RULES

MEANING An essential part of social life is the ability accurately to read other people's emotions and to respond to them in an appropriate manner. At the same time, it is also necessary to be properly aware of one's own emotions and be able to present them in a socially acceptable way. Children need to acquire such emotional competence, the term used to designate –

all those abilities involved in coping appropriately both with one's own and with other people's emotions.

What is regarded as 'appropriate' depends in part on the culture in which the child is reared; it depends also on the child's age and individuality and the extent to which allowance is made for both these factors.

Emotional competence is an umbrella term that covers a range of different components. The principal of these are the following (Saarni, 1999):

- Awareness of one's own emotional state.
- Ability to discern others' emotions.
- Ability to use the vocabulary describing emotions commonly used in one's culture.
- Capacity for sympathetic involvement in others' emotional experiences.
- Ability to realize that inner emotional state need not correspond to outer expression.
- Capacity for adaptive coping with aversive or distressing emotions.
- Awareness that relationships are largely defined by how emotions are communicated and by the reciprocity of emotions within the relationship.
- Capacity for emotional self-efficacy, that is, feeling in control of and accepting one's own emotional experiences.

There are complex interrelationships between these components; however, they do not necessarily come in one undivided package: being proficient in one does not guarantee proficiency in any other, and each may follow its own unique developmental course. Emotional competence is thus a multifaceted and not a unitary concept, but one that has nevertheless been found useful in drawing attention to an aspect of people's socio-cognitive life with profound implications for a wide range of psychological functions.

There is, however, one fundamental aspect that underlies several of the above listed components, namely **EMOTIONAL REGULATION**. Following Thompson (1994), this can be defined as –

> *the extrinsic and intrinsic processes involved in monitoring, evaluating
> and modifying emotional reactions, especially their intensity and duration.*

Emotions can be managed in various ways: by extrinsic means such as an adult's
soothing and distracting the child or by a change in the situational circumstances
that brought about the emotion in the first place, or by intrinsic means involving
the child's own efforts. It is the latter that is relevant to any discussion of emotional
competence; self-regulation, that is the capacity to exert control over one's own
emotions, is one of the main attributes singled out in everyday life as indicating an
individual's psychological maturity.

ORIGINS

The subject of emotions has fascinated writers since the days of the ancient Greek
philosophers (see Oakley, 2004, for a detailed historical account). It is Charles
Darwin (1872), however, to whom credit is due for a first attempt scientifically to
record emotional behaviour in children and to explain its origins. His interest lay
primarily in the facial expressions used by human beings to convey their inner feelings, and to this day the observations he made (many on his own infant son) are
widely regarded as invaluable both for proposing a classification scheme of emotional expressions and for the theoretical formulation whereby he placed human
emotions in an evolutionary framework.

Just how essential a part emotions play in people's lives was made very clear in
Freud's many writings. As his clinical work convinced him, emotional failure, whatever its form, can seriously disrupt people's lives and cause havoc with their social
relationships, and though individuals employ a variety of mental mechanisms to
defend themselves against these potentially destructive influences their psychological health may suffer and their ability to cope with the ordinary tasks of life dete-
riorate. Emotional failure is the opposite to emotional competence, but it was not
until the 1990s that serious efforts began with a view to conceptualizing the latter
term. This was in no small degree due to a popular book by Daniel Goleman
(1995), a New York Times journalist, entitled *Emotional intelligence*, which aroused
widespread interest by emphasizing the need to promote not only people's cognitive intelligence but also its emotional equivalent. Arguing that *emotional literacy*
(as Goleman also called it) is a vital quality to foster in children, he drew attention to the many undesirable consequences of neglecting this aspect of human
functioning by focusing only on conventional types of learning and thereby creating one-sided individuals – intellectually efficient but emotionally incompetent.
Various attempts to measure emotional intelligence and develop an EQ (emotional
quotient) for the assessment of individuals followed; however, the multifaceted
nature of this quality soon convinced psychologists that the development of a single index was not a fruitful enterprise and that instead detailed investigation of the
nature of emotional competence in all its diverse manifestations needed to be
undertaken.

CURRENT STATUS

Emotional competence continues to attract the attention of research workers, though as a result of their efforts the concept has become somewhat blurred around the edges. This is largely because of the lack of a clear boundary between emotional and **social competence** – a point emphasized by Halberstadt, Dunsmore and Denham (2001), who have proposed the term *affective social competence* to do justice to the overlapping nature of the two concepts. There are certainly many indications that skill in dealing with one's own and others' emotions is central to interacting with others, and this is especially apparent in peer relationships where popularity and friendship depend to a considerable extent on children's ability sensitively to link their own emotions to those of others. Social interactions are mostly accompanied by emotional arousal, and the ability to read the nature and extent of this in others and manage it in oneself is crucial to interactions running a reasonably smooth course (Denham, Von Salisch, Olthof, Kochanoff & Caverly, 2002).

How that ability is expressed depends largely on three types of influence: culture, temperament and age. As to culture, each society has evolved certain acceptable ways of coping with emotions and will bring up its children to behave according to these norms. The Utku Eskimos, for example, disapprove of all displays of anger; much of their socialization efforts are thus devoted to channelling children's negative emotions in other directions (Briggs, 1970), and as a result from a quite early age aggression in peer groups is an astonishingly rare phenomenon. The Yanonamo Indians of South America, on the other hand, value fierceness above all other qualities in their interpersonal relationships, and foster this quality by bringing up their children with little affection and much aggressiveness (Chagnon, 1968). As anthropological observations such as these make clear, what is judged as 'mature' behaviour in one social setting may not be so in another.

Temperament, as a biologically based expression of individuality, exerts its influence on such characteristics as the ability to inhibit impulses and the intensity of emotional responsiveness. Emotional competence, insofar as it involves the regulation of one's feelings, is clearly more difficult to attain by some children than by others. This becomes especially evident in cases of pathology such as Down Syndrome children: their emotions are often hard to arouse in the first place yet, once aroused, the children may have considerable difficulty in exerting control over their feelings and displaying them at acceptable levels (Cicchetti, Ganiban & Barnett, 1991). Emotional deficits also play a large part in autism, in that children with this disorder have repeatedly been found to lack the capacity for empathy with other people, being unable to recognize the meaning of the emotional messages that others send them by facial expression, gesture or vocalization (Rutter, 1999).

The influence of age on emotional competence is perhaps the most obvious effect of the three types we have mentioned, and is certainly the one that has attracted the most research attention (for details see Denham et al., 2002). As demonstrated by many studies, the various components of emotional competence first clock in and subsequently reach maturity at different stages of development.

For example, the ability to discriminate emotions in others is already evident in infancy; at that stage, on the other hand, children still have to rely on their caretakers to provide guidance as to what emotion they themselves should display in particular settings. This is well illustrated by what has come to be known as **SOCIAL REFERENCING**, a concept denoting –

> *the use of caretakers' emotional expressions as a guide to the child's own emotional response.*

As shown in experimental situations (e.g. Feinman, 1982), a 1-year-old, confronted by an unfamiliar person or object, will look to the mother to check her reaction and only then act, adopting a similar response. If the mother looks calm or happy the child is also likely to behave positively; if she adopts an anxious or bewildered expression the child will become wary and back away. Another person's interpretation is thus needed to direct the child's understanding of the situation; only later on in development will children become independent agents when confronted by strangeness and ambiguity.

A particularly fertile area of developmental research has been children's understanding of emotions – what causes them, why they may be expressed differently in different people and what strategies can be adopted to manipulate, control and hide them (Harris, 1989). As studies of age comparisons have shown, considerable progress is made in this respect during the preschool years – a period when children become increasingly competent in using language as a means of understanding. Being able to talk about emotions means that children can stand apart from them, think about them and discuss them with others, and so objectify their own feelings as well as those of other people. At the same time they are also becoming more proficient in generating theories that will help them to predict the nature of other people's feelings (see **theory of mind**). As a result, emotional competence in the 5-year-old is a vastly more powerful mental tool than it is in the 2-year-old.

It is not only emotional understanding but also emotional expression that changes over age. Let us pick out one aspect, namely the tendency to express emotions in increasingly more subtle ways as the child learns to react in a socially approved manner by acquiring **EMOTIONAL DISPLAY RULES**. These refer to –

> *the cultural norms for the overt expression of emotion, including both the kind of emotions displayed and the circumstances under which they should be displayed.*

These rules are a further instance of the influence of culture; they ensure that children learn 'manners' as defined by their particular social group. This means that children may be taught to display feelings that they are not actually experiencing, as seen in such parental exhortations as 'boys don't cry'; 'kiss your baby sister'; and 'remember to say thank you to auntie even if you don't like the present'. As Saarni (1984) has shown, at the age of 6 children still have considerable difficulty in hiding their true feelings; only when they get to 9 or 10 years do they show signs of being able to master their emotions and behave 'politely'. At the same time children also learn that other people do not always really feel what they appear to feel – this being yet another constituent of emotional competence that needs to be acquired in the course of development.

As to emotional regulation, this has become a very busy area for research (e.g. Eisenberg & Morris, 2002). Questions asked include the ages when children become capable of exerting various forms of control over their displayed emotions, the kinds of strategies they employ to this end, the influence of family and other social agents that foster or impede development and the various cognitive abilities that are the key to success. However, it has become evident that there is by no means unanimous agreement among researchers on precisely what is meant by emotional regulation and how to define it; even the differentiation of emotional regulation and emotion raises a host of conceptual problems (for a detailed discussion see Cole, Martin & Dennis, 2004 and following commentaries). There is clearly a danger of different studies allegedly examining the same characteristic but in fact looking at different phenomena.

Further reading

Denham, S. (1998). *Emotional development in young children*. New York: Guilford Press. Referring mainly to the preschool period, the book gives an informative account of research on the nature of emotion in the early years.

Saarni, C. (1999). *The development of emotional competence*. New York: Guilford Press. A lucid explanation of emotional competence and its components, with special attention paid to developmental failures and malfunctioning.

See also **social competence; temperament; theory of mind**

RELATIONSHIP FORMATION 7

SEVEN

The formation of interpersonal relationships is one of the most vital developmental tasks in childhood. There is a widespread belief that the very first relationships set the tone for all subsequent close relationships, and that differences among children in the nature of the ties they form early on can have profound implications for the particular developmental pathway each child embarks upon. So far the evidence for such an assertion is by no means decisive; any attempt to demonstrate the existence of simple one-to-one connections between early relationships and later ones ('men always marry their mothers') is doomed to failure. What cannot be disputed is that relationships form the context in which all of a child's psychological functions develop: it is there that the child is first introduced to the outside world, provided with learning opportunities and constraints, finds out what is significant and worth attending to, acquires labels and means of communicating and, in the process, develops some degree of emotional security and a sense of self.

Given the importance of relationships it is curious that it is only lately that a start has been made to investigate their nature and development objectively and systematically – to establish a *science of relationships*, as Robert Hinde (1997) has named it. We all know about relationships from our personal experience and spend a lot of time thinking about them, yet they are of an elusive nature which makes it difficult to determine their constituents and agree upon the dimensions along which they can be ranged. In part, this is because relationships are not directly perceived but inferred. What we are aware of are *interactions* between people, that is, the overt behaviour that people show towards each other – a level of analysis that is distinct from the level of relationships though the two are often confused (Hinde, 1979). It is only when interactions form consistent patterns over time that one can conclude a relationship exists. Thus interactions are here-and-now phenomena whereas relationships imply temporal continuity. Moreover, as Hinde (1979, 1997) has repeatedly stressed, a relationship is more than the sum of the interactions which gave rise to it: each of the two levels has characteristics of its own that cannot be found in the other. For descriptive purposes it therefore becomes essential to keep the two levels distinct.

How children form relationships, especially their primary ones, and the significance these have for other aspects of development, have become an active field of research in the past few decades. The following concepts have emerged as widely used foci in this enterprise:

INTERSUBJECTIVITY
and: **Joint attention**
ATTACHMENT
and: **Secure base**
    Goal corrected behaviour
    Internal working models
BONDING
PEER GROUP STATUS
and: **Social withdrawal**
    Social information processing model
SOCIAL COMPETENCE

INTERSUBJECTIVITY
and: **JOINT ATTENTION**

How does a young baby begin the highly complex task of establishing relationships with other people? One answer is built around the concept of intersubjectivity – an extension of the term *subjectivity* which refers to an awareness of oneself as a thinking, feeling being and is thus a phenomenon occurring *within* individuals. Intersubjectivity, on the other hand, occurs *between* individuals and is – **MEANING**

> *a joint pattern of awareness among people of each other's thoughts and feelings, based on a common focus of attention.*

It thus refers to a natural rapport that can be found among individuals, which exists whenever two or more people reach a mutual understanding and purpose and a mutually felt emotion – or, to put it in popular terms, whenever the participants are 'on the same wavelength', bringing about a meeting of minds.

Intersubjectivity, according to its principal protagonist Colwyn Trevarthen (e.g. 1977, Trevarthen & Hubley, 1978), is 'an exceedingly complex innate mechanism foreshadowing the cooperative intelligence of adults' that forms the foundation of interpersonal communication. Its use is generally (though not necessarily) accompanied by twin assumptions, namely that it is evident from the early weeks on in the exchanges of parent and infant and that it is inborn, part of all human beings' biological heritage. It is thus said to explain the social precocity that even very young infants manifest in their exchanges with adults.

To achieve intersubjectivity a common referent needs to be established – a topic, that is, to which the partners attend simultaneously. In the early months of life, during parent–infant interaction, that topic lies entirely within the dyad itself, namely in the facial expressions, gestures and vocalizations each partner emits and to which the other one responds. Somewhat later in the first year a change takes place: external objects and events are simultaneously attended to by both partners, thus incorporating a third party in the dyadic exchange. These two kinds of interaction have been labelled by Trevarthen (1979; Trevarthen & Hubley, 1978) as *primary intersubjectivity* and *secondary intersubjectivity* respectively. The former describes those social situations where the participants interact directly with each other; the latter those where the interaction takes place around an external topic.

Secondary intersubjectivity is closely associated with another concept, one that has become the subject of much interest to investigators of early development, namely **JOINT ATTENTION**. This refers to –

> *the complex of social skills whereby interacting partners ensure that they incorporate a common referent in their exchange.*

Pointing to an object or following another person's gaze are among the most common nonverbal means employed to this end; once children acquire language words increasingly also serve this function. Joint attention is regarded as a topic of considerable significance, in part because it is one of the first clearly interpersonal competencies to emerge and in part because it is thought to have some definite implications for the development of other psychological functions such as language.

Let us note one source of confusion in the use of the term intersubjectivity. It is sometimes referred to as though it is an ability that individuals possess, and at other times as a state existing among individuals. Murray (1991), for example, describes infant intersubjectivity as a rudimentary capacity to apprehend the emotional and interpersonal significance of another's behaviour which is to be found in an infant; whereas others subscribe to the definition given above and stress the *mutual* awareness of interacting partners. It is thus useful to apply a distinction made by Gomez (1998) between *one-way intersubjectivity* and *two-way intersubjectivity*, the former denoting what individuals are capable of while the latter describes an essentially dyadic characteristic.

ORIGINS   The ideas behind intersubjectivity have a long history, though the term itself only became common in the latter half of the last century. It first appeared in writings about the phenomenology of language, where it was used to underline the importance of mutual understanding between speakers engaged in dialogue. Thus Habermas (1970), in his attack on the 'monologic' model of verbal communication, found the concept useful to express the idea that both hearer and speaker share the same code and are thereby enabled to home in on the same topic – an idea also taken up and further developed by proponents of Speech Act Theory (e.g. Searle, 1969) in their endeavour to analyse the nature of verbal utterances in terms of their communicative intent by speakers and their comprehension by listeners (see **speech acts**).

However, the main credit for introducing the term to developmental psychology is due to Trevarthen (see 1988, for a comprehensive statement). His minute analyses of filmed interactions between infants of all ages and their mothers convinced him that from the beginning one can observe a 'remarkable adaptation of infants for interpersonal communication' (Trevarthen, 1980). Two-month-olds, for instance, show an apparently purposeful orientation towards the mother in face-to-face interactions, exhibit patterns of excitement not found in response to toys, and emit purely communicative movements such as facial expressions and gesture-like hand actions as well as lip and tongue movements that 'are evidently precursors of verbal expressions'. Moreover, these actions are interlinked with those of the mother in an intricate sequential pattern resembling a dialogue – something the infant is said to be just as responsible for bringing about as the mother. Infants, that is, from an early age actively seek to engage in reciprocal to-and-fro communicative exchanges, demonstrating thereby their motivation not only preferentially to respond to other people but also to coordinate their actions with those of the other person. Even the earliest interactions, according to Trevarthen, thus involve genuine, two-party communications.

Trevarthen, in his many publications, has produced a rich descriptive body of social interactions between adults and infants, which has been found most useful in providing a basis for understanding the nature of infants' early encounters with the outside world. At the same time he has proposed an explanatory framework for the phenomena observed – one that considers intersubjectivity (using Trevarthen's own phraseology) to be 'an inborn capacity for interpersonal understanding', based on an 'innate self-regulatory brain system which, in effect, is composed of primitive concepts of persons and how to communicate with them'. This gives rise to a 'clear commitment to intentional communication' and to a tendency to 'link their subjective evaluations of experience with those of other persons'. Thus all along infants show a 'well-formed, if rudimentary purposiveness' in behaviour towards others, whom they perceive from at least 2 months onwards as 'intentional agents with feelings' and with whom they can share the mental states that they themselves experience.

It is by no means always easy to see how these conclusions about inner processes are derived from outer manifestations of behaviour, and especially so as some of the processes are discussed as though they were directly accessible to observation. It is therefore not surprising that intersubjectivity, at least as applied to young infants, has become a topic of marked contention.

CURRENT STATUS

Used in a purely descriptive sense to denote mutual understanding among individuals, intersubjectivity is a relatively non-controversial concept. Thus it has been applied, for instance, to Vygtosky's proposal of a **zone of proximal development** in order to describe the nature of interactive processes between adult and child: help by the former can only be effective if it is closely geared to the latter's existing state of knowledge – the teacher, that is, must start where the child is. In that sense, however, a term like sensitivity is probably sufficient, in that it does not carry the extra conceptual baggage that intersubjectivity brings with it.

It is this extra baggage that has given rise to considerable debate, with particular reference to two aspects. The most contentious refers to the origins of intersubjectivity, that is, how the fine mutual adjustment between infant and adult, that all observers agree is evident from the early weeks of life, is brought about. Trevarthen's view is that intersubjectivity is an inborn tendency, that it is based on some (unspecified) brain mechanism and that as a result even very young infants are already equipped to play an equal part in communicative exchanges with adults. The opposite view (Kaye, 1982; Schaffer, 1984) points to the evidence that early interactions are essentially asymmetrical in character: it is up to adults to 'carry' the infant, allow them to set the pace and determine the topic of the exchange and to fit in with their response patterns. Such asymmetry is seen, for example, in mother–infant vocal exchanges: the turn taking pattern which these take may give the impression of a 'conversation', but it is produced by the mother's close attention to the bursts of the infant's vocalizations and then inserting her vocalizations in the pauses between them (Schaffer, Collis & Parsons, 1977). The exchange ought therefore to be characterized not so much as a dialogue as a pseudo-dialogue, and only at later stages of infancy will children begin to assume a more equal role. There is thus a dispute as to when infants become capable of engaging in truly reciprocal give-and-take and begin deliberately to coordinate their interpersonal behaviour with a partner:

is it from birth on, presumably as a result of an inborn preparedness, or at some subsequent age after a more or less prolonged period during which adults provide them with plenty of experience of being involved in interaction?

The second point of contention refers to Trevarthen's assertion that the communicative behaviour of even the youngest infants is intentional in nature. As he has put it, both mother and infant are 'mutually reactive intentional agents', and all along infants have a 'clear commitment to intentional communication'. As the criteria for this assertion are not spelled out in operational terms it is difficult to link it to the empirical data presented. Most other writers have located the first signs of clearly intentional behaviour towards the end of the first year rather than at the beginning. Piaget (1952), for instance, argued that intentionality appears around 9–12 months, that is, in sensorimotor stage 5, when the infant becomes capable of differentiating means from ends and can therefore employ particular actions not for their own sake but in order to obtain some specified goal. He agreed that this milestone does not arise out of the blue but is dependent on a sequence of developments in the preceding months; nevertheless, the ability to hold a goal in mind, select the most appropriate means to obtain it and flexibly switch to some other means if an obstacle arises (all criteria for intentionality) are not evident until the last quarter of the first year. Similarly Bowlby (1969/1982), in his account of attachment development, picked out the end of the first year as the time when the infant's behaviour is no longer purely reactive but becomes *goal corrected* – the term used by him to designate actions that are continually adjusted in the light of prevailing circumstances and show a flexibility and purposiveness absent from earlier behaviour (see **goal corrected behaviour**). Infants, that is, when distressed can now adjust their cries according to whether the mother is near or far, coming or going. Thus the emergence of goal corrected behaviour appears to coincide with the onset of means–ends differentiation as described by Piaget: both accounts draw attention to infants' growing ability to plan their behaviour in the light of anticipated outcomes, that is, to behave intentionally, and both place its onset at the end rather than the beginning of the first year.

There is, on the other hand, comparatively little controversy as far as the status of *joint attention* is concerned. It is widely accepted that this is a useful concept, and a considerable body of research on the nature of young children's attention sharing confirms this conclusion (see Moore and Dunham, 1995, for examples). The research has dealt mainly with three questions:

1 By what means are joint attention episodes brought about?

2 How do children's joint attention abilities change in the course of development?

3 What role do joint attention episodes play in children's development?

The first question concerns the devices whereby children and adults establish joint attention. Direction of gaze, pointing, contacting an object and referential language all serve this purpose and each of these has received detailed attention. The last of these becomes in due course particularly important: words can stand for things, and by introducing them into a conversation the participants can share their particular interests, even in the physical absence of the relevant object. However, long before the onset of language the other devices are already in place: an infant's look at, pointing to or contact with an object enables the adult to home in on the same attentional focus, and in due course the child too will use them in order deliberately to draw the adult's attention to particular features of the environment. Two strategies have been distinguished when adults apply these devices in interacting with an infant: an *attention-following* strategy and an *attention-switching* strategy. The former refers to the adult following the existing focus of the infant's attention; the latter to the adult drawing the infant's attention away to a different object from that currently being examined. The distinction is important because attention-following has been found to be a more effective technique in furthering children's language acquisition: learning what an object is called is easier when the child has spontaneously selected the object as interesting than when the adult decides what should interest the child (Carpenter, Nagell & Tomasello, 1998).

As to the developmental course of children's joint attention abilities, most investigators point to the 9–12 month period as the crucial time when infants become able to follow another person's gaze and pointing gesture. It is in fact not possible to give a precise age for the emergence of these skills, for this depends greatly on the particular task demands of the test situation employed and the criteria used for defining the existence of the skill (Schaffer, 1984). Following another person's pointing, for example, is easier for nearby than for more distant targets, and also for targets that are in the same sector of the visual field as the pointing hand than for those in a different sector. Similarly with the production of pointing: when this gesture first appears it takes the form of 'pointing-for-self', in that there is no indication that the infant is thereby attempting to communicate something to the adult. Only several months later will infants gaze back at the other person in order to check that she has followed the gesture, thereby showing that the infant is capable of 'pointing-for-others'.

Regarding the third question concerning the influence of joint attention on other aspects of behaviour, it is widely agreed that the occasions when a child is simultaneously engrossed with an adult in some object or event are potentially a context for enriching experiences, with positive developmental implications (Schaffer, 1992). Young children jointly engaged with an adult perform at a more advanced, complex level than when on their own – a point made not only by Vygotsky in relation to his concept of the **zone of proximal development** but by numerous more recent studies involving functions such as problem solving, play, attention and language. The latter in particular has been subjected to detailed scrutiny: for example, Carpenter et al. (1998) demonstrated that the amount of time infants spend in joint engagement with their mothers predicts the infants' development of skills in both verbal and non-verbal communication. Language, that is, emerges in social contexts made meaningful by joint attention to an interesting topic; the more of these the child experiences the greater the chance that skills like word learning are fostered. Most dramatically, however, the role joint attention abilities play in development is illustrated by studies of autistic children, for in these children such abilities have been found to be deficient (Sigman and Kasari, 1995) – a deficiency that various writers believe to be linked to the difficulty in developing communicative and other forms of interpersonal competence that characterizes autism.

The fact that joint attention abilities normally emerge around the end of the first year does not mean, however, that sharing of attention is not possible before then. The difference is that earlier on it is mainly up to the adult to convert the infant's spontaneous interest in particular environmental features into one of mutual interest. The mother, that is, employs an attention-following strategy: having established the child's focus on some specific feature she is likely not only to look there too but also then to extend the child's interest by such means as pointing to it, labelling it and commenting on it (Collis & Schaffer, 1975), thereby getting some teaching in on the sly. Thus, initially, joint attention episodes tend to be one-sided: the infant leads, the mother follows. Only towards the end of the first year will the other person's direction of gaze become a meaningful signal to the infant, and with further development the onus for topic sharing will increasingly become an evenly shared affair, with the child also assuming an active role in directing the other person's attention to outside entities. As a result, both the frequency and duration of joint attention episodes increase over age.

Further reading

Braten, S. (Ed.) (1998). *Intersubjective communication and emotion in early ontogeny.* Cambridge: Cambridge University Press. A variety of authors, including Trevarthen, join together to present the many different facets of intersubjectivity, including developmental, evolutionary, comparative and philosophical considerations.

Moore, C., & Dunham, P. (Eds.) (1995). *Joint attention: its origins and role in development.* Hillsdale, NJ: Erlbaum. Provides a clear indication of the state of research on joint attention and its theoretical underpinnings.

See also **zone of proximal development**

ATTACHMENT
and: SECURE BASE
GOAL CORRECTED BEHAVIOUR
INTERNAL WORKING MODELS

MEANING As a result of John Bowlby's highly influential writings (especially 1969/82), attachment has become one of the central concepts in developmental psychology, signalling a very different approach to accounts of children's social development to those that prevailed before. The term is used somewhat loosely in everyday speech to denote affection or devotion (*Concise Oxford Dictionary*), but in psychology has come to be endowed with special meaning, backed up by a great body of research. Following Ainsworth (1979), we will define attachment as –

> *a deep-seated emotional tie that one individual forms with another, binding them together in space and enduring over time.*

Attachment, so conceived, is more than mere affection; for young children in particular it is a highly significant emotional experience with profound implications for their self-development and trust in the world. Though initially used almost exclusively to denote the tie infants form with their parents, attachment is a life-long phenomenon covering a range of close relationships, including in particular the parent's tie with the child. Nevertheless, it is the initial attachments formed in early childhood that have attracted most attention.

There are several aspects of attachment that need to be differentiated:

- *Attachment system* is one of a number of behavioural systems with which human beings are endowed (examples of others are those concerned with exploration, caregiving, affiliation and sexual mating). Systems are inferred from their outer manifestations, these being a range of behaviour patterns which may be very different in form but identical in function. Crying, smiling and following, for example, are overtly very diverse phenomena but all may be used by the child for the same end, namely to attain and maintain the parent's proximity. It is the function that gives meaning to the system.
- *Attachment behaviours* are the outer expression of the system. They are activated and deactivated by situational conditions: when, for example, the young child encounters something frightening he or she will call, cry or run to restore the usual level of security. In young infants activation is automatic; in older children the response is chosen according to circumstances.
- *Attachment bonds* refer to the feelings one individual experiences for another. They are one type of the general class of affectional bonds, all of which are statements about individuals and not about relationships. Thus a child may have an attachment bond towards the mother even though the latter does not reciprocate it.
- *Attachment relationships* are those relationships where both partners are attached to one another. Thus, unlike attachment systems, behaviours and bonds, relationships are dyadic in nature and exist between, not within, individuals.
- *Attachment figures* are the objects of an individual's attachment. They are not interchangeable with other people; thus an infant may refuse to be comforted by anyone except the mother. In many cases hierarchies of attachment figures become established: if, say, the mother is not available the father will be used for security purposes.

The term attachment is sometimes used so widely that it is virtually equivalent to the whole of the child–parent relationship. This is a misuse; the child is equipped with other behaviour systems implicating the parent such as exploration and fear of the strange, and it is the interplay of the various systems that expresses the reality of the child–parent relationship as a whole. It is this interplay, moreover, which highlights a basic feature of early attachment behaviour, namely the disposition to treat the parent as a **SECURE BASE** from which to explore the environment and to which the child can return whenever made afraid by something threatening. The concept of secure base thus denotes –

> *the use that young children make of the parent (or some other attachment figure) in order safely to explore the environment and to obtain comfort and security in the face of perceived danger.*

ORIGINS The secure base concept has assumed great importance in that it has led to a widely used procedure, the Strange Situation (see below), for assessing infants' attachment security, making it possible to observe the manner and extent to which young children make use of the parent whenever the balance between exploration and proximity seeking deviates from the optimum.

The attachment theory that Bowlby (1958, 1969/1982) formulated was in many respects a radical departure from previous accounts of children's development of ties to their mother (see Bretherton, 1992, for a detailed historical description). Previous accounts, put forward by both psychoanalysis and learning theory, were based on the *secondary drive hypothesis*, namely the belief that children are born only with primary, physiological drives such as hunger, thirst and pain, but as the mother is almost invariably associated with relief of the tensions arising from these drives infants will in due course come to love her for her own sake. Love of mother, that is, is cupboard love in origin – it must therefore be seen as a secondary drive not grounded in any biological preparedness for social interaction.

Bowlby put forward a markedly different view – a change that he signalled by dropping the term *dependence* formerly used to designate the child's tie to the parent and substituting *attachment* instead. His *evolutionary-ethological theory* (as it came to be labelled) rejected the belief that the tie is merely a secondary phenomenon – largely because of the mounting evidence that from the beginning infants are powerfully motivated to interact with other human beings. The bonds infants form with their caretakers, according to Bowlby, have an evolutionary basis because in humanity's distant past, at a time when predators spelled real danger, a mechanism was required whereby offspring could keep close to their caregivers and so obtain protection, thus enhancing their chances of survival. Crying, clinging, following and other such means serve this purpose; they are **fixed action patterns**, 'wired into' the baby's response repertoire from birth and ensuring that infants can gain and maintain the proximity of their caretakers. This would, of course, only work if the parent reciprocates the child's behaviour, hence the parallel development of a parental attachment system that ensures that parents for their part are programmed to respond to the child's signals.

The need for proximity is a powerful tendency seen in many species, and Bowlby was especially influenced by the work of Konrad Lorenz and other ethologists on the *imprinting* phenomenon in geese, ducks and chicks (see **critical periods**). Different species express their need for proximity in different ways, and Bowlby set out to describe in detail the various means used by the human infant to this end and the way these change over age. In brief, the developmental course of attachment formation goes through various phases, starting with indiscriminate social responsiveness in the early weeks when the various attachment behaviours can be elicited in a purely automatic manner and directed to anyone, and proceeding to gradually more discriminate, flexible, purposive and organized behaviour (see Schaffer, 2004, for a somewhat more extended outline or Bowlby's 1969/1982 book for the full account). Here we shall refer to two concepts used to characterize certain features of the developmental course, both of which play a prominent role in attachment theory, namely goal corrected behaviour and internal working models.

GOAL CORRECTED BEHAVIOUR is the term used by Bowlby to denote –

> *children's ability deliberately to plan their behaviour*
> *in the light of some specific goal.*

For much of the first year infants still lack this ability, behaving as though unaware of the possible outcome of their actions; only from about 9 or 10 months will they begin to plan their behaviour with the clear purpose of achieving an intended goal. Thus the young infant will cry as an automatic reaction to pain; the 2-year-old will cry in order to summon the mother to deal with the pain and, moreover, adjust the cry according to the mother's perceived distance and availability, substituting if need be some other attachment behaviour such as calling or following. The precise actions carried out are then continuously adjusted in the light of feedback – hence Bowlby's assertion that behaviour systems like attachment can be thought of as *control systems*, that is, devices somewhat like a thermostat designed to maintain a steady state, such as staying within the proximity of the mother: as long as the mother is near the attachment system is quiescent; when the mother disappears from view the system springs into action in order to restore the status quo. The capacity for such adjustive behaviour continues to develop; thus from the age of 2 children also understand that other people have goals and start taking these into account in planning their behaviour. They can now enter into a *goal corrected partnership* with the other person in which both partners can adjust to one another.

INTERNAL WORKING MODELS are a further development to characterize the emergence of more mature attachments. An internal working model is –

> a hypothetical internal structure whereby the child mentally
> represents the attachment relationship and the partners
> involved in it, self as well as other.

From the end of the first year children become increasingly able to represent the world in symbolic form (see **symbolic representation**), and as a result they begin to construct mental models of their attachment-related experiences embodying the kinds of interactions and emotions encountered day by day with attachment figures, as well as the pertinent attributes of each attachment figure and of themselves as participants. Bowlby considered these models to be long-term phenomena; although by no means impervious to change as a result of further experience the earliest models, by virtue of being formed outside consciousness in infancy, are most likely to persist and thus affect any future close relationship even in adulthood, and especially so that formed by parents with their own children.

As a clinician, Bowlby was acutely aware of the need to allow for children's individuality, but it was largely due to Mary Ainsworth, his one-time colleague, that this aspect also came under scrutiny and has since become a major focus of research. For this purpose Ainsworth devised both a procedure for investigating individual differences in attachment formation and a classification scheme for describing them (Ainsworth, Blehar, Waters & Wahls, 1978). The procedure has come to be known as the *Strange Situation*, which consists of a sequence of somewhat stressful episodes, including being confronted by a stranger, left by the mother with the stranger, left alone and being reunited with the mother, and all occurring in an unfamiliar environment. The episodes are designed to activate attachment behaviour and to highlight the way in which children make use of the mother as a source of security. A complex system of coding the children's behaviour can then indicate the various ways in which children's attachment behaviour manifests itself in different children – differences that have been classified by Ainsworth and her followers in terms of four basic attachment patterns, that is, *securely attached*, *avoidant*, *resistant* and *disorganized* (the last three are generally grouped together, though somewhat loosely, as insecure). Investigating these patterns – their characteristics, their origins and their implications for further development – has now developed into a major industry (see Cassidy & Shaver, 1999).

CURRENT STATUS There is no doubting the enormous influence that attachment theory has come to exert not only on developmental psychology but on psychology generally. Its immediate aim was to shed light on the nature of children's primary relationships; however, in doing so it also provided new insights into the psychological make-up of human beings generally and their functioning in the real world. People, it asserted, are not motivated by drive reduction but by evolutionarily based regulating mechanisms; these (as seen for instance in the infant's proximity seeking) are continuously active in their interplay with the environment to ensure the individual's survival and personal comfort and security. A much more dynamic conception of human functioning thus replaced the previously held mechanistic view.

The first studies to investigate aspects of Bowlby's theory set out primarily to demonstrate that the attachment concept could in fact be empirically examined (e.g. Ainsworth, 1967; Schaffer & Emerson, 1964). In doing so they confirmed many aspects of the theory – the usefulness of viewing the mother as a secure base, the existence of a range of interchangeable action patterns to bring about proximity, the developmental course of attachments in infancy and so on. They also showed the need for certain modifications of Bowlby's ideas – for example, his belief that selective attachments are invariably *monotropic* in character, that is, focused on only one person (usually the mother), was not supported when observational data showed infants capable of selecting several individuals as attachment figures (Schaffer & Emerson, 1964). Also Bowlby's one-time suggestion that there is a critical period in the formation of attachments, with a cut-off point in the third year beyond which it was no longer possible to reverse the effects of previous deprivation, could not be supported by studies of late-adopted children (see review in Schaffer, 2002). However, the thrust of most subsequent work was to extend the Bowlby/Ainsworth scheme along various lines, among which the following deserve emphasis (in view of the voluminous body of relevant reports we shall not cite individual studies; interested readers are directed to the *Handbook of attachment* by Cassidy & Shaver, 1999, which covers all the required material).

- *Validity issues.* Given the extent to which the Strange Situation came to be used as an assessment tool for attachment security patterns, it is clearly important to investigate its validity – does it measure what it purports to measure? Construct validity has mostly been claimed to be good, as indicated by the predictive power of the classification system. Rather more uncertainty arises when considering reports about the use of the procedure with samples different from the Western, family-reared children as originally investigated by Ainsworth and her collaborators. For example, the distribution of attachment patterns in Japanese children is markedly different from that among most Western samples – a difference, however, that is not a true reflection of these children's attachments but rather due to the far more stressful nature of the Strange Situation for children accustomed to very close and continuous contact with the mother in everyday life. In day care children the opposite situation prevails: these children are used to separation from the mother, and hence react to the Strange Situation in a different, 'atypical' way compared to family-reared children. Both these cases raise questions about the psychological equivalence of the Strange Situation when applied to children from different backgrounds and therefore about the validity of the procedure as a 'pure' measure of attachment sensitivity.
- *The role of temperament.* Another possible influence that might detract from the Strange Situation as an attachment test is temperament. Some investigators have argued that children's differential reactions to stresses such as separation from the mother are largely due to their constitutional make-up;

for example, children of negative emotionality are more likely to show behaviour patterns associated with insecurity. However, in the light of a considerable number of studies it now seems unlikely that temperament is a major factor in Strange Situation behaviour, and though the precise part played by it in attachment formation remains to be ascertained it clearly cannot account on its own for attachment classification.

- *Stability of attachment patterns.* Short-term stability in infancy is known to be high; longer-term stability involving gaps of several years less so. To some extent the need to compare Strange Situation findings on infants with those obtained from different assessment tools developed for older ages (see below) introduces a complicating factor; nevertheless it must be concluded that changes in classification can occur, and this applies especially to those children whose family environment undergoes some drastic change as a result of stresses such as divorce or abuse. Infancy attachment patterns, it appears, are thus not necessarily for ever but can be modified by later experience.

- *Antecedents of attachment patterns.* According to Ainsworth, the main reason why children are secure or insecure in their attachments lies in the mother's sensitive responsiveness to them in the early months of life. The mother who responds promptly and appropriately to the infant's signals conveys that she is readily available as a haven of safety, especially when the child is in distress, and so fosters a feeling of security; failure by the mother so to react gives rise to insecurity. The link between maternal sensitivity and attachment security is, however, not as firm as Ainsworth had suggested; according to further research it is only one factor, albeit an important one, among a variety of other parenting qualities that shape the child's attachment to the mother.

- *Consequences of attachment patterns.* Do early attachments affect later development? Considerable claims have been made, in that children classified as secure in infancy have been said to be more competent, better adjusted and more mature in subsequent years in a range of psychological functions than insecure children. However, the conclusions emerging from research indicate a more complex picture. The closest links have been found with respect to socio-emotional development: securely attached infants tend to become more socially competent than insecurely attached infants, as seen in areas such as peer popularity, friendship, empathy and anger management. As far as cognitive functions such as intelligence and language abilities are concerned, there are few indications that early attachments play a decisive role. The same conclusion applies even more markedly to the emergence of broad personality attributes such as self-esteem and agency.

- *Development of other attachment measures.* The Strange Situation is only applicable to a very narrow age range around the start of the second year. As attachment is a life-long phenomenon, the need for measures suitable for older individuals became increasingly apparent and gave rise to a variety of proposals, of which two have received the most attention, namely the

Attachment Q-Sort (AQS) and the Adult Attachment Interview (AAI). The former covers the preschool range up to about 5 years, and assesses children's use of the mother as a secure base by means of observations collected in the natural environment of the home. The AAI consists of a series of questions put to adults in the course of a semi-structured interview, designed to elicit the individual's experiences of attachment relationships in early childhood and the way that person believes these experiences to affect present functioning. The answers are used to assign each individual to one of a number of categories summarizing their state of mind with respect to attachment. Both these measures are currently in wide use.

- *Intergenerational continuity.* Do children's Strange Situation classifications resemble those of their parents as assessed by the AAI? Are parents' attachments to their children of the same kind as their own attachments to parents in childhood? As far as both such comparisons are concerned most studies agree in finding a substantial degree of concordance; there are even indications that some degree of continuity is maintained across three generations, that is, grandmothers, mothers and children. However, the continuity is far from complete; discontinuity also exists and especially among those assessed as insecure.

- *Clinical application.* Increasingly the implications of attachment theory for clinical practice are now coming under scrutiny. Two lines of enquiry are being followed. The first concerns childhood disorders in which attachment constitutes a principal feature, one example being the syndrome typical of institutionalized children and distinguished by an apparent inability to form selective attachments. The second asks whether certain types of infants' attachment patterns are likely to lead to psychopathology in later years. While various associations have been found between insecure attachment and subsequent maladjustment (especially conduct disorders), the correlations are rarely more than modest and in any case do not justify cause-and-effect statements. The most that can be said at the present state of knowledge is that attachment insecurity may be a risk factor for psychopathology, while security may act as a protective factor.

Work on attachment has grown up in recent years, in the sense that there is no longer an almost exclusive preoccupation with infancy and instead, thanks to the availability of measures other than the Strange Situation, an extension of research to older children and adults. As a direct result, the concept of internal working models has become increasingly recognized as a useful tool for describing and understanding the processes underlying the development of attachments. In particular, it has come to be seen as a helpful guide to research on topics such as the continuity, and also the discontinuity, of specific attachment ties, the role of early security patterns in the formation of later relationships and the possible link of the various patterns with later psychological competence.

Further reading

Cassidy, J., & Shaver, P.R. (Eds.) (1999). *Handbook of attachment: theory, research and clinical application*. New York: Guilford. A massive book that provides a mine of information on all aspects of attachment.

Goldberg, S. (2000). *Attachment and development*. London: Arnold. A rather more compact summary of attachment work than the above *Handbook*.

See also **bonding; critical (sensitive) periods; fixed action patterns; symbolic representation**

BONDING

MEANING While the term *bonds* is used by attachment theorists to describe interpersonal emotional ties, the term *bonding*, denoting a special kind of process said to bind parents to their children immediately after birth, has not found a place in their writing. Attachment formation and bonding are sometimes treated as though they are synonymous; in fact attachments refer to the ties that children form to their parents while bonding has been used for –

> *the process whereby parents form emotional ties to their children.*

As such, the term has become closely associated with one particular view and one set of findings, namely those by two paediatricians, Klaus and Kennell (1976), who propounded what has come to be known as the *bonding doctrine*, that is, the belief that immediately after birth the mother must have skin-to-skin contact with her baby in order to become emotionally tied to the infant; if deprived of such contact her bond will be inadequate, possibly irreversibly so.

ORIGINS In their book *Maternal–infant bonding*, Klaus and Kennell (1976) presented the results of an experiment, in which one group of mothers experienced the rather limited amount of contact with the newborn infant that was customary in most Western maternity units at that time, whereas mothers of the other group were given 16 hours of additional contact during the first three days following birth. Seen again on a follow-up visit to the hospital one month later, the extra-contact mothers spent more time in eye contact with their babies, showed more soothing behaviour and fondling and reported greater reluctance to leave the baby with someone else than mothers of the standard-contact group. The difference between the two groups was maintained at further follow-up investigations. One year later extra-contact mothers again showed more soothing behaviour, remained closer to the baby and appeared to be more preoccupied with it. At age 2 their children received more varied and elaborated speech input from their mothers, and at age 5 the children not only obtained more advanced scores on language tests but also had a significantly higher mean IQ than the other children.

These findings led Klaus and Kennell (1976) to conclude:

> There is a sensitive period in the first minutes and hours of life during which it is necessary that the mother and father have close contact with their neonate for later development to be optimal.

This *maternal sensitive period*, as they named it, is said to be a unique time during which events may have lasting effects on the family. Lack of close contact interferes with the parent's bonding process; it will thus prevent the child from receiving the necessary emotional affection and support and hence have adverse effects on the child's socio-emotional development. In putting forward this view Klaus and Kennell were very much influenced by observations of such other species as goats and sheep, where separation of the mother from her young had been found to result in drastically adverse effects – indeed so much so that reuniting the couple after a given period following birth produced hostile rather than nurturant behaviour in the mother.

The bonding doctrine received widespread publicity in the years following the Klaus and Kennell book and had one very positive effect: it drew attention to the rigid procedures prevailing then in many maternity units, involving the separation of mother and baby for most of the day other than for feeding periods. Changes in hospital routine were instituted as a result, and the need to support a mother's confidence in handling her new baby from as early a time as possible was widely acknowledged. However, the notion of a **sensitive period**, let alone a **critical period**, with implications for long-term development of the mother–child relationship and the child's adjustment in later years, began to attract increasing criticism when studies by other research workers produced results that almost unanimously failed to replicate the Klaus and Kennell findings.

CURRENT STATUS

The bonding doctrine made assertions that were of interest not only to practitioners but also to developmental psychologists investigating the establishment of early relationships. In the years following the original Klaus and Kennell publication a number of attempts were consequently made to check their findings. For example:

- Carlsson et al. (1979) found that giving mothers up to 2 hours' extra contact with the newborn following birth produced more affectionate behaviour while feeding during the following four days. However, when observed again six weeks later these effects had disappeared.
- Grossmann, Thane and Grossmann (1981) separated out the effects of type of early contact (tactile or not) and duration of contact (several hours daily or routine only), and found some effects initially but, regardless of experimental condition, none that was still evident after 8–10 days.
- Svejda, Campos and Emde (1980), in a double-blind experiment, randomly assigned mother–infant pairs to either routine contact or to 10 hours' extra contact in the first 36 hours after birth. Observations of feeding and free play sessions yielded no differences in any of a large number of response measures.
- Rode, Chang, Fisch and Sroule (1981) investigated the effects of minimal contact and prolonged separation in a group of premature and seriously ill full-term infants on their **attachment** security patterns at 12 months of age. No indications were found that their early experience in any way affected the kind of attachments these infants developed to their mothers.

Why the difference between the Klaus and Kennell findings and those of other investigators? One possibility concerns the various methodological shortcomings in the original study, especially in the way measures were chosen, applied and interpreted. Subsequent studies were very much more rigorous in their design and procedures, and consequently more credible in their conclusions (Myers, 1984). It may well be that extra contact between mother and her newborn baby does produce beneficial effects by boosting familiarity and the mother's confidence; it is highly unlikely, however, that this is a lasting effect, that is, a *must* without which the relationship is put in jeopardy. Otherwise, what about babies that need immediate special attention because of prematurity, or mothers too ill to have extended contact with the newborn, or children adopted after the critical period, and what about fathers? Are all these condemned?

In the light of the criticisms they encountered, Klaus and Kennell have somewhat amended their original position and toned down their claims (see Klaus, Kennell & Klaus, 1995). They now agree that the whole course of the bonding process cannot depend on just a single process in the postpartum period, that early contact is not an easy cure-all and that even parents who miss out on the postpartum period generally become bonded with the infant. Among developmental psychologists the bonding doctrine has been abandoned; on the other hand it still prevails among some professional workers, especially those in paediatrics and social work, and to some extent among the general public. The notion that bonding is a kind of superglue process, an all-or-none event that must take place at the very beginning of the baby's life, is still to be found. Replacing such a simplistic picture with a view of the parent–child relationship that is shaped by a multitude of factors and so assumes a highly complex form has not been an easy undertaking.

Further reading

Sluckin, W., Herbert, M., & Sluckin, A. (1983). *Maternal bonding*. Oxford: Blackwell. Despite being somewhat dated now, the book presents an easy-to-read account of all the relevant issues, including the practical implications arising from work on this topic.

See also **attachment; critical/sensitive periods**

PEER GROUP STATUS
and: SOCIAL WITHDRAWAL
SOCIAL INFORMATION PROCESSING MODEL

Interpersonal relationships have been categorized as either *vertical* or *horizontal* (Hartup, 1989). The former refer to relationships between two partners of unequal knowledge and power, such as that between parent and child; the latter to egalitarian relationships where the participants have similar social powers, as found among same-age peers. In the past most attention has been given to the former, in the belief that these are the only ones with a decisive influence on children's development, and it is only comparatively recently that the latter too have come to be acknowledged as important determinants – indeed, according to some (e.g. Harris, 1998), as more important in the socialization of children.

MEANING

The two kinds differ in form and function, and one of the challenges to research on peer relationships has been to develop descriptive schemes that do justice to the particular nature of such relationships. There is a long-standing tradition in psychology of classifying people according to their specifically individual characteristics – intelligence, anxiety level, artistic ability and so forth. Classifying them according to their interpersonal characteristics, such as the way in which they function as group members, has been less common, yet whether children have 'good' or 'bad' relationships with other children is clearly of importance in assessing their adjustment and prospects. The concept of peer group status draws attention to one attempt to describe children as group members rather than as individuals, and can be defined as –

children's social status in any given group, with respect to such characteristics as acceptance or rejection, popularity and isolation.

171

Traditionally, peer group status has been investigated by means of *sociometric techniques*, which set out to assess an individual's standing in the group by quantitative methods, usually based on information provided by members of the group (for example, nominating the most liked and the most disliked children). Hence the term *sociometric status* has also been used to designate this concept; the rather vaguer term *social status* can also be found. In any case, group status is defined in terms of a set of interpersonal categories, the number, nature and boundaries of which have been the subject of much discussion and research.

ORIGINS   The study of peer relations was slow to get started, despite the pioneering work of certain individuals such as Parten (1932), who evolved a means of classifying children's social participation in play that made it possible to plot the way preschool children become increasingly able to integrate their own activities with those of their companions rather than pursuing entirely separate interests. However, the main impetus for work on social groups came from an Austrian psychiatrist, Jacob Moreno (1934), whose work with institutionalized adults convinced him of the need to understand how human beings operate in groups, as these provide the main context in which people function and from which they derive meaning for their individual behaviour. He therefore proposed a technique of quantitatively analysing interpersonal relationships in groups in such a way that they could be plotted in diagrammatic form, referred to as a *sociogram*, whereby it is possible to determine which group members are leaders, which are isolates and which are 'stars'. Moreno himself was primarily concerned with the structure and dynamics of groups as entities in their own right – an unusual perspective at a time when the focus was almost wholly on individuals. However, when developmental psychologists discovered the potential of sociometry they too saw it mainly as a means of assessing the peer group status of individual children, and with rare exceptions this state of affairs still prevails (see Bukowski & Cillessen, 1998, for a detailed account of developments in sociometry).

Moreno focused mainly on three basic dimensions of group members' responses to fellow members: *attraction*, *repulsion* and *indifference*. Most subsequent work dealt initially with the former two, that is, liking and disliking. However, the need for more refined distinctions soon became apparent, and particularly influential in this respect was a paper by Coie, Dodge and Coppotelli (1982), which distinguished between five types of status: *accepted* (highly visible and well liked), *rejected* (highly visible and not liked), *neglected* (low visibility and neither liked or disliked), *controversial* (highly visible and both liked and disliked) and *average* (around the mean for both visible and being liked). Thus instead of a simple distinction according to likeability, a two-dimensional model was substituted which included visibility (or impact) as well, to bring greater precision to the way in which children differ in terms of their social status. While the need for yet further refinements became evident subsequently, this categorization scheme did stimulate a considerable amount of research into the antecedent and consequent conditions associated with the various types of peer group status.

A great deal of research is now being conducted on peer relationships, and a **CURRENT** considerable part of it makes use of the concept of group status. Several topics in **STATUS** particular have attracted attention, namely the further refinement of the categorization system proposed for peer status, the antecedents and consequents of various types of status, and the underlying processes that distinguish the types (see Hymel, Vaillancourt, McDougall & Renshaw, 2002, and Rubin, Bukowski & Parker, 1998, for detailed accounts).

As to the categorization system, a familiar story unfolds: dimensions that were thought to be simple continua turn out on further investigation to be multifaceted. Thus according to more recent findings acceptance and rejection (or being liked and being disliked) do not represent the two poles of a single continuum: separately obtained acceptance scores and rejection scores show little of the negative correlation that one would expect, and each is associated with different sets of behaviour and antecedent conditions. They thus represent two distinct dimensions, each of which needs to be assessed in its own right.

In addition, a further subdivision has been proposed for rejected children into rejected-aggressive and rejected-withdrawn children – a distinction that draws attention to the need to account for the antecedents of the different status types. In particular, given the importance that nearly all children attach to being liked by other children, why do some children fail to become assimilated into groups? Two reasons have been given, indicating distinct pathways to rejection and leading respectively to rejection-aggression and rejection-withdrawal. In the former case children are too disruptive and uncooperative to be tolerated as group members and are therefore ostracized; it is the group, therefore, that takes the initiative in rejecting the child. In the latter case, on the other hand, the child takes the initiative as a result of a general personality tendency to avoid involvement in interpersonal activities and a preference for solitary pursuits – a characteristic referred to as **SOCIAL WITHDRAWAL**, which has attracted a considerable amount of attention from research workers.

Social withdrawal has been defined by Rubin, Burgess and Coplan (2002) as –

> *the consistent display across situations and over time of all forms of solitary behaviour when encountering familiar and/or unfamiliar peers.*

Children, that is, isolate themselves from the peer group. Just why certain children adopt such a pattern of behaviour has given rise to much speculation but also to a lot of research. The most common explanation is that this reflects an inherent personality disposition which is biologically rooted and evident from infancy onwards, forming part of the child's **temperament**. According to Kagan (e.g.1997), certain quite young infants tend to become inhibited in response to anything novel: any unfamiliar person, object or event elicits responses that may vary in intensity from wariness or shyness to outright fear. Such a tendency is associated with a unique pattern of electrical brain activity, apparently confirming the belief in its innate origin. However, follow-up studies indicate that the tendency can be changed subsequently within certain limits by experience and that it is only in its more extreme form that it shows stability, in that such infants grow up remaining shy, withdrawn and disinclined to join social groups (see **developmental continuity**).

Most attention has been given to the consequences of peer status, that is, the idea that a child's standing in the peer group makes it possible to predict psychological characteristics in subsequent years, with particular reference to socio-emotional adjustment. There is general consensus that accepted and (surprisingly perhaps) neglected children are most likely to develop into well-adjusted individuals; whereas rejected children are at greatest risk for subsequent psychological disorders. In rejected-aggressive children this takes the form of *externalizing* problems, such as delinquency, truancy, violence, bullying and poor educational achievement; in rejected-withdrawn children *internalizing* problems are more likely, such as anxiety, depression and loneliness. Rejection by peers thus appears to be a warning sign for possible future maladjustment, and it is no wonder that the establishment of positive peer relationships has been regarded as a central task for childhood. However, one cannot as yet firmly conclude that peer group status is a *cause* of later difficulty; it is rather a sign of possible problems to come.

One other approach to understanding the differences between peer status groups is to investigate the mental processes children employ when interacting with others. In this way one can, for example, determine whether rejected children have some kind of social skills deficit that accounts for their failure to establish positive peer relationships and, by specifying the nature of the deficit, make it more likely that some form of appropriate remedial action can succeed. To this end Dodge (1986) put forward a **SOCIAL INFORMATION PROCESSING MODEL**, namely –

> *a means of analysing the cognitive mechanisms used in processing the social cues provided by a child's partners in peer interaction.*

Several steps are hypothesized as being involved in such processing:

1 Encode the cues.

2 Interpret the cues.

3 Access or construct appropriate responses.

4 Evaluate the likely effect of the responses and select the most suitable.

5 Enact the chosen response.

The underlying assumption behind the scheme is that the way in which a child behaves in social situations is a function of the manner in which social cues are dealt with by that child. The model has mostly been used to locate the precise problems rejected-aggressive children have when interacting with peers, and there is evidence that it is also useful with regard to other kinds of peer problems and their correction (Crick & Dodge, 1994).

Further reading

Bukowski, W.M., & Cillessen, A.H.N. (Eds.) (1998). *Sociometry then and now: building on six decades of measuring children's experiences with the peer group.* New Directions for Child Development, No. 80. San Francisco: Jossey–Bass.

Cillessen, A.H.N., & Bukowski, W.M. (Eds.) (2000). *Recent advances in the measurement of acceptance and rejection in the peer system.* New Directions for Child Development, No. 88. San Francisco: Jossey–Bass. The various chapters in these two linked books give an insight into the way Moreno's work on sociometry has influenced research on peer groups.

Hymel, S., Vaillancourt, T., McDougall, P., & Renshaw, P.D. (2002). Peer acceptance and rejection in childhood. In P.K. Smith, & C.H. Hart (Eds.), *Blackwell handbook of childhood social development.* Oxford: Blackwell. A useful summary of theory and research dealing specifically with children's peer group status.

See also **emotional competence; social competence; temperament**

SOCIAL COMPETENCE

MEANING One of the most frequently used concepts in the social development literature, social competence is also one of the vaguest and most ill-defined. The idea that children should be 'good with people', and that deficits in this respect are warning signs for maladjustment, has a lot of intuitive appeal; translating this into objective indices that can be used in research and intervention has, however, encountered a great many obstacles and generated much controversy.

Here are just some of the definitions of social competence provided in the past: the attainment of relevant social goals; the ability to engage effectively in complex interpersonal interaction; behaviour that reflects successful social functioning; the attainment of relevant social goals in specified social contexts; the ability to perform culturally defined tasks; the possession and ability to use appropriate social skills; a judgement by another that an individual has behaved effectively; and the formulation and adoption of personal goals that are appropriate and adaptive to specific social situations. In addition, social competence has also been equated with social maturity, social skilfulness and adequacy of social performance. As Dodge put it in 1985, the number of definitions of social competence seems to approach the number of investigators in the field – a situation that has changed little today. Different theoretical assumptions and different research goals account largely for such divergence; in addition, particular value judgements underlie some of the choices. This is seen especially in one of the most common operational definitions adopted in research, namely one that expresses it in terms of acceptance by peers (see **peer group status**), the unspoken assumption being that the child who is extraverted, active and popular with other children must therefore be socially competent, whereas any child of a more introverted disposition is condemned as relatively incompetent. However, for one thing the use of such an index focuses on just one particular domain of behaviour and disregards many others that, a priori, could also be taken into account. And for another, it neglects the culture-specific nature of the value placed on being extraverted and outgoing (see Chen, Hastings, Rubin, Chen, Cen & Stewart, 1998, on the belief in Far Eastern countries that shyness is a positive attribute and that it is shy rather than assertive children who should be regarded as competent).

It is apparent that social competence is an umbrella term that covers a wide variety of different kinds of behaviour. In a very thorough review of the relevant literature Rose-Krasnor (1997) has found it useful to distinguish between four different approaches to the operational definition of social competence, referring respectively to social skills, sociometric status, relationships and functional outcomes. Each of these has certain advantages and disadvantages, but a central component in all which seems to express the essence of the concept is *effectiveness in interaction*. This still begs the question of how we judge 'effectiveness' – something that clearly cannot be done without taking into account the context within which the child is operating. In the light of these considerations, and at the risk of adding yet another item to the existing long list of definitions, it appears to be useful to think of social competence as –

effectiveness in interaction, as assessed in relation to the child's age, culture, situation and goals.

ORIGINS   'Being good with people' has always been recognized as an important characteristic of individuals, but from about the mid-twentieth century this became increasingly evident in the light of the many studies pointing to a link between interpersonal characteristics and a range of mental health indicators. At the same time it also became clear that fairly early on in childhood it is possible to differentiate those who are proficient in their relationships with others from those who are not, giving rise to the hope that by fostering the various social skills involved in relating to others one can prevent or at least mitigate children's adjustment problems. A term was required to act as a label for the particular relationship quality desired, and from the 1960s onwards 'social competence' was increasingly acknowledged as suitable for this purpose.

The concept quickly became a topic for study in its own right, as various investigators grappled with the task of defining, conceptualizing and measuring this quality (for early examples see White, 1959; Weinstein, 1969; Anderson and Messick, 1974). As Hubbard and Coie (1994) point out, two distinct approaches were adopted, one of which conceived of social competence in terms of social skills while the other stressed the social outcomes achieved by such behaviour. The first resulted in efforts to compile lists of skills that constitute competence – empathy, cooperating, helpfulness, interactive play abilities, conversational skills and many more. The second adopted a functional approach, asking what purposes social competence serves and proposing, for example, popularity, having friends and achieving influence over others as desirable outcomes. Both approaches are still being used as guidelines for research, though the second has become very much more common, with particular reference to the use of popularity as an index for competence.

For a concept that has attracted so many diverse meanings social competence continues to act as the focus of a surprisingly large body of work. Unfortunately there is still no consensus as to what operational definition to employ in its study, and while various theoretical models have been proposed in an effort to bring order to the field (e.g. Meichenbaum, Butler & Gruson, 1981; Rose-Krasnor, 1997) none of these has succeeded in gaining general acceptance. A proposal by Waters and Sroufe (1983), that any model of social competence must portray it as a process – one that organises social behaviour patterns and is not tied to age- or situation-specific criteria – is widely quoted with approval, though when it comes to the choice of operational definitions in designing research projects it too has not led to consensus.

CURRENT STATUS

There have been various efforts to examine the coherence of social competence as a concept by investigating the interrelationships between the different aspects proposed as its constituents. The results add up to a rather mixed picture. Comparing **peer group status** with various specific social skills (for example, group entry ability, conflict resolution, interactive play and the different forms of prosocial behaviour), popular children's behaviour in these social situations has generally been found to be more mature than that of unpopular children. However, the relationship is rarely more than moderate in magnitude (Cillessen & Bellmore, 2002) – a finding that also applies to the correlations between different social skills: being good at one task does not necessarily guarantee being good at another, suggesting that the totality of such skills does not represent a unitary entity.

While a lot of useful material has emerged from the analysis of individual skills, shedding light on how children function in various specific social settings, so far the findings do not take us further in understanding how social competence as a whole is organized. And yet it has also been reported that social competence, however assessed, bears certain orderly relationships to other psychological characteristics. It is, for example, associated with **temperament**; thus children classified as *difficult* are more likely to be unpopular with peers and to manifest lower levels of social skills (Sanson, Hemphill & Smart, 2002), in part because such children tend to show deficiencies in regulating their own emotions and in their awareness of others' emotions – giving added impetus to efforts to integrate social competence with **emotional competence** (Halberstadt, Dunsmore & Denham, 2001). Furthermore, socially competent children have been found to be more likely to manifest superior coping strategies and problem solving techniques in a range of cognitive situations; the processes responsible for this association, however, are not well understood as yet.

One of the main reasons why the topic of social competence has attracted so much attention is the hope that it can provide leads to helping children deficient in this respect. A considerable number of intervention programmes have been developed to this end (for adults as well as children), most involving the training of certain specific skills found to be deficient in particular individuals and using peer acceptance as the criterion for success – a focus that has been criticized as too narrow for evaluation purposes (Ladd, Buhs & Troop, 2002). A rather different approach is that based on the **social information processing model** developed by Dodge (1986), which analyses the mechanisms involved in processing interpersonal information and describes these in terms of a five-step sequence. The aim of intervention is to locate the precise point in this sequence where a child has difficulties and to direct training efforts accordingly. The approach has been used primarily with aggressive children and is said to have achieved an encouraging measure of success.

Further reading

Rose-Krasnor, L. (1997). The nature of social competence: a theoretical review. *Social Development*, *6*, 111–135. A thorough discussion of the various approaches adopted in the study of social competence, together with a proposed model to guide future work.

Cillessen, A.H.N., & Bellmore, A.D. (2002). Social skills and interpersonal perception in early and middle childhood. In P.K. Smith & C.H. Hart (Eds.), *Blackwell handbook of childhood social development*. Oxford: Blackwell. A critical review of work done on the various skills that many regard as making up social competence, pointing to what we do not know yet as well as what we do know.

Ladd, G.W. (1999). Peer relationships and social competence during early and middle childhood. *Annual Review of Psychology*, *50*, 333–359. Considers what research has achieved in recent years in understanding how children form relationships to peers and how such relationships can provide an insight into the nature of social competence.

See also **emotional competence; peer group status; social information processing model**

SOCIALIZATION

8

EIGHT

The term socialization is used to cover *the multitude of processes that enable children to become integrated into their community, by adopting as their own the values and customs prevailing therein.* This is a central task for all children, in that they need to acquire the beliefs, attitudes and rules of behaviour of those around them in order to function effectively as members of society. Socialization is thus a generic label covering a wide range of topics, and though it assumes greatest importance in the early years it is by no means confined to childhood: adults too need to be socialized (or re-socialized) in order to keep up with changes in the particular society in which they live or to which they have relocated. Socialization occurs primarily in a relationship context, that is, through interaction with other people who, in the case of children, are mainly the child's parents. It is therefore no wonder that the study of parent–child interaction constitutes an essential ingredient in our thinking about socialization.

Among the various specific questions that have been asked by developmental psychologists about socialization are the following. What are the aspects of children's behaviour repertoire that become the main target of parental socialization? How can one differentiate change resulting from socialization from that brought about by maturation? Who are the agents of socialization and what is their respective influence? How do socialization practices vary from one developmental period to another? In what way do diverse cultures differ in the goals of socialization and in the manner in which it is accomplished? How do children contribute to their own socialization and in what way is this contribution integrated with that of their caretakers? At one time the main interest lay in the products of socialization such as honesty, dependence-independence and conformity, in order to establish age norms, individual differences and antecedents; more recently, however, a shift in focus has occurred from outcome to process, so that it is much more the intra-individual and interpersonal mechanisms underlying socialization that are now the main topics of investigation.

The following concepts will be described here:

CHILD EFFECTS
and: **Bidirectionality**
PARENT EFFECTS
PARENTAL BELIEF SYSTEMS
SHARED AND NONSHARED ENVIRONMENTAL INFLUENCES
INTERNALIZATION
and: **Compliance**
MORAL, CONVENTIONAL AND PERSONAL CONDUCT RULES

CHILD EFFECTS
and: **BIDIRECTIONALITY**

MEANING The notion that parents affect their children is widely accepted. However, the idea that the influence process can also go in the opposite direction, from child to parents, has only comparatively recently been acknowledged, giving rise to the concept of child effects, defined as –

> *the influences children exert on their caretakers by virtue of their particular characteristics.*

For long, parents were thought to play the sole role in socialization: they are, after all, more powerful and more knowledgeable than their children and therefore should be able to impose on them whatever standards they choose. Socialization was accordingly regarded as a unidirectional process, analogous to clay moulding, in which passive children are moulded by parents to assume any shape that the latter decide upon. Recognizing the existence of child effects, however, has transformed our ideas about what goes on between parents and children: socialization is not so much something that is done *to* children as something done *with* children (Maccoby & Martin, 1983). Both partners contribute; the parent–child relationship is co-constructed; and socialization needs to be conceived in terms of **BIDIRECTIONALITY** (Russell, Mize & Bissaker, 2002). This concept expresses the idea that –

> *in the course of dyadic interaction the behaviour of each partner affects the behaviour of the other partner.*

Thus even the youngest children are active participants when interacting with another person; moreover, each child has an individuality that affects the parents' choice of rearing practices – what works for one may not work for another. Socialization is therefore the result of *both* partners' contributions.

ORIGINS Historically the view of the child as a passive recipient of adults' rearing practices is of long standing, but is usually associated with the seventeenth-century philosopher John Locke and his belief that the child's mind is like a *tabula rasa* (blank slate), to be inscribed by experience, this constituting the sole source of mental content. Insofar as experience is mostly provided by caretakers, it is they who determine how the child's mind is moulded.

The clay moulding view was given apparent academic respectability by John Watson, the father of behaviourism, who once referred to the newborn infant as 'a very lowly piece of unformed protoplasm, ready to be shaped by any family in whose care it is first placed' (1928). This view became the starting point for much of the research by developmental psychologists in the following decades, in that they approached the study of child rearing from a behaviourist point of view, with its emphasis on training and learning, its faith in the shaping influence of reward and punishment and its assumption that in reinforcement and association we find the mechanisms to account for child development. Socialization, as Bijou (1970) once put it, is simply the product of the individual's reinforcement history.

The research that followed this conception aimed to show what sort of connections there are between particular child rearing activities of parents and the developmental characteristics of their children. The former were seen as antecedents, the latter as outcomes, and any correlations obtained were assumed to demonstrate cause-and-effect sequences proceeding from parent to child (probably the best known of these studies is that by Sears, Maccoby & Levin, 1957). However, two points need to be made about this approach. One is that the correlations obtained were often low and gave little ground for believing in the all-powerful role of parental influence. The other is that correlation is not causation, that correlations can be brought about in many different ways and that it is therefore not justified to use correlational methods to demonstrate causal mechanisms. To understand what transpires between parents and children a different approach needs to be adopted.

This came about in the 1960s and 1970s as a result of two developments. One was a seminal paper by Richard Bell (1968), in which he marshalled the evidence then available to argue that the influence of children on parents plays as big a part in their socialization as parents' influence on children, and that such *child effects* (as he was the first to call them) must be considered alongside **parent effects** if we are to gain an insight into the way developmental outcomes are brought about. Children's individuality, that is whatever distinctive characteristics a child brings to the interaction, will play a part in shaping the parent's actions, and outcomes are thus invariably a joint product of the two sets of effects. The details of this process were further spelled out in subsequent publications (e.g. Bell & Harper, 1977; Bell, 1979; Bell & Chapman, 1986).

The other development came from the wave of microanalytic studies of social interaction that made use of films and video recordings to examine in minute detail what transpires between mothers and infants in everyday face-to-face encounters such as play and caring routines (see Schaffer, 1977, for examples). These made it abundantly clear that any notion of mothers being solely responsible for setting the tone, pace and content of these interactions could not be upheld: child effects were evident in that infants, at least as frequently as mothers, appeared to initiate behaviour sequences by such means as vocalization, touch and gaze, to which the mothers replied in ways judged by them appropriate in terms of the infant's ongoing state and interests. Analysing such a sequence of intricately linked, reciprocal actions in terms of cause and effect has encountered considerable conceptual and statistical difficulties, giving rise to the view that dyads should be treated as entities in their own right without attempting to tease apart the contributions of the individual partners. What has become amply clear is that in these encounters even the youngest infants are active, not passive, and that the flow of influence is bidirectional, not unidirectional.

CURRENT STATUS   Highlighting the existence of child effects has necessitated some radical rethinking of the way we conceptualize socialization and parent–child interaction. Initially, however, much of the research that followed was aimed primarily at identifying these effects. A substantial number have been listed; they can be grouped into three categories:

1 *Individual attributes.*   Included here are such aspects as the child's gender, physical attractiveness, impulse control, disability and temperament. The last in particular has received considerable attention: mothers of children with *difficult* temperaments respond to them with more restriction, more punishment and less stimulating contact than is found in mothers of children with *easy* temperaments.

2 *Discrete behaviours.*   These are especially evident in microanalytic studies of adult–child interaction and refer to brief actions such as smiles, cries, vocalizations, gaze and gestures. Each of these, in the course of the interaction, may induce a particular reaction from the adult, giving the impression that in some limited sense at least the infant is 'driving' that part of the interactive sequence.

3 *Age-related characteristics.*   Child effects refer not only to static characteristics; developmental change, as an influence in its own right, must also be acknowledged. As children get older new characteristics emerge to which parents must respond appropriately: the impulsive toddler exerts a different influence on the parents than the emotionally much better controlled 10-year-old. Moreover, any one child characteristic may change its meaning in the course of development: 'babyish' behaviour is tolerated in babies but not in older children.

Identifying child effects is one thing, but to prove conclusively that they indeed affect the other person's behaviour has proved far from easy. One of the most conclusive ways is to disentangle these influences experimentally, as done by Anderson, Lytton and Romney (1986) in a study of two groups of mothers, one with conduct-disorder children and one with non-problem children. Each mother was observed both with her own child and with a child from the other group. The results highlight the marked difference of a mother's behaviour according to the nature of the child with whom she is interacting: mothers with non-problem children, for example, became much more controlling and negative when interacting with a conduct-disorder child, thus showing behaviour typical of these children's own mothers. It can be concluded that the mothers were 'driven' by the aggressiveness and lack of impulse control characteristic of conduct-disordered children and that these really do act as child effects.

While the reality of child effects cannot be doubted, there is still considerable uncertainty as to the way in which their role in social interaction should be conceptualized. Clearly it is insufficient merely to add another unidirectional arrow, that from child to parent, to the parent–to–child arrow. Bidirectionality is not simply the sum of two sets of unidirectional influences: the core of this concept lies rather in the way in which the two sets of influences mesh, so that they can be treated as one unitary entity. A shift from individuals to dyads as the unit of analysis has thus taken place in the socialization literature as one result of the introduction of child effects, and terms such as mutuality, reciprocity and synchrony are accordingly used to describe the relationships existing *between* people rather than the people themselves (Hinde, 1997). A picture has consequently emerged of the parent–child dyad as a system (see **dynamic systems**), the nature of which is not due to any one partner nor to the sum of their individual contributions but to their joint transactional history (Kuczynski, 2003).

The *transactional model* of development has become the most common way of viewing the parent–child dyad (Sameroff, 1975). A transactional process is one in which one person's behaviour in a dyad affects the other person's behaviour which in turn influences the first person's behaviour, and so forth. Applied to parent–child interaction, the model views child development as the outcome of reciprocal, circular interchanges that occur over time between child characteristics and parental influences. The time interval may be very brief, such as some specific interaction episode, or encompass the whole of childhood. The model thus attempts to do justice to the merging of the two sets of causal arrows into one unitary process, in which each partner's behaviour is contingent on the other's and where both partners become changed as the recursive cycle proceeds.

The transactional model may be seen as a step beyond bidirectionality, in that it draws attention away from the two separate sets of causal influences to the dynamics of their meshing. The model is not without shortcomings, however, as seen for instance in its vagueness in explaining precisely how change in the parent–child relationship occurs over time. Attempts are therefore under way to construct more comprehensive explanatory models of parent–child relations, such as Granic's (2000) proposal to apply the principles of **self-organization** to this area. The usefulness of these new approaches remains to be established.

Further reading

Kuczynski, L. (Ed.) (2003). *Handbook of dynamics in parent–child relations*. Thousand Oaks, CA: Sage. Contains a number of chapters directly relevant to child effects, such as the first one by the editor and the epilogue by Maccoby.

Russell, A., & Russell, G. (1992). Child effects in socialization research: some conceptual and data analysis issues. *Social Development*, *1*, 163–184. Especially useful in its discussion of methodological problems and solutions.

Schaffer, H.R. (1999). Understanding socialization: from unidirectional to bidirectional conceptions. In M. Bennett (Ed.), *Developmental psychology: achievements and prospects*. London: Psychology Press. Provides a historical account of the models adopted to account for the socialization process.

See also **dynamic systems; parent effects; self-organization; temperament**

PARENT EFFECTS

MEANING Unlike **child effects**, the case for parent effects has never had to be argued. By parent effects we mean –

all the various ways in which parents influence the behaviour and development of their children.

It has always been taken for granted that children's development is to a considerable extent a function of the behaviour and attitudes of their parents – an assumption reinforced by the deviant development of children deprived of parental care. Thus there has rarely been any doubt that parenting is all about steering children's development in certain socially approved directions, and inadequate parenting (however defined) is widely considered to be a major cause of children's maladjustment.

From a scientific point of view, however, there are various uncertainties surrounding parent effects (O'Connor, 2002a). Two in particular stand out. One is the extent to which parents actually do influence their children's development as opposed to the part which such other forces as genes and peers play; the other refers to an understanding of the processes whereby parent effects can cause changes in children's behaviour. It is perhaps ironic that a phenomenon as ubiquitous as parenting is still shrouded in so much mystery, despite the huge amount of theorizing and research it has attracted. Even the identity of the different constituents of parenting remains a matter of debate.

Parents have always been considered to play a significant role in their children's lives, but historically the nature of that role has been thought about in different ways. Four models have dominated thinking at various times, each based on a particular concept of the nature of children and hence also of the role their parents play in their development (Schaffer, 1996):

ORIGINS

1 *Laissez-faire model*. According to this view parents have just a limited part to play in their children's upbringing. Much influenced by the writings of the eighteenth-century French thinker Jean-Jacques Rousseau, the assumption is that children arrive in the world preformed, with all basic aspects of personality already laid down and ready merely to unfold. Parents' task is therefore one of *laissez-faire* (leave alone), that is, of providing an environment suitable for the unfolding process to occur; anything more active can only do harm. It is noteworthy that this view has resurfaced in more modern form in the writings on **maturation** by Gesell (1954), who also saw parents' role as confined to ensuring that children's potential could be realized by the kind of setting provided for them. It is also found in the assertion by Scarr (1992), writing on the role of genes in development, that as long as children receive 'good-enough' parenting their development is primarily determined by inherited characteristics.

2 *Clay moulding model*. As pointed out under **child effects**, this model prevailed for a large part of the twentieth century. It depicts the newborn infant as formless and passive, like a lump of clay that the parents can mould into any shape they decide upon. In time the shape will set, and the form it takes will then be wholly explicable in terms of whatever the parents did during the child's impressionable years. Parent effects are thus all-powerful determinants of children's development, with a direct causal link proceeding from the former to the latter.

3 *Conflict model*. According to this view, children are active from birth but in pursuance of goals that are antagonistic to those of their parents. Infants, it is alleged, are self-centred, require instant gratification and are incapable of controlling their primitive emotional impulses. It is therefore the task of parents to compel them to give up these undesirable tendencies and instead comply with the standards of society. Freud espoused such a model, in that he saw child and parent as protagonists on opposite sides of the conflict, which the more powerful parent has to win to be an effective socializing agent. Development is thus a painful process, for it requires resolution of the basic antagonism of child and society. The picture that emerges of the parent–child relationship is thus a thoroughly negative one, with parents determined to ensure that their children should adopt 'civilized' ways of behaving that are, initially at least, unnatural to them. A more recent version of the model is to be found in Hoffman's (1977) proposal that the *discipline encounter* represents the primary context in which parents bring about change in children's behaviour – an encounter in which there is a clash of wills, with parent and child having different aims and where the conflict element is seen as providing the motive power for the child's eventual conformity.

4 *Mutuality model.* This represents the most recent view, based on the notion of **bidirectionality** in the influence pattern of parent and child. Even the youngest infants are far from being inert recipients of parental influence; from the beginning they are active participants in their own socialization. And parents, for their own part, are neither passive bystanders nor all-powerful shapers nor ruthless enforcers but more like sensitive negotiators who facilitate their children's development on the basis of warmth and collaboration. Far from being antisocial beings who must be coerced into sociability, children share a common heritage with their caretakers that impels them to adopt the same social goals. Mutual adaptation is thus the basic theme that runs through the course of parent–child interaction.

CURRENT STATUS

The way we think about and study parenting has undergone some radical changes in recent times (see Collins, Maccoby, Steinberg, Hetherington & Bornstein, 2000, for details). Above all, we have come to acknowledge it as a far more complex activity than had previously been suggested – one that involves a multiplicity of functions, that forms one part of a network including other influences rather than constituting a unique effect, and that does not act in a direct causal fashion but in conjunction with moderating effects such as characteristics of the individual child.

As to multiplicity of functions, parent effects manifest themselves in a considerable variety of ways, both direct and indirect. Direct ways rely on face-to-face interaction: commands and prohibitions, instructions, guidance and modelling are examples. Some of these are more forceful than others, but as work on parental **scaffolding** has shown, the more a parent can take account of the child's current state of knowledge, skill and orientation the more likely it is that their action will be effective – another demonstration of the importance of adopting a mutuality model in thinking about parent–child relationships. However, much of what parents do is accomplished by more indirect ways: as Parke et al. (2003) have described, parents also act as managers, organizers, facilitators and gatekeepers of social opportunities and thereby influence their children's development. Parents, for example, decide what kind of neighbourhood the family will live in, choose the school the child should attend, arrange for the child to mix with certain kinds of peer groups and in general regulate access to a range of resources and social contacts. Here again they do not usually act in a purely arbitrary manner but in conjunction with the child, taking into account the child's characteristics and inclinations.

For long, a child's development was regarded as wholly due to the parents (or rather to the mother), with no attention paid to any other possible influence. This is no longer the case: the parents may be the child's primary socializing agents but other sources too have come to be acknowledged – siblings, the extended family, peers, teachers and the media. There are even those, like Harris (1995), who have proposed that such other agents as peers play a greater part in shaping children's personality development, though most writers have fiercely resisted this argument. What cannot be doubted is that parents are by no means the only ones who constitute the child's socialization environment: their effects need to be seen in the broader context of a network of influences to which the child is exposed; the parental role cannot therefore be treated in isolation. This becomes a particularly important consideration when different sources provide different messages: what this means to children and how they resolve such conflicts is an area to which attention is now beginning to be paid (e.g. Padilla-Walker and Thompson, 2005).

There is one further set of influences which must be considered in conjunction with parent effects, namely those denoting the child's individuality. As described in the discussion of **child effects**, these set limits to what parents do and channel their rearing practices in certain directions appropriate to the particular child. Take one instance to which a considerable amount of attention has been paid, namely children's **temperament**. In a number of studies carried out by Grazyna Kochanska (summarized in Kochanska & Thompson, 1997) temperamentally fearful children were found to respond readily to their parents' disciplinary measures even when these were of a mild nature; on the other hand, children who by nature were of an imperturbable disposition required more forceful techniques before they conformed to their parents' requirements. Temperament, it appears, acts as a moderating variable without which one cannot understand how parental practices bring about developmental outcomes for children.

While there are other factors, such as the child's age and gender, which also moderate the impact of parenting, the role of temperament is significant because it is to a large extent genetically determined, and draws attention to the intricate intertwining of genes and environment (see **gene–environment effects**). To investigate parent effects in isolation from child effects is thus misleading (O'Connor, 2002b) – a consideration that alone is responsible for an extensive transformation of the study of parenting, making it a much more complex enterprise, conceptually and methodologically.

Further reading

Bugental, D.B., & Goodnow, J.J. (1998). Socialization processes. In W. Damon (Ed.), *Handbook of child psychology*, vol. 3 (N. Eisenberg, Ed.). New York: Wiley. An overall account of research on socialization, with particular reference to the role of parenting.

O'Connor, T.G. (2002a). The 'effects' of parenting reconsidered: findings, challenges and applications. *Journal of Child Psychology and Psychiatry*, *43*, 555–572. Concerned specifically with parent effects, outlines the changes in thinking about the parent–child relationship that have taken place as a result of recent research.

See also **child effects; gene–environment interactions; maturation; scaffolding**

PARENTAL BELIEF SYSTEMS

MEANING Parents are not merely bundles of child rearing practices – as well as act they also reflect upon, plan and evaluate what they are doing with children, choose particular goals they want to achieve and the means of accomplishing these, and develop theories about the nature of children and their own role as parents which are not necessarily conscious but which can act as guides to action and thus become indirect determinants of child outcomes. To cover all these functions the term *parental belief systems* is used, meaning thereby –

> *the sets of ideas that parents hold about the nature of children's socialization.*

Various other terms have also been used in the same sense as parental beliefs, such as parental cognitions, ideas, thoughts, constructs, representations and (when comparing the beliefs prevalent in different cultures, see Harkness & Super, 1996) ethnotheories. No clear case has been made as to whether one or another term is preferable; all, however, refer to mental constructs that give parents some direction as to what they ought to do in their parenting capacity and help them to make sense of what they actually do in that capacity. Parental beliefs may thus be thought of as a type of **folk theory**, that is, a naïve version of psychology as applied to the way parents think about their children and themselves.

Parental beliefs cover a wide range of topics, indicated by the kind of questions to which parents seek answers (Goodnow & Collins, 1990). What is the basic nature of children – are they born good, bad or unformed? What are the respective influences of nature and nurture? How should the course of development be viewed – smooth, irregular, step-wise? At what ages can one expect particular new achievements to appear? What role should parents play in furthering their children's development? What form of discipline works best? These are just some of the issues parents attempt to resolve, which they do on the basis of a mixture of preconceived ideas, other people's advice and their own experience, but which they may then come to regard as obvious truths or valid statements of facts.

There are indications that parents do not approach each question anew but that there are certain consistencies in their views across a range of topics. Some parents, for example, have a definite preference for nature as an explanatory principle for their children's characteristics, whereas others favour nurture, each applied to any situation where the question of causation of behaviour arises (Miller, 1988, 1995). The use of the term *systems* in connection with parental beliefs is thus justified, in that beliefs concerning a diversity of topics appear to be organized in clusters that provide a formal structure to the separate pieces. The systems are open, in that they are not set once and for all but can be modified by the individual's experience, and how they change and why are thus some of the questions that need to be asked about them.

ORIGINS

As long as a behaviourist ethos prevailed in psychology parents were seen only in terms of the overt actions they perform and not as thinking beings. The notion that they may hold certain beliefs about what they do and what they ought to do and that these beliefs are conceptually separate from and yet closely associated with their practices is thus of very recent origin, spurred on by the growth of work on cognition and information processing (Goodnow & Collins, 1990). As a result of the 'cognitive revolution' developmental psychologists became interested in the role that cognition plays in family interaction (Bugental & Johnston, 2000), and for this purpose began work on a range of mental concepts such as **attribution, scripts, internal working models** and knowledge structures generally, and these in turn fuelled interest in the theories, goals and values that lay behind their rearing practices and indicated the need for a concept such as parental belief systems as a general label for parents' cognitions.

The shift of focus from parental behaviour to parents' cognitions was heralded by the first volume specifically concerned with parental beliefs, edited by Sigel and published in 1985. Initially learning about parental beliefs was seen primarily as a means of improving the prediction of child outcomes (Miller, 1988, 1995), and only subsequently did the topic assume importance in its own right.

CURRENT STATUS

For a long time a search has been going on for the most useful ways of describing parenting – useful, that is, in that the dimensions chosen should represent the essential context in which children experience their family life. Most attention has been given to parental attitudes to child rearing – warmth, hostility, acceptance, protectiveness and other wide-ranging predispositions that could be assessed by questionnaires and were expected to bear an orderly relationship to children's development. However, as described by Holden and Buck (2002) in a detailed review, over the past two decades parental attitudes have been ousted from their pre-eminent status, partly because of definitional uncertainties, partly because of methodological problems in their measurement, partly also because of their failure to predict child outcomes but mainly because the *Zeitgeist* has moved on to a more cognitive orientation and consequently to a search for social cognitive concepts, capable of describing how parents represent to themselves the nature of childhood and the nature of child rearing.

Parental belief is one of the concepts (**attributions** and **internal working models** are other examples) that have become prominent as a result of this change. The amount of research devoted to the topic has steadily increased (for reviews see Goodnow & Collins, 1990, and Sigel & McGillicuddy-DeLisi, 2002), mostly guided by four general questions:

1 What are the sources of parents' beliefs?
2 What are the links between parents' beliefs and their child rearing practices?
3 What are the consequences of parents' beliefs for children's development?
4 What is the nature of parents' beliefs?

As to the first of these, parents obtain their ideas about child rearing from many sources. Some of these derive from their personal experience, especially that accumulated from being parented themselves in childhood and stored as mental representations or **internal working models** (Grusec, Hastings & Mammone, 1994). Others are shaped by the opinions expressed by relatives, neighbours and friends, and (increasingly so these days) by the media. A rather more subtle influence, but nevertheless a powerful one, are the beliefs and values prevailing in the particular culture to which parents belong – the *ethnotheories*, as Harkness and Super (1996) have labelled them, an area to which probably more research has been devoted than to any other source. Cross-cultural data on child rearing have shown up the considerable differences that exist among societies in this respect, expressing the often widely divergent goals held with regard to the qualities which each society wants to foster in its members (for an example see LeVine et al., 1994 on a comparison of child rearing practices among the Gusii people of Kenya and American parents).

The second question, that concerning the relationship between parents' beliefs and practices, has not yielded the unequivocal answer that was looked for originally. Correlations have been found, but on the whole the evidence is far from overwhelming. There are two possible reasons for this. One is that the relationship between belief and practice is by no means a straightforward, unidirectional one from the former to the latter, but involves a complex interaction between the two in which they mutually modify each other over the course of time, neither remaining static (Goodnow & Collins, 1990). The other reason concerns the complexity of both beliefs and practices: each is made up of a great many different constituents, and no easy generalizations can therefore be made about a link between the two when each is conceived as a unitary whole. It appears that the only possibility of finding meaningful relationships is to study specific constituents, selected because on theoretical grounds they may be linked. So far, however, there are still only a few studies of this nature.

As to the third question, the link between parental belief and child outcome, this is, if anything, even more tenuous, in that neither close nor consistent relationships have clearly emerged. This is perhaps not surprising, for beliefs, being internal constructions, can influence child behaviour only indirectly via parents' overt actions. Moreover, children's development is determined by a great many factors, and beliefs must therefore be seen as forming just one part of a network of interacting influences. In any case, many of the relevant studies are correlational, so here too the direction of influence remains uncertain. This is especially important because of the now widely acknowledged role of **child effects**, in that experience of 'what works' with any given child may well determine the nature of beliefs about child rearing adopted by the parent. Longitudinal studies are better equipped to sort out the direction of effects problem, though the few that have taken this form have so far not yielded firm conclusions (Sigel & McGillicuddy-DeLisi, 2002).

These various considerations make it all the more important to give attention to the fourth question, that is, the nature of parental beliefs. It is widely agreed that greater specificity is required in isolating and defining the components of belief systems, but no one scheme has yet found general acceptance (though see Sigel & McGillicuddy-DeLisi, 2002, for a recent proposal). It is also agreed that beliefs come into being as a result of the individual's active construction as determined by multiple influences, and that such construction is an ongoing process because beliefs, being open systems, remain susceptible to the influence of experience. What is more, beliefs do not operate in isolation from other social cognitive domains: when Mize, Pettit and Brown (1995) investigated the impact on child rearing practices of three such domains, namely parents' perceptions of their children, their knowledge of socialization strategies and their beliefs, they found that practices were best predicted by the *joint* effect of the various domains – a finding that explains why beliefs alone have generally been found to be only moderately related to behaviour. Both parental practices and child outcomes are multi-determined; it must be concluded that to understand them we need to treat beliefs as just one amongst a number of co-determinants.

Further reading

Goodnow, J.J., & Collins, W.A. (1990). *Development according to parents: the nature, sources and consequences of parents' ideas.* Hillsdale, NJ: Erlbaum. Remains one of the best examinations of theoretical and empirical aspects of research on beliefs, together with suggestions regarding trends, gaps and future directions of research.

Harkness, S., & Super, C.M. (1996). *Parents' cultural belief systems: their origins, expressions and consequences.* New York: Guilford. Various authors provide accounts of the way in which cultural influences affect parental beliefs, backed up by observations of the manifestations and the consequences for children's development of these influences.

Sigel, I.E., & McGillicuddy-DeLisi, A.V. (2002). Parent beliefs are cognitions: the dynamic belief systems model. In Bornstein, M.H. (Ed.), *Handbook of parenting*, vol. 3 (2nd ed.). Mahwah, NJ: Erlbaum. Contains a summary of findings regarding the determinants and outcomes of parental beliefs, as well as proposal for a theoretical framework to understand belief systems.

See also **child effects; dynamic systems; parent effects**

SHARED AND NONSHARED ENVIRONMENTAL INFLUENCES

MEANING As a result of research by behavioural geneticists, two kinds of environmental influences on children's development have been distinguished. On the one hand there are shared influences, referring to –

> *those environmental experiences that are common to all children in a given family.*

Marital break-up, overcrowding, parental alcoholism, social class and poverty are examples, in that they are family-specific and act to make the siblings in that family more similar to one another. On the other hand, nonshared influences refer to –

> *environmental experiences that impinge differently on each child in the same family.*

These are experiences such as a child's hospitalization, joining some particular same-age peer group and differential treatment by parents as seen in favouritism and scapegoating. The effect of experiences such as these is to make siblings different from one other. Thus, whereas shared influences contribute to familial resemblance nonshared influences are those that contribute to differences in the same family (further details in Plomin, DeFries, McClearn & McGuffin, 2001).

  In the past research has focused almost exclusively on shared influences and regarded these family-wide experiences as the salient forces that shape development.

Such research generally took the form of *between-family* comparisons, selecting one child from each family for this purpose and regarding these as representative of all children in that family. If nonshared influences are as important as many now claim, a different research strategy is required, one that is based on *within-family* comparisons in that it takes several children in the same family and asks what makes each of these children unique.

ORIGINS

The distinction between the two kinds of environmental influences is a very recent one, dating back to 1981, when two behavioural geneticists, Rowe and Plomin, argued that the portion of variation in psychological characteristics which is not accounted for by genetic factors is made up of two distinct types of environmental factors, shared and nonshared, and that of the two the latter is the predominant influence in accounting for individuals' development. Their paper was followed a few years later by one with the provocative title 'Why are children in the same family so different from each other?', in which Plomin and Daniels (1987) provided a much more detailed version of the argument and were able to back up their case with a substantial amount of new research.

The first surprise for many readers of these papers was to discover that genetics is not solely about nature but that it also has a contribution to make to our understanding of nurture, that is, to an analysis of experiential factors and their relative influence on children. However, as behavioural geneticists were able to point out, all psychological characteristics, even those like schizophrenia and autism that are heavily dependent on inherited forces, are influenced by experience too (see **gene–environment effects**), and moreover that the methodologies used by them for studying genetic influences lend themselves also to the investigation of experiential factors. The second surprise was the claim that nonshared influences are considerably more important than shared ones in accounting for child outcome, and that much of past research on socialization processes was therefore misleading in its sole concern with the effects of social class, parental styles and other shared characteristics and therefore in the assumption that parents affect all children in any one family equally. Being brought up in the same family need not, by itself, result in sibling similarity; the fact that adopted children reared from birth by parents with other children, biologically related to the parents or also adopted, are no more alike to their siblings than non-related children, was one piece of evidence advanced to bolster this case. It was thus proposed that a major shift in socialization research was called for: instead of treating the family as a monolithic force in its effect on children's development it is necessary to look inside the family and examine children's differential experience within it. In addition, any unique experiences outside the family must also be taken into account. This does not mean that families do not matter (as some have interpreted this proposal); rather, it stresses that families can provide many experiences that are specific to each child. Environmental measures should therefore be specific to particular children, not to particular families.

Plomin and his colleagues went on to map out a programme of research to advance our understanding of nonshared influences, consisting of the following stages:

1 Establish the magnitude of nonshared influences.

2 Identify specific nonshared influences.

3 Explore the relationship of these influences with child behaviour.

These aims have guided all subsequent work in this area.

CURRENT STATUS

There is plenty of evidence from both anecdotal reports and systematic research (Dunn & Plomin, 1990) that siblings brought up in the same family can be strikingly different from each other in all sorts of ways. Moreover, it is also apparent that siblings often receive surprisingly different treatment from their parents, as borne out by observations, interviews with children or parents and questionnaires such as the specially constructed Sibling Inventory of Differential Experience (or SIDE, Daniels & Plomin, 1985). At the same time it needs to be borne in mind that what matters are children's *perceptions* of their differential treatment rather than the objective facts of such treatment, hence the importance of obtaining information from the children themselves as to how they view their experience. Children's individuality and how events are subjectively interpreted have emerged as essential factors to take into account.

Identifying specific environmental effects has been a slow task and conclusive evidence is still scarce. Some have argued that experiences outside the family provide the richest sources of nonshared influences – siblings mixing with different peers, attending different schools and encountering unexpected traumatic events like accidents and hospitalizations. The company of peers in particular, according to some, constitutes a powerful influence. As Plomin et al. (2001) point out, siblings differing genetically may well be impelled to seek out different peer groups, so that it is ultimately genetic factors rather than the company of peers as such to which one must look for an explanation of developmental outcome.

Whether nonshared influences, of whatever source, are related to differences in children's development is a further point of debate. There are a number of studies that have shown parents' differential treatment of their children to be associated with varying patterns of adjustment (O'Connor, 2002b). For example, Deater-Deckard and Petrill (2004) have found that the extent of mutuality established between a mother and her child can differ from child to child within the same family, and that these differences tend to be correlated with adjustment problems: the lower the level of mutuality the greater the severity of such problems. There is, however, the ever-present problem of direction of effects: does differential treatment by parents cause children to be different or is the particular treatment of each child the result of pre-existing characteristics in that child? Longitudinal investigations will help to resolve this question in due course.

While the distinction between shared and nonshared influences has proved to be valuable and productive, the further assertion that it is nonshared influences that are crucial in accounting for children's development and that shared influences play a negligible role is now no longer considered to be tenable as a general proposition (Rutter, 2002). For one thing, there are too many exceptions to this claim when comparing results for different child functions. For example, whereas nonshared influences are predominant in the areas of cognition and psychopathology, shared influences play a notable role with regard to quality of attachment, aggression and anxiety (O'Connor, 2002b). Even within particular areas there are qualifications: with respect to cognition, for instance, shared influences are more important during childhood than from adolescence on. For another, there are variations according to children's individual susceptibility to environmental influence: experiences such as divorce or a parent's death are shared by siblings, but some children are much more affected by these traumata than others. Shared influences, we have to conclude, can lead to nonshared effects. There are thus two sources of differences between siblings: different experiences and different susceptibilities. A much more analytic perspective needs therefore to be adopted, in order to examine in detail how specific experiences impinge on each individual child in a family (Turkheimer & Waldron, 2000). At present any claim about the relative importance of shared and nonshared influences appears to be premature.

Further reading

Dunn, J., & Plomin, R. (1990). *Separate lives: why siblings are so different*. New York: Basic Books. A highly readable account of the rationale for distinguishing shared and nonshared influences, based on the conviction that the latter matter more than the former.

Hetherington, E.M., Reiss, D., & Plomin, R. (Eds.) (1994). *Separate Social worlds of siblings*. Hillsdale, NJ: Erlbaum. A more specialized account of the reasons for regarding nonshared environment as important, together with various research reports dealing with different aspects of this topic.

Plomin, R., DeFries, J.C., McClearn, G.E., & McGuffin, P. (2001). *Behavioral genetics* (4th ed.). New York: Worth. Chapter 15 sets out to show how genetic research can contribute to our understanding of environmental influences on development, with reference especially to nonshared effects.

See also **child effects; gene–environment effects; parent effects; temperament**

INTERNALIZATION
and: **COMPLIANCE**

MEANING It is widely believed that one of the primary goals of socialization is to ensure that children adopt the values, standards and rules of conduct of the community in which they live – something considered to be essential for the functioning of society. As far as individuals are concerned, failure to be socialized in this respect is usually seen as a serious sign of maladaptation. Thus an important theme in childhood is the progression from other-control to self-control, from a state where the child's behaviour is regulated by external agents to behaviour being the responsibility of the individual him- or herself. This progression is referred to as internalization, more formally defined as –

> *the processes whereby individuals acquire the standards and values laid down by others and adopt them as their own.*

Behaviourally, individuals show that they have succeeded in this task by, for example, spontaneous willingness to stick to social standards, resistance to temptation and signs of guilt after not following the rules laid down. One can then credit them with having acquired a *conscience*, that is, a psychological mechanism that will guide their actions in the absence of control by external agents. The latter is the crucial point about internalization, namely that it results in individuals themselves regulating their behaviour in socially approved ways and not relying on pressure from others present at the time.

Developmentally, however, children first require external controls in order to learn what the standards are to which they are meant to conform. This is seen in compliance situations, where caretakers make requests ('Drink your juice', 'Don't touch that vase') and expect prompt obedience from their child. **COMPLIANCE** is –

> *a child's willingness to follow another person's request to carry out, or to desist from carrying out, some particular action.*

Control is thus exerted by someone else and conformity is expected here-and-now rather than being carried forward to future behaviour. There is evidence (see below) that compliance is a necessary antecedent to internalization, in that children must acquire the ability to comply in the early stages of development before they become capable of the more sophisticated skill of internalizing instructions and following that 'still, small voice' inside them.

Socially, both compliance and internalization are highly valued qualities, hence the considerable attention they have received in the developmental literature (see, for example, Grusec & Kuczynski, 1997). This is especially in societies where **collectivist** values prevail and children are early on expected to act for the common good. Obedience is thus a more important socialization goal than in countries with a more **individualist** orientation, yet it is noteworthy that in the West too noncompliance has been found to be one of the most frequent reasons for psychiatric referral of young children (Forehand & McMahon, 1981).

ORIGINS

There has always been speculation about how standards and values are passed on from one generation to another. Mostly it was assumed that the transmission process is a didactic one: parents teach children what behaviour is acceptable and children, by following their instruction, gradually learn the rules and adopt them as their own. Even when psychology emerged as a scientific discipline the same orientation prevailed, as seen in the emphasis of social learning theory on reward and punishment as the principal motives for children's development of conformity to social norms. Accordingly, by pairing reward with approved acts and punishment with disapproved acts it gradually becomes possible to extinguish the latter but retain the former, and though strict behaviourists shied away from openly using mentalist terms like conscience it was tacitly understood that such entities simply refer to the accumulation of children's learning experiences and their lasting effects.

A very different account was provided by psychoanalytic theory. Children, according to Freud (1930), love their parents but also fear and hate them, for they are not only sources of comfort and security but also of prohibition and frustration. To resolve the ensuing conflict children take over their parents' commands and internalize them as though they were their own. Conscience is thus based on *identification with the aggressor*, though as this results in a highly emotionally charged structure of a largely unconscious nature Freud preferred the term *superego* to the more rational 'conscience'. In this way children retain their parents' affection and at the same time develop a mechanism whereby they punish themselves whenever transgression gives rise to feelings of guilt. The hostility previously felt towards the parent is now directed inward, and fear of guilt rather than fear of punishment ensures that children act in accordance with social standards.

The details of Freud's account have received little support from research (Hoffman, 1988); on the other hand it has led psychologists to view the process of internalization as a much more complex and less mechanical development than the learning theory account would suggest. A more down-to-earth approach than relying on any megatheory therefore appeared indicated. This took two forms. One, initiated by Martin Hoffman (e.g. 1975, 1988), asked about the kinds of disciplinary techniques that parents use to socialize their children, describing them in detail and examining their effectiveness in the development of children's moral internalization. According to Hoffman, it is possible to distinguish three general types of techniques: (1) *love-orientated*, where the threat of withdrawal of love is used to get the child to conform; (2) *power-orientated*, including punishment, withholding of privileges and various verbal means of parents imposing their will; and (3) *inductive*, referring to all those techniques relying on reason and explanation. Although most parents use all three types at one time or another, parents relying mostly on inductive means were found by Hoffman to have children most advanced as far as the internalization of standards is concerned. Unlike Freud's emphasis on fear Hoffman thus considered the role of reason to be the most important aspect in parents' transmission of standards.

The other approach was to start with children rather than parents and ask about the developmental course of the ability to comply with requests and commands. According to Claire Kopp (1982), children pass through a series of phases of increasingly sophisticated skills in becoming able to understand another person's demands and to regulate their own behaviour accordingly, thus achieving congruence between what the adult wants and how the child responds. Five such phases were outlined; it is in the third of these, beginning at the start of the second year, that children show signs of deliberate control over their actions in response to adult demands and that genuine compliance therefore becomes possible. Insofar as children may choose either to comply or not to comply a definite advance in self-regulation is indicated, though as yet this is tied to the here-and-now directives of the adult and internalization remains to be achieved at a later phase. Developmental progress is dependent on certain cognitive prerequisites; however, the social context also plays a vital, though facilitating rather than causative, role in so far as caretakers are required to provide support for the child's fragile control capacities and thereby help them to progress to the next phase. How that support is offered, and more generally the precise nature of the social interactive context for compliance development, is one line that further research has pursued; the relationship between compliance and internalization is another.

CURRENT STATUS

It is now widely recognized that the concept of internalization is in need of greater specification than it has received in the past. Even Vygotsky (1978), who used it in his account of children's acquisition of learning (see **zone of proximal development**), conceded that 'as yet, the barest outline of this process is known'. Examination of the mechanisms involved in internalization has thus become a major focus of attention.

One notable result is seen in the recognition that the previous conception of children passively assimilating *in toto* the messages of their parents is in need of revision. Such a view was part of the legacy of the unidirectional approach to socialization; however, as Lawrence and Valsiner (1993) have pointed out, children are not mere recipients of messages but challenge, question and actively adapt them to their own mental structures, and may even deliberately break rules in order to test the limits. Socialization cannot therefore be conceived of just as a process of *transmission* where one generation simply passes on its own set of values to the next, but must also be seen in terms of *transformation* of culturally provided input which children set about incorporating into their own conceptual systems. What is more, parents are far from the rigid enforcers depicted in the past; as Goodnow (1997) has shown, parents frequently adapt their messages to the specific characteristics of their children, attempt to make them more acceptable and are prepared to negotiate rather than engage in conflict. Internalization, as Goodnow has stated, is more than the conversion of external into internal control: desirable standards can be conveyed by parents in any one of a number of ways considered appropriate in the light of particular children and particular situations, and children, even fairly young ones, can appraise what they are told and accept or change accordingly. Discontinuity from generation to generation is thus as noteworthy as continuity.

Such a view is based on the **bidirectionality** concept of socialization, in that children are seen as active processors of parental messages and parents as showing sensitivity in their choice of the most appropriate techniques with respect to any one child (Grusec & Goodnow, 1994). Take the influence of child temperament on the socializing practices parents employ: as a series of reports by Kochanska (e.g. 1997), have shown, children who by nature are anxious tend to be more responsive to their parents' disciplinary efforts and to show signs of guilt as a consequence of even quite mild reprimands; children who are temperamentally unperturbable, on the other hand, will not be affected by such low-key measures and require more forceful methods. Parental sensitivity to child individuality is thus a key factor in helping children towards internalization – a conclusion supported by findings from a range of studies. Compliance to parental controls, for example, is obtained more easily from infants if the parent works within the child's frame of reference: a request to carry out some action on an object will be more successful if it is sensitively timed to coincide with the child's interest in the object rather than having to redirect attention from elsewhere (Schaffer & Crook, 1980). The effectiveness of discipline depends less on the specific technique chosen than on the parent's willingness to be flexible in the choice of techniques judged suitable for particular occasions (Grusec & Goodnow, 1994) – an argument against the search for the single most effective method. And, as found repeatedly, when as a result of the mother's sensitivity in the early stages of development children establish a secure attachment with her, they are more likely to be open to her requests and cooperate with her and in due course to internalize her goals as their own (Bretherton, Golby & Cho, 1997).

The other major focus of attention in recent years has been the developmental course of internalization, with particular reference to its relationship with early compliance. Compliance, as we noted, refers to elicited conformity in the presence of caretakers; internalization to spontaneous conformity not requiring any form of surveillance. Suggestive evidence that internalization gradually emerges from compliance in the course of the first few years is provided by an extensive programme of research by Kochanska and her colleagues (e.g. 1995, 2001), based on a follow-up investigation of children from infancy onwards. However, Kochanska found it necessary to distinguish between two forms of compliance:*situational* and *committed*. Situational compliance requires the sustained control of parents and is characterized by the child's superficial cooperation; committed compliance, on the other hand, is seen when the child appears to endorse, embrace and accept the parental agenda as his or her own. Measures developed for these two types indicate, first, that their developmental course differs in that situational compliance decreases but committed compliance increases over the first few years, and secondly that committed but not situational compliance is positively related to measures of later internalization. Committed compliance would thus appear to be a first step in the unfolding of internalization, the latter being a more sophisticated ability that requires the necessary cognitive underpinnings to develop before it becomes established. The distinction between the two types of compliance, according to this proposal, is therefore an important and productive one.

One other point concerning our conception of compliance refers to the way we view noncompliance. Conformity to parental demands has generally been regarded as a valuable, indeed essential quality, accompanied by the assumption that all instances of failure in this respect must be viewed in a negative light. Yet Spitz (1957) once identified the ability to say 'no' in the second year of life as 'beyond doubt the most spectacular intellectual and semantic achievement of early childhood'. There is now recognition that at least some degree of non-compliance can serve a positive function, in that it indicates an expression of autonomy and leads to the development of an array of strategies whereby children can assert themselves in increasingly sophisticated ways (Kuczynski & Kochanska, 1990). Thus not only compliance but also noncompliance is an ability that needs to develop in early childhood.

Further reading

Grusec, J.E., & Kuczynski, L. (Eds.) (1997). *Parenting and children's internalization of values*. New York: Wiley. A considerable number of approaches to the topic of internalization are brought together in this volume and between them cover the area thoroughly.

Grusec, J.E., & Goodnow, J.J. (1994). The impact of parental discipline methods on children's internalization of values. *Developmental Psychology, 30*, 4–19. This paper has become an important guide to our thinking about socialization techniques, and the comments from three other writers following the paper are also well worth noting.

See also **bidirectionality; child effects; parent effects; zone of proximal development**

MORAL, CONVENTIONAL AND PERSONAL CONDUCT RULES

The concept of **internalization**, described above, refers to the processes whereby **MEANING** children acquire the standards and values regarded as appropriate to social living. But what is the nature of these internalized entities? One answer, given by such influential writers as Piaget (1932) and Kohlberg (1969), is to group them together as constituting the realm of morality, that is, a more or less homogeneous set of principles which provide individuals with rules enabling them to judge what is right and wrong and which will thus govern the way they conduct themselves in everyday life. The task of developmental psychologists is therefore to investigate how this system comes into being and what form it takes at different ages.

More recently a different view has emerged – one that asserts that there is not a single system but several different ones, each constituting a domain in its own right, with its own rules of conduct and distinctive course of development (see Turiel, 1998, for a detailed discussion). Three such domains have been distinguished, respectively covering moral, conventional and personal rules. Taking these one by one –

> *Moral rules pertain to matters of fairness, welfare, rights and harm, and express the individual's conception of what is just and what is unjust.*

Such rules are primarily concerned with interactions between people; seriousness of violations, as seen in such actions as hitting, insulting, stealing and breaking a promise, are judged by children by their consequences for the victims and not because the perpetrator may be punished if found out. Moral rules thus have certain characteristics, namely:

- The individual has a feeling of inner obligation to follow the rule and does not act because of fear of detection and punishment for transgression.
- The rule is independent of any specific authority figure or social group.
- It holds across all relevant situations.
- It cannot arbitrarily be altered by any individual or group of individuals.

Such characteristics serve as criteria whereby it is possible to distinguish moral from the other two types of rules.

> *Conventional rules pertain to the norms that groups of individuals arbitrarily decide upon in order to regulate the behaviour of their members.*

Thus driving on the right or on the left side does not refer to any absolute, universal principal but is decided by specific communities. What matters is that everybody follows the rule that has been set in that community; infringement would have serious consequences. Similarly, children's games have certain rules that all participants must follow; they can, however, be changed if there is a consensus within the peer group to do so. Thus the characteristics of conventional rules are:

- They are determined by authority figures (parents, teachers, etc.) or specific groupings of people (e.g. governments, sport ruling bodies, peer groups, families).
- They express the customs that particular groups of people wish to follow. Etiquette (e.g. how to address another person), manners (at table, or expressing thanks for a gift) and family routines such as church attendance are examples.
- Their function is to produce uniformity of behaviour within particular groups, thus making the actions of individual members more predictable.
- Unlike moral rules, conventional rules are context dependent, that is, they do not necessarily hold across all situations (a child's table manners, for example, may differ radically when eating with unfamiliar adults as compared with peers).

Thus conventional rules are not as universal and generalized as moral rules, and the seriousness of their violation is judged in relation to the rule rather than to issues of fairness or the welfare of others.

> *Personal rules are those that have consequences only for the individual.*

These are rules that concern matters such as choice of friends, hairstyle or musical taste – spheres that are regarded by all as personal and, except for the youngest children, as falling within their own decision making sphere without interference by authority figures. The characteristics of such rules may be summarized as follows:

- It is up to each individual to determine how his or her conduct is regulated.
- The rules may be changed willy-nilly by the individual, without reference to anyone else.
- Any negative consequences of violating such a rule are the individual's responsibility.

Despite these characteristics individuals do not make choices in total isolation. They are influenced by the actions of others, peers especially, when confronted with similar choices; moreover, for children the boundaries of the personal domain and its content are ultimately constrained by such parental matters as cost and the parents' own preferences and are therefore first established through negotiation with the parents. Perhaps it is not surprising that the personal domain has been found to give rise to a lot more conflict between child and adults than the moral or the conventional domains.

The three kinds of conduct rules are distinguished from quite an early age, as shown by children's answers when asked to make judgements about particular hypothetical actions, generally involving violations of a rule. It is these differences in judgement that are said to point to the existence of different domains of thought within individuals whereby their conduct is regulated. For example, children as young as 2½ judge moral transgressions to be more wrong, more serious and more deserving of punishment than conventional transgressions. However, it must also be added that not all rules fall neatly into one or the other of the three categories: some are multifaceted in that they entail components of more than one domain, as seen, for example, in India where people are arranged in a caste system according to convention, which can then lead to such moral problems as injustice and harm to those on the lowest rungs of the social order (Smetana, 1993).

ORIGINS

Philosophers and theologians have for long speculated about the nature of morality and discussed how we come to make distinctions between what is right and what is wrong. In more recent years they have been joined by sociologists, anthropologists, psychoanalysts and psychologists, each discipline providing its own perspective and empirical data. The most useful contribution that psychologists have made is with respect to the development of morality in childhood, asking questions such as when children begin to distinguish right from wrong, how morality is acquired, what form moral judgements take at different ages and how developmental change is brought about.

Much of the thinking about these issues was due initially to the groundbreaking work of Piaget and Kohlberg. In his book *The moral judgement of the child*, Piaget (1932) provided not only a wealth of empirical material regarding the way children think about moral issues but also a theory about how their thinking is transformed in the course of development. After an initial premoral stage during the first four years or so children progress from what Piaget referred to as a *heteronomous* orientation to one based on *autonomous* thinking. The former is characterized by being dependent on the dictates of authority: whatever rules parents lay down are regarded as fixed, absolute and to be obeyed literally. In the latter stage children free themselves from external authority and become independent in their thinking about everyday morality – a development largely due to the increasing experience of participation in peer groups, where they have the opportunity to learn about rules concerning such general issues as fairness, cooperation and sharing. Thus they become able to move on from a reliance on externally imposed rules to an appreciation of general principles of justice, applied by the child as an autonomous agent.

Kohlberg (e.g. 1969) also proposed a stage sequence for the development of morality, though his account involved three levels, each with two substages. He saw morality as initially interpreted by children in terms of power and punishment, as opposed to Piaget's view of reverence for others' rules: whatever avoids punishment is regarded as 'right'. This *preconventional* level is succeeded by a *conventional* level, at which it is the collective feelings of others that becomes the primary criterion. Finally, at a *postconventional* level objective principles of justice become detached from subjective feelings: 'right' is defined in terms of universal standards. Kohlberg followed Piaget in seeing children as actively thinking about matters of right and wrong; like him, he believed that their conceptions of morality must therefore be constrained by the cognitive level they had reached. And both writers did not differentiate morality from any other rule domain: thinking about moral issues in terms of justice was seen as a developmentally advanced stage following thinking about rules as being authority imposed.

It is this domain general approach which was subsequently challenged by Elliot Turiel (1983) and his colleagues. Basing their proposal on a series of studies of children's responses to vignettes of rule violation, presented in stories, drawings or doll play, and subsequently also taking into account their comments on real incidents they had observed, they found evidence that from an early age children distinguish between two sets of conduct rules, referring respectively to moral and social conventional issues; a third set, concerning personal issues, was added by Nucci (see 1996). Such an orientation is in keeping with the general move towards **domain specificity** in the cognitive area, and though the details of the distinction may not yet be fully established there is now widespread agreement that this is the right step to take in moving beyond Piaget and Kohlberg.

CURRENT STATUS

The domain specific approach to conduct rules has stimulated a considerable amount of research, much of it aimed at showing that the differentiation between the three types of rules is justified (for an overview see Turiel, 1998). This applies especially to the distinction between morality and convention, the personal domain having so far attracted rather less attention. The distinction is in place from at least the third year on and by age 4 it is reliably established. Thus some acts are judged to be wrong because they cause harm, other acts because the child's caretakers disapprove of them. Preschool children will even indicate that they would not follow a parent's command to engage in some behaviour that violates a moral rule such as stealing; on the other hand, if told to act in some unconventional way such as changing the rules of a game in the course of play, they show no hesitation to do so. On the whole moral transgressions are judged by young children to be more wrong and deserving of punishment than conventional transgressions, though at a surprisingly early age children will also take other considerations such as extenuating circumstances into account when comparing the seriousness of the two kinds of acts. Furthermore, what limited evidence there is concerning personal rules suggests that even preschool children regard these to be at the discretion of the individual and that violation is therefore of no consequence for any other person. With age, children become able to generalize the distinctions they make to an ever-increasing range of situations: thus at first these are applied mainly to familiar experiences; by mid-childhood they are also evident in the way children judge unfamiliar situations and eventually are extended to abstract, hypothetical events.

As to the developmental origins of the three-some distinction, there are three possible explanations (Smetana, 1993): that the distinction is learned in the course of adults' socialization; that it is a biological given and potentially available from the beginning; and that it is the result of children actively constructing it from their experiences of social interaction. The three are by no means mutually exclusive; thus the specific domain approach has generally favoured a genetic view (see **domain specificity**), but it is also conceded that biological givens need a particular environment to convert the potential into the actual. How such a conversion occurs is not yet established, though one possibility advanced is that the different rules arise from different kinds of adult–child interaction and that children can then readily evaluate and construe these in distinctive terms. Quite a number of studies (listed by Smetana, 1993) indicate that there are indeed differences in the social contexts in which moral, conventional and personal transgressions occur. For example, adults' responses to children hitting or not sharing generally highlight the consequences of the act, such as the harm done to the victim or the lack of fairness, whereas in the case of conventional transgression the adult is more likely to point out the need to obey rules and regulations. These various experiences may then lead children to form intuitive theories as to how specific actions are to be assigned to different categories of judgement.

One further line of research concerns the influences that account for individual differences in the nature of children's conduct rules. It is clear that children derive their ideas from a multitude of experiences, and while most studies have examined parental influences Piaget's insistence on the importance of peer relationships has considerably extended the scope of enquiry. But it is also widely recognized that all these experiences occur in a particular cultural context – hence the need to investigate how children in cultures other than the West categorize their experiences. The evidence suggests that in all cultures so far examined the three-domain hypothesis can be upheld: in all of them children assign the do's and don'ts they have learned to the three different kinds of categories and view the respective rules in different ways. However, the content between the three domains may differ: in India, for example, certain acts judged as conventional or personal in the West, such as not eating particular kinds of food, are closely tied to religious beliefs and transgression are consequently judged in moral terms (Miller & Bersoff, 1995). Qualitatively distinct types of conduct codes will therefore characterize different cultures, in that the boundary lines between the three domains may vary from one to the other.

Further reading

Helwig, C.C., & Turiel, E. (2002). Children's social and moral reasoning. In P.K. Smith & C.H. Craig (Eds.), *Blackwell handbook of childhood social development*. Oxford: Blackwell. A brief overview, covering most of the issues that have been raised concerning this topic.

Nucci, L.P. (2002). The development of moral reasoning. In U. Goswami (Ed.), *Blackwell handbook of cognitive development*. Oxford: Blackwell. Reviews current research trends in this area, with particular emphasis on the roles which culture, socialization and emotion play in the establishment of social rules.

See also **domain specificity; internalization**

LINGUISTIC AND COMMUNICATIVE DEVELOPMENT 9

NINE

The ability to use language is surely the single most important achievement human beings have attained. It enables us to form a system of symbols which we can use creatively for thinking and problem solving, for recalling the past and anticipating the future and for forming concepts and other abstractions. It is a means whereby we can control our emotions and regulate the actions we take. And above all it is a highly flexible way of communicating with others, as the particular system of symbols we use is shared by every one else in our community.

The relationship between language and communication is not a straightforward one. On the one hand, language is more than communication in that it is employed not just *between* individuals but also *within* individuals as a tool for thought. And on the other hand, communication is more than language, for there are many nonverbal ways of letting others know our feelings and wishes. Thus infants, long before they begin to use speech, are already capable of conveying their requirements for food and company to their caretakers and have no difficulty in letting them know whatever emotions and discomforts they are experiencing. A complex system of gestures, facial expressions and vocalizations is in place quite early on to serve all these functions. Whether these act as precursors to language, that is, whether the ability to use words has its developmental origins in such early nonverbal behaviours, is a matter of contention. On the one hand, Chomsky (1991) was convinced that 'language is not intrinsically a communicative system' but a 'computational-representation system, which exists in its own right irrespective of any function it may serve'. And on the other hand, there are those who believe that there is a definite connection between prelinguistic and linguistic expressions and that this is due to the communicative purpose which both forms serve. This latter view is presently held by the majority of writers, though how to prove or disprove that such a connection exists remains a problem.

A number of explanations for the origins of language have been put forward, but all must acknowledge the fact that children acquire the ability to use words in meaningful ways with great ease. This is despite the fact that language is not only a highly complex, multifaceted system which is more than a collection of words, but is also a *coherent* system where there are rules for combining the words in particular order. Children, that is, need to acquire not only a vocabulary but also a grammar. It is customary to distinguish between four aspects of language:

- *Phonology*, which is the study of the sound systems that make up language.
- *Semantics*, that is, the branch of linguistics concerned with the meaning of words and how we acquire them.
- *Syntax*, which refers to the rules whereby words are combined to make up meaningful sentences, that is, a grammar.
- *Pragmatics*, namely the rules that determine how we use language for practical purposes.

Acquiring language involves competence with respect to all four aspects, and each covers a considerable number of skills. Many concepts and technical terms are employed with respect to all aspects, and we shall discuss the following below:

UNIVERSAL GRAMMAR
and: **Language acquisition device**
      Surface structure and deep structure
PROTO-LANGUAGE
and: **Proto-conversations**
      Proto-declaratives
      Proto-imperatives
MOTHERESE
and: **Language acquisition support system**
SPEECH ACTS
and: **Locution, perlocution and illocution**
LINGUISTIC COMPETENCE
and: **Communicative competence**
      Conversational maxims

UNIVERSAL GRAMMAR
and: **LANGUAGE ACQUISITION DEVICE**
SURFACE STRUCTURE and **DEEP STRUCTURE**

The single most influential account of language acquisition is that provided by **MEANING** Noam Chomsky (e.g. 1957, 1965, 1991). In some crucial respects it is actually a series of accounts, for the original version has been revised on several occasions, as a result of which the role and prominence of some of the concepts Chomsky employed have also changed. Nevertheless, those mentioned here have all played an important part in the development of the theory.

Chomsky is generally labelled as a nativist, for he was convinced that children are equipped from birth with some wired-in 'knowledge' of the structure of language, and that their task is to use that knowledge to make sense of the speech they hear in their particular community. To explain the nature of children's inborn equipment, Chomsky made use of two particular concepts, those of universal grammar (subsequently abbreviated to UG) and language acquisition device (see below).

Universal grammar refers to –

> *a genetically specified awareness of those rules of grammar that are to be found in all languages.*

According to Chomsky, it is necessary to postulate such an inborn tendency so that young children, confronted by the considerable complexities of grammar, get a headstart in acquiring **linguistic competence** and relatively speedily begin to speak in correct sentences. The mechanism responsible for this was envisioned by Chomsky as a mental module (a 'mental organ', as he referred to it), that is, as a self-contained feature not influenced by such other modules as cognition. In this respect he was one of the first to espouse a **modularity** view of the mind. In a subsequent revision to his theory, however, he decided that only part of the UG is innate and that there are certain aspects that are dependent on experience.

UG thus designates a type of grammar that is of such abstraction that it is able to characterize all languages, actual and potential. Languages do share quite a number of structural characteristics; for example, they all make distinctions between past, present and future; they all require both a subject and a predicate to make up a complete sentence; and they all divide words into grammatical categories such as nouns and verbs. If children already have some innate knowledge about such aspects the acquisition task is very much easier, in that they are provided with an implicit set of rules to guide both the comprehension and production of speech.

Whereas UG can be thought of as the storehouse of grammatical knowledge, the **LANGUAGE ACQUISITION DEVISE** (LAD) is the agent whereby that knowledge is used. Chomsky did not specify the exact nature of this concept; however, we may think of it as –

> *the means whereby children set about constructing the grammar of their native language from the speech they hear.*

Thus the stream of speech to which children are exposed is filtered through the LAD, which extracts whatever regularities occur in it (for example, add *ed* to a verb to indicate the past tense), and so provides children with the guidelines required for talking in their native tongue. It is an essential part of the language acquisition process that children, without being aware of it, are continuously engaged in generating hypotheses about acceptable ways of expressing themselves. Whatever regularities may occur in others' speech are then used to construct rules – a procedure, however, that is not always foolproof, as seen in children's use of words like *goed* or even *wented*.

Two other concepts of importance in Chomskyan theory are **SURFACE STRUCTURE** and **DEEP STRUCTURE** (abbreviated to s-structure and d-structure), used at the level of individual sentence construction. These concepts are linked in a two-tier mental organization, which Chomsky employed in order to explain how speakers, even quite young children, can put together grammatically correct sentences.

> *Surface structure is the actual sequence of words we hear or speak, arranged in a grammatically correct manner to convey a particular message.*

> *Deep structure is a hypothetical entity located in the brain which contains the basic constituents of sentences and their various possible grammatical relationships.*

Each sentence is represented at the deep structure level but in a grammatically unexpressed form, which can then be transformed into any one of several syntactic constructions at the surface level. 'Can eat it', for example, may become 'I can eat it' or 'Can I eat it?', depending on the speaker's purpose. Producing an utterance thus begins with a basic sentence form at the deep structure level which undergoes linguistic processing to ensure it is grammatically correct and is then expressed at the surface level. Various *transformational rules* are said to be part of the total apparatus; the rule 'move', for instance, is applied to the deep structure representation of a sentence in order to change the order of words to a particular sequence. Thus the active form 'the dog chased the cat' and its passive equivalent 'the cat was chased by the dog' are the different surface results of moving the constituents of the basic sentence as represented at the deep structure, though both forms retain the same intent.

Language, according to Chomsky, is more than its overt manifestation; it is based on a system of rules which stipulate its grammatical form. It is unlikely that children can acquire complex grammatical rules merely by learning them: in part because of young children's limited cognitive capacity and in part because other people's speech is often too ill-formed for a child to discern regularities. Another mechanism is therefore necessary for children to sample the surface utterance they hear – hence the hypothesized deep structure which is largely innate and provides a tacit understanding of language.

ORIGINS

How children acquire language has always been a matter of fascination, though it is only in the last century or so that speculation has given way to empirical enquiry. Initially this took the form of descriptive studies, aimed at establishing age norms such as for children's first word or the beginning of sentence formation, thus tracing the growth of vocabulary over age and ascertaining when particular grammatical categories are first used. Explanations of *how* children learn to speak came later, and for much of the first half of the twentieth century were heavily influenced by behaviourism, which regarded language as essentially *learned* behaviour. The most detailed account of the mechanisms of learning was provided by B.F. Skinner (1957), who used *operant conditioning* as the principal vehicle to account for children acquiring the use of words. Infants, that is, are reinforced by parental praise or attention when they make sounds that approximate words; as a result they are more likely to repeat these sounds and will also learn to associate them with the appropriate context and, in due course, with each other to form sentences. On the other hand, sounds that are ignored become extinguished and drop out of infants' repertoire. Thus infants' spontaneous vocalizations come to be shaped into acceptable speech by the action of their caretakers; the child, on the other hand, is merely the passive recipient of these efforts (see **environmental learning**).

Skinner's book received what must be one of the most devastating book reviews ever published, written by Noam Chomsky. As Chomsky put it, 'I have been able to find no support whatsoever for the doctrine … that slow and careful shaping of verbal behavior through differential reinforcement is an absolute necessity.' On the contrary, parents are very tolerant of their children's grammatical errors and rarely correct them, focusing instead on the factual truthfulness of what they say. Yet children do not retain these erroneous utterances but soon learn to correct them on their own initiative. What is more, adults are imperfect models from whom children can learn, for their speech input tends to be full of false starts, errors and ambiguities, making it virtually impossible for children to learn the complexities of grammatical expressions through imitation. And most of all, Chomsky criticized Skinner for being unable to explain children's creativity in forming utterances that they have never heard before. Children, that is, bring something to language acquisition that they could not have picked up from the environment; instead they appear to be endowed by nature with the propensity of generating increasingly complex utterances that are derived from knowledge of an underlying rule system.

Chomsky's book *Syntactic structures* (published in 1957, the same year as Skinner's) set off a revolution in the study of linguistics. It did so by proposing a *generative grammar*, that is, a set of rules that determine the form and meaning of spoken utterances and that make it thereby possible to generate an infinite number of sentences. Speakers are thus seen as essentially creative, though within the constraints imposed by native endowment. The task of linguists is to work out these rules and thus to concentrate not so much on what speakers actually do (their performance) but on what they are potentially capable of doing (their capacity). It was therefore the mental grammar which underlies people's overt speech that Chomsky set out to elucidate.

Insofar as Chomsky was mainly interested in ideal speakers he depended largely on adult speech samples. It was left to Roger Brown (1973) to assemble a corpus of child language, which he did by periodically sampling the speech of two young children, Adam and Eve (a third child, Sarah, was subsequently added) as they went through the early stages of acquiring language. These samples provided a rich source of support for many of Chomsky's proposals; in particular they showed clearly just how active children are in searching for regularities in other people's speech to provide them with rules to apply to their own (for example, add *s* to English nouns to indicate the plural), and how various abilities emerge quite spontaneously in the course of the first years, such as being able to rearrange the sequence of words in a sentence according to whether it serves the purpose of a statement, a question or a negation.

Many other samples of children's early language use have since been collected, most inspired by Chomsky's writings and by the vision of children as creative, actively rule-searching beings. The behaviourist view of language development as a matter of passive rote learning has been well and truly left behind.

CURRENT STATUS

The package of concepts described here and the theory from which they stem have brought about a drastic change in our thinking about the nature of language and its origins in childhood. We no longer see language as a bundle of responses acquired through learning from parents; instead, it is viewed as an orderly system that is, in some way and to some extent at least, dependent on an innate propensity that enables children to acquire linguistic competence relatively early and speedily.

This does not mean, of course, that Chomskyan ideas have been accepted uncritically. There is, for example, debate as to whether both UG and LAD are required and, if so, where the dividing line between them should be drawn (Morgan, 1990). Chomsky himself abandoned the notion of LAD as part of one of his theory revisions, though others continue to use it, even without resorting to UG as well. Some have questioned the very idea of a truly universal grammar: according to Slobin (1986) there is far greater diversity among the world's languages in the grammatical rules they employ than Chomsky's proposal would allow. The basic notion of a 'language organ' is certainly in keeping with the current emphasis on **modularity**; on the other hand, there are arguments as to whether there is just one language module or several, each concerned with a distinct aspect of language.

Most of all, however, there is concern among many that Chomsky has swung the pendulum too far from nurture to nature and not done justice to the considerable help and support children get from the language input received in the course of everyday social interaction (see **motherese**). Admittedly, Chomsky himself in his later writings changed his position somewhat in this respect, as is most evident in what has come to be known as his *principles and parameters theory* (see Chomsky, 1986). According to this formulation, UG should be regarded as a two-tier system: an innate basis of universal *principles* which characterize all human languages and a second layer of *parameters* referring to those features that distinguish one language from another. The latter can be thought of as a series of on–off switches which are set by experience: in one language environment one particular set of switches will be set to the on position, in another a different set will be switched on, depending on the particular linguistic conventions (for example, how to order words to make up an acceptable sentence) that prevail in each of them and which the child learns about through exposure to other people's speech. Therefore, as Chomsky (1986) put it: 'We may think of UG as an intricately structured system, but one which is only partially wired-up.'

The nature–nurture issue as it applies to language is far from settled. On the one hand there are those like Steven Pinker (1994), who in his provocatively entitled book *The language instinct* amended Chomsky in certain respects but fiercely defended the need for a nativist approach to language acquisition. And on the other hand, there is the increasing number of social interactionists (e.g. Bruner, 1983), who believe that learning about language occurs first in the context of everyday routines carried out jointly with other people well before the first word appears (see **proto-language**). Also noteworthy is the recent use of **connectionist networks** as a technique to throw light on the origins of language – an approach that emphasizes children's learning of language to a much greater extent than is found in any of Chomsky's writings (e.g. Plunkett, 1995).

Further reading

Messer, D.J. (1994). *The development of communication: from social interaction to language*. Chichester: John Wiley. A generally very informative book in which Chapters 10 and 11 are especially relevant to the above discussion.

Owens, R.E. (2005). *Language development* (6th ed.). Boston: Allyn & Bacon. An introductory textbook in which Chapter 2 provides an overview of Chomsky's theory and an evaluation of his contribution and limitations.

Pinker, S. (1994). *The language instinct*. London: Penguin. A lively though partisan argument for the nativist approach to language.

See also **linguistic competence; motherese; proto-language**

PROTO-LANGUAGE
and: **PROTO-CONVERSATIONS**
PROTO-DECLARATIVES
PROTO-IMPERATIVES

MEANING Is there continuity from the prelinguistic to the linguistic stage in early childhood? Is the former in some way relevant to the latter, so that what takes place before children are able to say their first word sheds light on the origins of language? This is certainly a different approach to Chomsky's (see **universal grammar**), for he took little notice of the transition from prelinguistic to linguistic functioning and based his account only on individuals who had at least attained the stage of two-word sentence formation. It is, however, a direction followed by a number of writers who have looked for possible antecedents of language and communication in the first year or so of life and used the concepts of proto-language and proto-conversation for this purpose.

Proto-language refers to –

> *strings of idiosyncratic sound patterns that indicate a particular intent or expression but cannot be recognized as words.*

These become increasingly prominent in the first year but are most evident at the post-babbling stage just before the child's first recognizable word. According to protagonists of continuity they imply a readiness to acquire language and are a necessary step towards this end; according to others they are discontinuous with language and form a separate system that disappears once speech becomes dominant.

Language is essentially a communicative tool; as Bruner (1983) has put it, 'Entry into language is an entry into discourse.' To understand how children become proficient at verbally communicating with others a search for the precursors of this ability has also been undertaken. **PROTO-CONVERSATIONS** are –

> *the vocal and gestural interactions of a preverbal infant with an adult that in certain respects resemble the verbal exchanges found in mature conversations.*

These early dialogues are regarded by some as relevant to later linguistic conversations because some of their formal characteristics (e.g. turn taking) are similar, so that once a child starts to acquire verbal skills it is possible for words to be simply slotted into an existing format. The transition from non-linguistic to linguistic exchanges is thus facilitated – an argument taken a step further by those who believe that certain types of proto-conversations, namely those surrounding parent–infant games, enable children easily to acquire the rules of grammar. The significance of both proto-language and proto-conversation may therefore be that infants become acquainted with certain formats in a nonverbal form which can then be relatively easily transferred to verbal forms.

For centuries those interested in the origins of language began their accounts only with the onset of the ability to speak recognizable words. The non-linguistic period was regarded as irrelevant; infant vocalizations were seen as belonging to a different order. It was largely due to Roman Jakobson (1941) that the gap began to be closed and the notion of continuity came to be considered. In his book *Kindersprache* (Child language) Jakobson proposed that the babbling noises of infants contain all the speech sounds of the world's languages, and that it is not till the last months of the first year that they narrow down to only those sounds that are contained in the language of their own speech community. Since then other attempts to bridge the gap have been made, benefiting from the technological advances in sound recording and filming made in recent decades. Notable is Trevarthen's (1979) description of a syndrome he labelled *prespeeech*, referring to a pattern of lip and tongue movements resembling those of adults while speaking. These patterns are present from birth, become very evident from 3 months on, and appear mostly in the presence of other people. They are said to be an embryonic form of real speech. **ORIGINS**

Most of the driving force in the past few decades in the search for precursors has come from work on infant communication. A book entitled *Before speech*, edited by Margaret Bullowa (1979), contains some of the first systematic analyses of infants' attempts to communicate with another person, accomplished by gesture, gaze, posture, facial expression and vocalization. A chapter by Mary Bateson on 'the epigenesis of conversational interaction' is particularly relevant here, for in it she uses the term proto-conversation to characterize some of the early exchanges occurring between mother and baby. These exchanges are described as already indicating a highly complex interweaving of infants' multi-modal behaviour patterns with the adult's behaviour, and are said to show the kind of sequencing and temporal spacing typical of conversations among adults. The contribution infants make to these exchanges are said to indicate that from early on they have the potential of becoming involved in dialogues with other people.

It is generally accepted that the development of language is dependent on a range of skills emerging in the preceding months – skills that relate to perceptual, motoric, neural, cognitive, social and affective functions (for details see Locke, 1993). For example, in the course of the first few months infants become able to distinguish speech from nonspeech; preferentially to orient to the former; to discriminate different intonational patterns; and to distinguish between contrasting **CURRENT STATUS** phonemes. Such developments are clearly necessary to prepare the ground for entry into language.

However, there is less certainty as to whether the various manifestations of proto-language are relevant to subsequent speech sound production. Take Trevarthen's (1979) claim that the phenomenon of prespeech is a prototype for the real thing. His observations indicate certain similarities in mouth movements, from which he concluded that these are patterned early on specifically for speech even though the infant is as yet incapable of producing reliably controlled sound. However, whether the infant is thereby expressing 'a rudiment of intention to speak', and whether there is any functional continuity with the emergence of language production several months later, remains unproven.

As to the relationship of babbling to speech, this too is still an unsettled issue. Babbling starts around the middle of the first year and often occurs in sentence-like sequences with rising and falling intonation that, apart from content, are so like real talk that parents frequently respond as though the infant had in fact spoken. But is this stage a *prerequisite* for speech development? Several studies have found significant correlations between age of onset, amount and various qualitative indices of babbling on the one hand and subsequent rate of lexical development on the other hand (Locke, 1993), suggesting a relationship. However, conflicting results have come from studies examining speech development in infants on whom a tracheotomy had been performed just before the babbling period. This operation is carried out when the upper respiratory tract is blocked and involves the insertion of a tube through the skin of the throat to permit breathing. It prevents all vocalizations at the time but is subsequently reversed when the condition is cured. If this occurs after the usual end of the babbling period we have an experiment of nature whereby the influence of babbling has been eliminated and one can determine whether speech development is thereby affected. Frustratingly, the findings are mixed: in some studies a definite adverse effect is seen; in others there are short-term effects and in still others the effects are of a long-term nature. Thus no definite conclusions are as yet possible.

Turning to proto-conversation, a comparable situation arises. Some pronounced similarities are to be found between early nonverbal dialogues and later verbal conversations, but so far any contention that the one is functionally continuous with the latter and acts as a prerequisite is merely an act of faith, based largely on analogy and not proof. A large body of evidence accumulated over the years (e.g. Reddy, Hay, Murray & Trevarthen, 1997; Schaffer, 1996) has shown that parent–infant dialogues, like adult conversations, are characterized by features such as turn taking, joint topic attention and use of multi-channel expression (for example, looking, gestural and facial as well as vocal). It is tempting to conclude that the infant is already intentionally communicating with the partner, albeit nonverbally, and that developments from the second year onwards merely signify a change from various bodily to verbal expressions. Children, that is, learn how to conduct a conversation with another person before they can use and understand words to conduct such an exchange. However, the dialogues observed in early infancy do differ in one crucial respect from their successors: the intricate synchronization that occurs between the two partners' contribution is not a mutual product but is largely the work of the adult only. Thus the turn taking pattern in their vocalizations is brought about by the mother allowing herself to be paced by the infant, filling in the pauses between vocal bursts by virtue of great sensitivity to the temporal flow of the child's behaviour. The dialogues are really *pseudo-dialogues* (Schaffer, 1979), and the infant is not yet an intentional communicator.

Descriptively, it seems that the experience of being involved in structured non-verbal exchanges leads in due course smoothly and in an orderly manner into similarly structured conversations, as indicated by several follow-up studies that have observed infants repeatedly over the transition from the non-linguistic to the linguistic period. Several of these have focused on certain specific communicative features, and especially those expressing the functions of requesting and directing. At a prelinguistic stage infants are already quite able nonverbally to make requests for objects and to direct the adult's attention to some feature of the environment, that is, to use **PROTO-DECLARATIVES** and **PROTO-IMPERATIVES**. Proto-declaratives can be defined as –

> *preverbal request forms such as gestures like pointing and reaching, used to convey a wish to the adult for something out of reach.*

Proto-imperatives are –

> *preverbal means of obtaining the adult's attention to something by, for example, showing or giving.*

Thus proto-declaratives are a prelinguistic way of saying 'I want', proto-imperatives are equivalent to 'Look at that'.

Most attention has been given to proto-declaratives – see in particular Bates, O'Connell & Shore, 1987; Bruner, 1983). These have shown how infants from the end of the first year use their actions quite intentionally for communicative purposes by not only looking at the desired object but also switching their gaze to the adult to check that their message has been received. In addition, an increasing proportion of these actions are accompanied by vocalizations (Messinger & Fogel, 1998), which at the beginning of the second year assume a phonetic form that is unique to request making (for example, making a noise like a car engine, to stand for 'I want my toy car'). This is a forerunner of a word-like sound, that is, a *proto-word*, which in turn subsequently gives way to a recognizable linguistic expression. Whether a child could progress straight to linguistic requests without going through the prelinguistic phase (analogous to the above example of tracheotomized children) is not known and would be difficult to investigate; in that sense proof that one is a prerequisite for the other is not available.

Let us mention one other proposal concerning the role of prelinguistic experiences in the development of language. This is a suggestion by Bruner (1977) that the joint games that parents play with their infants such as 'peek-a-boo' and 'this little piggy' provide the preverbal child with a valuable opportunity to learn about the nature and use of rules, which can then be applied to the acquisition of the rules of grammar. Such games have a well-defined task structure, as seen in the provision of particular slots for actions and for words and in the allocation of turn taking roles for the participants – just as found in conversations. According to Bruner, this structure of games helps to shape the structures of initial grammar, and it is therefore in the context of joint parent–child actions that 'the child is learning what might be properly characterized as the prelinguistic prototype of case grammar: who is the Agent, what is the Action, the Object, the Recipient of Action and how these may be exchanged and substituted'. This is an intriguing idea; once again, however, we are confronted by an argument based on analogy and a virtually untestable hypothesis. As Flavell, Miller & Miller (1993) put it in their verdict on the role of preverbal exchanges: 'Probably helpful, but very probably not necessary, and in any case far from sufficient.'

Further reading

Messer, D.J. (1994). *The development of communication: from social interaction to language*. Chichester: Wiley. A detailed and informative account of the transition from preverbal to verbal communication.

Reddy, V. (1999). Prelinguistic communication. In M. Barrett (Ed.), *The development of language*. Hove: Psychology Press. Gives an outline of communicative development in infancy, including the emergence of proto-language and the continuities that appear to exist with language.

See also **developmental continuity**

MOTHERESE
and: LANGUAGE ACQUISION SUPPORT SYSTEM

MEANING Also known as *child directed speech* (CDS) or as *adult to child speech* (A–C), motherese is –

> *the distinctive style of speech used when talking to a young child.*

The distinctiveness is found in all four major aspects of language, as given below with a few examples for each:

- *Phonology*: e.g. higher pitch, slower speech, exaggerated intonation.
- *Syntax*: e.g. shorter utterance length, sentences well formed, few subordinate clauses.
- *Semantics*: e.g. limited range of vocabulary, 'baby talk' words, reference mainly to here-and-now.
- *Pragmatics*: e.g. more attention devices, repetition of child's utterances, more questions.

Dozens of such characteristics have been described (see Gallaway & Richards, 1994 for review); in sum, they make speech to young children simpler, briefer, more repetitive and more attention-worthy than speech to adults. The extent to which they are used depends on the age and linguistic comprehension of the child being addressed: thus the younger the child the more marked they tend to be. Such *fine-tuning* is found in the speech of almost anyone confronted by a young child, including fathers, adults with little experience of children and even 4-year-olds talking to 2-year-olds. It is usually quite unconscious and unplanned, and has been reported for a wide range of languages. Because it is not just the prerogative of mothers, the label *motherese* is perhaps somewhat misleading and is often now replaced by CDS or by A–C speech; however, there is something warmer, more human about motherese, and this is the term that we shall use here.

The need to examine the language used by adults when addressing children arose as part of the *social interactionist* response to Chomsky's theory (see **universal grammar**). One of the reasons put forward by Chomsky for an innate basis to language development was his belief that the linguistic input to which infants are exposed is impoverished, as seen in the unclear, ambiguous and often confusing speech of their caretakers, that therefore infants cannot learn to speak grammatically by listening to others and that consequently they must be biologically equipped to acquire the basics of language. However, social interactionists such as Snow (1972) and Bruner (1983) have taken issue with this argument, pointing out that language arises in the context of communicating with others and that these others initially bear the burden of such communication – a task that they generally accomplish successfully. How they do so must therefore be examined systematically – something that Chomsky failed to do, relying on impressions only. A large body of studies, beginning in the 1970s and still continuing, has addressed itself to this issue, aimed at describing the full range of adults' help and support to language acquiring children. Motherese is one form such help is said to take, but let us also note a few examples of other forms:

ORIGINS

- *A responsive, accepting style* which adults adopt to their children's attempts to use words, marked by being prompt, contingent and appropriate in their replies. This is the opposite of a controlling, intrusive style where the parent sets out to take charge of how the child should express itself. As has repeatedly been shown, the former is considerably more successful in fostering children's linguistic competence than the latter (Masur, Flynn, & Eichorst, 2005).
- *Taking part with the child in* **joint attention** *episodes*, in which both infant and adult are focused on the same object or activity. Once established, the adult is able to insert speech in the context of a shared interest, making the words more meaningful for the child (Schaffer, 1989).
- *Linking speech to the child's own current topic of interest*, by following rather than directing his or her focus of attention and then labelling, describing and commenting on what the child has spontaneously chosen as a significant feature in the environment (Tomasello & Farrar, 1986).
- *Embedding verbal messages in an action context*, which the adult achieves by associating her utterances with such nonverbal cues as gazing at, pointing to, touching or manipulating the object referred to and so giving the child additional information whereby to decode the words used (Schaffer, Hepburn & Collis, 1983).

There is evidence that all such forms of support are associated with subsequent linguistic competence, prompting Bruner (1983) to propose a **LANGUAGE ACQUI-SITION SUPPORT SYSTEM** (LASS), which refers to –

> *all the various techniques adults employ to make it easier for children to acquire language.*

According to Bruner, language arises from and is embedded in social communication; to suggest, as did Chomsky, that its sole basis is to be found in innate structures such as the **language acquisition device** (LAD) is to neglect the additional part that the child's caretakers need to play in structuring the linguistic input and making it meaningful. Language development requires certain biological underpinnings, but social interaction activates these predispositions and provides the framework to enable the child to make use of language. LAD and LASS, as Bruner put it, go hand in hand.

CURRENT STATUS

All manifestations of language support have received attention from researchers, but by far the most has been given to motherese. Two aspects in particular have been the focus of investigation: more detailed descriptive specification of this style and its effects on children's language development.

As to further descriptions of motherese, these have been offered for virtually all its characteristics (see Gallaway & Richards, 1994, for details). For example, the distinctive use of prosodic features in motherese such as intonation and pitch have been investigated, in order to determine the part they play in conveying the adult's meaning (comforting, directing, questioning and so forth) and their effectiveness in eliciting and maintaining the infant's attention. Another focus has been the hypothesis that fine-tuning of speech varies according to children's age: while this has mostly been confirmed, the finding that speech to infants younger than 8 months is *more* complex than speech to older infants suggests that the adult's modifications depend on feedback from the child: before 8 months infants do not respond to the content of speech whereas from then on they can indicate the extent of their understanding. Thus the characteristics of motherese depend on the characteristics of the child – a point further emphasized by studies of speech addressed to such special groups as children with learning disability or hearing problems. Yet another example of research concerns the examination of motherese when used by individuals other than the mother. This has shown, for instance, that fathers and older siblings also fine-tune their speech to infants but do so in a less sensitive manner than mothers – a discrepancy, however, that according to some may have developmental advantages, at least at later ages, in challenging the child to learn skills to communicate with non-familiar interlocutors.

Of particular significance is the extension of studies to languages other than English and to cultures beyond the West. As a result it has become apparent that modifications in speech to children previously assumed to be universal – an apparently essential part of being a sensitive, helpful parent – are absent in certain societies (Ochs & Schieffelin, 1984). For example, in Samoa infants receive a great deal of physical contact from their parents but virtually no verbal interaction for most of the first year. Only with the onset of mobility will the mother begin verbally to address the child; yet even then speech is not simplified in any way but is in most respects like that used when talking to other adults. Motherese is thus totally absent from the child's language experience, and yet Samoan children are said to become fluent speakers at the usual time.

This leads us on to the second focus of current interest, namely the role of motherese in children's language development. As Snow (1994) has put it, is such a special style of talking to young children essential, facilitative or irrelevant? There have been many attempts to relate individual differences in the use of motherese to children's linguistic competence; the results have on the whole been mixed and inconclusive. The problem is largely methodological, in that these studies usually depend on correlational findings and do not allow any assumptions to be made about causation. As to the cross-cultural data, here too no firm conclusions can be drawn, for not enough societies have been investigated to make possible systematic comparisons of the nature and extent of motherese and its consequences for speech development. It may seem from societies like the Samoan that the experience of not being talked to in a simplified manner in the early years need not be a handicap; however, there are other explanations in such single-case instances which cannot be ruled out (Lieven, 1994). Yet what we cannot deny is that in the great majority of cases motherese is so natural a manner of relating to young children that its features appear even in mothers' signing to deaf children (Masataka, 1993).

The most likely way forward in clarifying the relationship of input to language development is to follow the direction indicated by Snow (1994), namely to stop treating motherese as though it were a unitary phenomenon that is in some way associated in a uniform fashion with all aspects of children's linguistic competence. Rather, it is apparent that different aspects of motherese have different functions, each predicting some particular characteristic of child language development. Thus, high pitched rather than low pitched voices attract the child's attention to adult speech; number of nouns heard under conditions of joint attention appears to facilitate the learning of nouns; contingent responding by the adult to the child's vocalizations encourages participation in conversations, and so forth. It is these specific input–output relationships that, according to recent research, are more likely to yield positive results than some global index of motherese that is then correlated with some more or less arbitrarily chosen index of child language.

Further reading

Gallaway, C., & Richards, B.J. (Eds.) (1994). *Input and interaction in language acquisition*. Cambridge: Cambridge University Press. Reviews the role of language input to children, as found in different cultures and family contexts and in typical and atypical learners.

Fletcher, P., & MacWhinney, B. (Eds.) (1995). *The handbook of child language*. Oxford: Blackwell. Chapter 3 by Elinor Ochs and Bambi Schieffelin on the impact of language socialization and Chapter 6 by Catherine Snow on issues in the study of input are highly relevant to the above discussion.

See also **joint attention; universal grammar**

SPEECH ACTS
and: LOCUTION, PERLOCUTION, and ILLOCUTION

MEANING Language is not just a highly intricate psychological system residing within individuals that one can study in its own right. It is also a device to be used for practical purposes, that is, to accomplish certain goals and especially so in communicative settings. This is the aspect of language known as *pragmatics*, and an essential concept in this area is that of speech acts.

Speech acts can be defined as –

verbally expressed communicative intentions.

As the philosopher J.L. Austin (1962), in his book entitled *How to do things with words*, put it, speaking is performing actions. This applies to every verbal utterance, the actions being such things as requesting, informing, promising, describing, asking and apologizing. Each speech act is thus a unit of communication which contains a meaningful message intentionally directed at others. The meaning behind a speaker's utterance needs to be interpreted by the listener, for one and the same meaning can be expressed in several different ways. 'You are standing on my foot' may sound like a piece of information but in fact must usually be understood as equivalent to 'Please get off my foot'. Thus there are direct and indirect speech acts, and indirect speech acts in particular depend on knowledge of the linguistic and social conventions that are shared by all members of the community.

According to Austin, speech acts have three components: **LOCUTION, PERLOCUTION** and **ILLOCUTION**. Locution refers to –

the linguistic form of a speech act (e.g. statement, question).

Perlocution denotes –

the effect the speech act produces on the listener.

Illocution is –

the speaker's intention behind the speech act.

The three-fold distinction has proved useful in that one can ask separate questions about each aspect of verbal utterances, and in particular has been helpful in tracing the development of speech acts when children are in the early stages of learning that words can be used to get things done.

ORIGINS

Speech act theory is largely the creation of two philosophers of language, namely J.L. Austin (1962) and John Searle (1969). Previously, little attention had been given to the pragmatics of language; however, these two writers between them ensured that prominence was given to this aspect of linguistics. Their thesis was that speaking was not just a matter of forming sentences but 'doing things with words'. Thus analysing an utterance without also taking into account the use to which the speaker means to put it is only a partial description of what is happening; to be complete it is also necessary to include the speaker's intention and the listener's interpretation of that intention. The form and content of a sentence on their own do not necessarily lead to an understanding of what the speaker means – the locutionary force, that is, may not convey the illocutionary intent. 'Can you pass the salt?' is on the surface in question form, but merely to answer 'Yes' without any further action is to neglect the conventional interpretation of such a sentence, namely that it means the same as the directive 'Pass the salt'. The basic units of linguistic communication are therefore not words or sentences but the production of words and sentences in the service of speech acts.

This way of looking at speech gave further impetus to the social interactionist approach to language, in that it emphasised communicative uses to which language can be put.

CURRENT STATUS The concept of speech acts has proved helpful as a means of understanding the pragmatic aspects of language, and in particular in finding out how children learn to make use of language in communicating with others. This is shown, for example, in the work of Elizabeth Bates and her colleagues (see Bates, Camioni, & Volterra, 1975), who examined the very beginning of this process in infancy, long before the onset of speech. Bates proposed a three-stage sequence to describe this development, making use of Austin's (1962) perlocution–illocution–locution distinction:

1 The *perlocutionary phase* lasts for the first 6–8 months, during which communication between infant and adult depends on the adult's interpretation of the gestures and vocal noises emitted by the infant without any deliberate intention of affecting the adult's behaviour.

2 The *illocutionary* phase takes place in approximately the last half or third of the first year. Infants are now becoming capable of intentional communicative acts, though these are still in nonverbal form.

3 The *locutionary* phase is to be found from about 1 year onwards, and is characterized by communication being not only intentional but also increasingly reliant on verbal means.

Thus the ability to use speech acts emerges gradually and in an orderly manner during the first year or two of life, each stage depending on the skills acquired in the previous one. In that sense there is functional continuity between them (see **proto-language**).

Other writers have examined the kinds of speech acts that children use and how the range of such acts develops over age. Thus in his book entitled *Learning how to mean* Michael Halliday (1975), on the basis of a very detailed study of his son's spontaneous speech from the end of the first year to the end of the second, compiled a list of seven communicative functions that emerge in order during this period, starting with the simplest, such as Instrumental (equivalent to requesting), and ending with the most abstract, like Imaginative (i.e. make-believe) and

Informative ('I have something to tell you'). He too believed that communicative functions can first be found in infants' nonverbal behaviour and gradually become expressed in the form of words. A function may remain the same, though the means of conveying it changes.

There have been other proposals for classifying speech acts, mostly designed to investigate how frequency and type of such acts changes over age (e.g. Ninio, 1995; Snow, Pan, Imbens–Bailey & Herman, 1996). Thus it has been shown that in the second year in particular there is a very substantial increase in the frequency with which speech acts are used and in the number of different kinds of speech acts that children become capable of using. Disagreeing, refusing and disapproving, for example, are added to the repertoire at this age; yet there are others such as promising which are not really fully understood until well beyond the preschool period. There have also been studies of the use of speech acts by children with pathological conditions such as autism and Down Syndrome (Adamson & Romski, 1999). In general, all these studies are based on the belief (as expressed by Halliday) that language is essentially a system for making meanings rather than a device for generating structures – in other words, that pragmatics rather than grammar explains why the human species developed the ability to speak.

Further reading

Ninio, A., & Snow, C.E. (1999). The development of pragmatics: learning to use language appropriately. In W.C. Ritchie & T.K. Bhatia (Eds.), *Handbook of child language acquisition*. New York: Academic Press. An overall review of pragmatic development, including research directly relevant to speech acts.

See also **continuity; proto-language**

LINGUISTIC COMPETENCE
and: COMMUNICATIVE COMPETENCE
CONVERSATIONAL MAXIMS

Various concepts concerned with competence have become popular in recent years in characterizing children's achievements. This is seen, for example, in the widespread use of **social competence** and **emotional competence**, despite problems in defining precisely what these terms mean and in translating definitions into objective measures. This applies to the concepts of linguistic and communicative competence as well.

MEANING

Linguistic competence refers to –

an individual's underlying knowledge about the system of rules determining the production of language.

Including the word *underlying* draws attention to the fact that the individual may not be able overtly to state the rules; rather, adherence to them is demonstrated by performance in speaking. Thus the knowledge is implicit, but it does result in being able both to produce and understand utterances that are phonologically, semantically and grammatically correct.

Yet linguistic competence on its own is not sufficient for communicating with others: further abilities are also required. As Hymes (1967) has put it:

A child capable of any or all grammatical utterances, but not knowing which to use, not knowing even when to talk and when to stop, would be a cultural monstrosity.

A distinction therefore needs to be made between knowing a language and knowing how to use it, and the concept of **COMMUNICATIVE COMPETENCE** is employed to denote the latter. It may be defined as –

the knowledge that enables an individual to make use of language effectively and appropriately in social settings.

The concept thus refers to the degree to which a speaker succeeds in getting messages across to listeners, and involves formulating the message in terms that are appropriate to the audience, adapting it if need be to the listeners' ability to comprehend (as illustrated by speaking **motherese** to young children) and to the environmental context (for example, talking louder in noisy environments). Communicating is consequently not just a matter of speaking correctly but also of using language as an effective means of sharing information with others, and the ideal measure of communicative competence is therefore some index of such effectiveness. There is some debate as to whether communicative competence includes linguistic competence or whether the two terms refer to separate domains. However, as spelled out below, there is evidence to prefer the latter alternative and that therefore communicative competence ought to be used exclusively for the pragmatic aspects of language while linguistic competence refers to phonological, semantic and grammatical aspects.

ORIGINS At one time linguistic competence was thought of as being largely a matter of accumulating a vocabulary and knowing what the words signify. The huge amount of work on language development in the past fifty years or so has changed all this and indicated how much more is involved in knowing and using language. Above all, the theory of **universal grammar** advanced by Chomsky (1957) shifted the focus from semantic to syntactic aspects: linguistic competence, according to Chomsky, refers to the innate knowledge we have of the basic grammatical rules that guide both the production and comprehension of speech, accounting for speakers' potential ability to generate an infinite number of sentences without any explicit tuition. It is the ability to apply the rules to combine single words into proper sentences and to create different forms of sentences (directives, questions, negative and passive constructions) from any one set of words that constitutes the essence of linguistic competence.

Such a formulation does not, of course, consider the use to which language is put, in that it views individuals in isolation rather than as participants in social interactions that demand communicative capabilities. As far as children are concerned, it is no wonder this was neglected, for right into the second half of the twentieth century there was still general agreement with Piaget's view that up to the age of 5 or 6 children are so immersed in their **egocentrism** that they are incapable of engaging in any meaningful communicative dialogue with another person. When two children talk together they are, according to Piaget, taking part in a *collective monologue,* and it is only well after the preschool period that they begin to take cognizance of their partner's point of view and to link their own verbal utterances to those of the other person.

However, as a result of new findings by socio-linguists and social interactionists, a different view came to prevail. These showed that even in the first two years the rudiments of communicative ability are present, and that long before the end of the preschool period children are in many respects very capable of communicating effectively with another person. The actual term 'communicative competence' was coined by Dell Hymes (1972), a social anthropologist who approached the topic via an interest in the varying styles of communication adopted in different societies. He argued that the language-learning child must acquire:

> knowledge of sentences not only as grammatical but also as appropriate. He or she acquires competence as to when to speak, when not, and as to what to talk about with whom, when, where, in what manner.

Although Hymes himself was primarily concerned with the mature form of communicative competence rather than with its manifestation in language-learning children, others readily took up the developmental issue in order to determine the various constituents of this ability in children, their emergence and rates of growth and the factors accounting for individual differences in competence (see the twin volumes edited by Schiefelbusch and Pickar, 1984 and Schiefelbusch, 1986). As a result of this growing attention to pragmatic aspects, a much fuller picture of the language acquisition process has gradually become available.

CURRENT STATUS A mass of descriptive findings have now been published which show what children are linguistically capable of at different developmental stages, giving rise to age-related norms with respect to such aspects as vocabulary size, word combination, formation of complex sentences and so forth. In addition, much has been learned about the development of such communicative abilities as different types of **speech acts**, adaptation of language to listener requirements (see **motherese**) and conversational skills like topic linking and repair of failed messages (see Hoff, 2001, for a review of this general area). What has also become evident from these findings is that the children most advanced in linguistic skills are not necessarily the same as those most advanced in communicative skills – a point further emphasized by children showing certain forms of language disorder. In autistic children, for example, a marked disparity can be found between the mastery of semantics and grammar on the one hand and communicative ability on the other (Tager-Flusberg, Calkins, Nolin, Baumberger, Anderson and Chadwick-Dias, 1990): whatever the level of intelligence, the ability of these children to use their acquired linguistic skills for social interaction is grossly impaired and may even be totally absent (Rutter & Schopler, 1987). There is thus a definite indication that linguistic competence and communicative competence refer to separate domains and that it is justified to make a clear-cut distinction between the two concepts.

The analysis of each concept into its components has been one of the main tasks of research, with a view to tracing each component over age and investigating the influences that determine the rate and nature of growth. Following on from this there have also been attempts to ascertain whether the developmental courses pursued by the different components are interdependent and coherent or independent from one another – one of the most hotly contested issues in linguistics according to Fenson and colleagues. These investigators (Fenson, Dale, Reznick, Bates, Thal & Pethick, 1994) examined the interrelationships during the early years of such aspects of linguistic competence as word comprehension, word production, use of verbs, sentence length and complexity and various indices of grammatical development, and found a considerable diversity of associations. The development of word comprehension and word production, for example, showed surprisingly low intercorrelations; indices of lexical and grammatical development, on the other hand, were associated to a strikingly close degree. Findings such as these are provocative but require further investigations before their implications can be clarified.

The study of communicative competence is of more recent origin than that of linguistic competence, but has also yielded lists of constituent skills encompassed by the concept. What is very apparent is that these skills emerge only gradually at different ages throughout much of childhood, with some in place quite early on – a very different picture from that painted by Piaget, with his emphasis on the fairly sudden release of the child from all-encompassing **egocentrism** at the end of the preschool period. As an example, take the skills needed to engage in conversation with another person. According to Grice (1975), a philosopher of language, taking part in a conversation involves knowledge of two basic principles: the need to take turns and the importance of being cooperative. The former is grasped by children at a very early age; the second is more complex and depends on four separate **CONVERSATIONAL MAXIMS**, by which Grice means –

> *the rules of conduct that speakers need to follow in order to bring about a successful exchange of information.*

There are four such maxims, relating to:

- *Quantity*: the need to give as much information to the other person as is required for understanding the message – no more and no less.
- *Quality*: the need to be truthful, though with certain permissible exceptions such as jokes, teasing and sarcasm.
- *Relevance*: the need for speakers to address the same topic, each following on from the previous speaker's contribution.
- *Manner*: the need to be clear and unambiguous.

Learning about these maxims is a long drawn-out process stretching over much of childhood. Again, some aspects appear surprisingly early: for example, 2½-year-olds already know that their messages need to be clear and are able to elucidate their utterances when the other person fails to understand them (Shwe & Markman, 1997). And at the same age children begin to make use of appropriate listener cues (for example, head nods, smiles, yeses) in response to a speaker to indicate their comprehension of what is said and so keep the conversation flowing (Miller, Lechner & Rugs, 1985). Yet even children aged 5 still do not as yet fully grasp the quantity maxim, that sufficient information must be given to their partner if the message is to be effective. This is illustrated by studies using the *referential communication technique* (e.g. Glucksberg, Krauss & Higgins, 1975), in which pairs of children are seated opposite each other at a table but visually separated by a screen, each provided with an identical set of objects. The task of one child is to describe a particular object so that the other child can pick out its duplicate. Right up to age 5 the information provided still includes phrases like 'this one here' or 'the one at the side' – hardly sufficient to be of communicative use. We have here just one illustration of the quite considerable difficulty children have in fulfilling all the requirements of being a participant in interpersonal dialogue and of the consequent time necessary to achieve mastery of all.

The term *competence* in all its various manifestations has been used both in an absolute and in a relative sense. The former refers to some end point of development when the fullest possible mastery of functioning has been achieved; anyone below that point is regarded as to some degree incompetent. Relative competence refers to individual differences, usually among members of a particular age group. Thus some 5-year-olds are further ahead in their mastery of grammar than others, and any scale measuring their competence in this respect would rank them accordingly. Individual differences in the rate of development of all aspects of language are enormous (Bates, Dale & Thal, 1996), and a lot of effort has gone into finding their determinants. Both environmental and child characteristics appear to play a part. As to the former, one important influence is the sheer amount of experience children have of being involved in interpersonal exchanges such as conversations with parents (Hoff-Ginsberg & Shatz, 1982); the quality of parental speech, such as whether it is supportive, rich and appropriate to the child's understanding, also plays a part. Among child characteristics **temperament** is one factor to take into account: thus children with outgoing temperament tend to be more advanced linguistically, presumably because such children are more likely to look for social contact and to have more talk directed at them (Slomkowski, Nelson, Dunn & Plomin, 1992). In addition, various cognitive skills have been found to show some interesting associations with both linguistic and communicative competence. Cognitive achievements are usually thought of as prerequisites for development in these two areas: the earlier the child becomes cognitively capable the sooner age-appropriate signs of competence appear. For example, children need to develop intentional control over their behaviour; only then can they target another person as a recipient of a communication designed to bring about some particular end such as help or comfort (see **illocution**). And likewise, there are intriguing suggestions that communicative competence is associated with **theory of mind** development – a relationship usually explained in terms of speakers needing to have some awareness of other people's likely thoughts and feelings if they are to tailor their own utterances appropriately. As yet, however, our understanding of the reasons why children differ so greatly in linguistic and communicative competence is still far from complete and badly in need of further research.

Further reading

Hoff, E. (2001). *Language development* (2nd ed.). Belmont, CA: Wadsworth. Chapter 6 deals specifically with the development of communicative competence and provides a very full account of the various topics that have been discussed under this heading.

Warren, A.R., & McCloskey, A. (1997). Language in social contexts. In J. Berko Gleason (Ed.), *The development of language* (4th ed.). Boston, MA: Allyn & Bacon. A chapter in an edited book which gives a usefully concise overview of pragmatic development.

See also **emotional competence; motherese; social competence; speech acts**

REFERENCES

Aboud, F., & Doyle, A. (1996). Parental and peer influences on children's racial attitudes. *International Journal of Intercultural Relations, 20*, 371–383.

Abramovitch, R., & Freedman, J.L. (1981). Actor–observer differences in children's attributions. Merrill–Palmer Quarterly, *27*, 53–59.

Adamson, L.B., & Romski, M.A. (Eds.) (1999). *Communication and language acquisition: discoveries from atypical development.* Baltimore, MD: Brookes.

Ainsworth, M.D.S. (1967). *Infancy in Uganda: infant care and the growth of love.* Baltimore, MD: Johns Hopkins University Press.

Ainsworth, M.D.S (1979). Attachment as related to mother–infant interaction. *Advances in the Study of Behavior, 9*, 2–51.

Ainsworth, M.D.S., Blehar, M.C., Waters, E., & Wahls, S. (1978). *Patterns of attachment.* Hillsdale, NJ: Erlbaum.

Anastasi, A. (1958). Heredity, environment and the question 'How?'. *Psychological Review, 65*, 197–208.

Anderson, K.E., Lytton, H., & Romney, D.M. (1986). Mothers' interactions with normal and conduct-disordered boys: who affects whom? *Developmental Psychology, 22*, 604–606.

Anderson, S., & Messick, S. (1974). Social competency in young children. *Developmental Psychology, 10*, 282–293.

Appleyard, K., Egelund, B., van Dulmen, M.H.M., & Sroufe, L.A. (2005). When more is not better: the role of cumulative risk in child behavior outcomes. *Journal of Child Psychology and Psychiatry, 46*, 235–245.

Archer, J. (1992). *Ethology and human development.* Hemel Hempstead: Harvester–Wheatsheaf.

Archer, J., & Lloyd, B. (2002). *Sex and gender* (2nd ed.). Cambridge: Cambridge University Press.

Aslin, R.N. (1993). Commentary: the strange attractiveness of dynamic systems to development. In L.B. Smith & E. Thelen (Eds.), *Dynamic systems approach to development.* Cambridge, MA: MIT Press.

Astington, J.W. (1994). *The child's discovery of the mind.* London: Fontana.

Atkinson, R.C., & Shiffrin, R.M. (1968). Human memory: a proposed system and its control processes. In K.W. Spence & J.T. Spence (Eds.), *Advances in the psychology of learning and motivation,* vol. 2. New York: Academic Press.

Austin J.L. (1962). *How to do things with words.* Oxford: Oxford University Press.

Baillargeon, R. (1987). Object permanence in 3½- and 4½-month-old infants. *Developmental Psychology, 23*, 655–664.

Baillargeon, R., & De Vos, J. (1991). Object permanence in young infants: further evidence. *Child Development, 62*, 1227–1246.

Baldwin, J.M. (1895). *Mental development of the child and the race.* New York: Macmillan.

Baltes, P.B. (1987). Theoretical propositions of life-span developmental psychology: on the dynamics of growth and decline. *Developmental Psychology, 23*, 611–626.

Baltes, P.B., Lindenberger, U., & Standinger, U. (1998). Life-span theory in developmental psychology. In W. Damon (Ed.), *Handbook of child psychology* (5th ed.), vol. 1 (R.M. Lerner, Ed.). New York: Wiley.

Bandura, A. (1977). *Social learning theory*. Englewood Cliffs, NJ: Prentice–Hall.

Bandura, A. (1986). *Social foundations of thought and action: a social cognitive theory*. Englewood Cliffs, NJ: Prentice–Hall.

Bandura, A. (1997). *Self-efficacy: the exercise of control*. New York: W.H. Freeman.

Banks, M.S., Aslin, R.N., & Letson, R.D. (1975). Sensitive period for the development of binocular vision. *Science, 190,* 675–677.

Baron-Cohen, S. (1995). *Mindblindness: an essay on autism and theory of mind*. Cambridge, MA: MIT Press.

Bartlett, F.C. (1932). *Remembering: a study in experimental and social psychology*. Cambridge: Cambridge University Press.

Bartsch, K., & Wellman, H.M. (1995). *Children talk about the mind*. Oxford: Oxford University Press.

Bates, E., Camioni, L., & Volterra, V. (1975). The acquisition of performatives prior to speech. *Merrill-Palmer Quarterly, 21,* 205–226.

Bates, E., Dale, P.S., & Thal, D. (1996). Individual differences and their implications for theories of language development. In P. Fletcher & B. McWhinney (Eds.), *The handbook of child language*. Oxford: Blackwell.

Bates, E., O'Connell, B., & Shore, C. (1987). Language and communication in infancy. In J.D. Osofsky (Ed.), *Handbook of infant development*. New York: Wiley.

Bates, J.E., & McFadyen-Ketchum, S. (2000). Temperament and parent–child relations as interacting factors in children's behavioural adjustment. In V.J. Molfese, & D. Molfese (Eds.), *Temperament and personality development across the life span*. Mahwah, NJ: Erlbaum.

Bateson, P. (1998). Ontogeny, communication and parent–offspring relationships. In S. Braten (Ed.), *Intersubjective communication and emotion in early ontogeny*. Cambridge: Cambridge University Press.

Bateson, P., & Martin, P. (1999). *Design for a life: how behaviour develops*. London: Jonathan Cape.

Bauer, P.J., & Mandler, J.M. (1990). Remembering what happened next: very young children's recall of event sequences. In R. Fivush & J.A. Hudson (Eds.), *Knowing and remembering in young children*. Cambridge: Cambridge University Press.

Bauer, P.J., & Mandler, J.M. (1992). Putting the horse before the cart: the use of temporal order in recall of events by one-year-old children. *Developmental Psychology, 28,* 441–452.

Baumeister, R.F. (1986). *Identity: cultural change and the struggle for self*. New York: Oxford University Press.

Beilin, H., & Pufall, P. (Eds.) (1992). *Piaget's theory: prospects and possibilities*. Hillsdale, NJ: Erlbaum.

Bell, R.Q. (1968). A reinterpretation of the direction of effects in studies of socialization. *Psychological Review, 75,* 81–95.

Bell, R.Q. (1979). Parent, child and reciprocal influences. *American Psychologist, 34,* 821–826.

Bell, R.Q., & Chapman, M. (1986). Child effects in studies using experimental or brief longitudinal approaches to socialization. *Developmental Psychology, 22,* 595–603.

Bell, R.Q., & Harper, L.V. (1977). *Child effects on adults*. Hillsdale, NJ: Erlbaum.

Belsky, J., Steinberg, L., & Draper, P. (1991). Childhood experience, interpersonal development, and reproductive strategy. *Child Development, 62,* 647–670.

Bennett, M., & Sani, F. (Eds.) (2004). *The development of the social self*. Hove: Psychology Press.

Berko Gleason, J. (Ed.) (1997). *The development of language* (4th ed.). Needham Heights, MA: Allyn & Bacon.

Bijou, S.W. (1970). Reinforcement history and socialization. In R.A. Hoppe, G.A. Milton, & E.C. Simmel (Eds.), *Early experience and the processes of socialization*. New York: Academic Press.

Birren, J.E., & Schaie, K.W. (1977). *Handbook of the psychology of aging*. New York: Van Nostrand Reinhold.

Bivens, J.A., & Berk, L.A. (1990). A longitudinal study of the development of elementary school children's private speech. *Merrill–Palmer Quarterly, 36*, 443–463.

Bjorklund, D.F. (Ed.) (1990). *Children's strategies: contemporary views of cognitive development*. Hillsdale, NJ: Erlbaum.

Bjorklund, D.F. (1997). The role of immaturity in human development. *Psychological Bulletin, 122*, 153–169.

Bjorklund, D.F., & Douglas, R.N. (1997). The development of memory strategies. In N. Cowan (Ed.), *The development of memory in children*. Hove: Psychology Press.

Bjorklund, D.F., & Harnishfeger, K.K. (1990). Children's strategies: their definition and origins. In D.F. Bjorlund (Ed.), *Children's strategies: contemporary views of cognitive development*. Hillsdale, NJ: Erlbaum.

Bjorklund, D.F., & Pelligrini, A.D. (2002). *The origins of human nature: evolutionary developmental psychology*. Washington, DC: American Psychological Association.

Block, J. (1971). *Lives through time*. Berkeley, CA: Bancroft Books.

Bloom, P., & German, T.P. (2000). Two reasons for abandoning the false belief task as a test of theory of mind. *Cognition, 77*, B25–B31.

Blurton Jones, N. (Ed.) (1972). *Ethological studies of child behaviour*. Cambridge: Cambridge University Press.

Boden, M.A. (1994). *Piaget* (2nd ed.). London: Fontana.

Bohman, M. (1996). Predispositions to criminality: Swedish adoption studies in retrospect. In G.R. Bock & J.A. Goode (Eds.), *Genetics of criminal and antisocial behaviour*. Chichester: Wiley.

Bolger, N., Caspi, A., Downey, G., & Moorehouse, M. (Eds.) (1988). *Persons in context: developmental processes*. Cambridge: Cambridge University Press.

Borke, H. (1971). Interpersonal perception of young children: egocentrism or empathy. *Developmental Psychology, 5*, 263–269.

Bornstein, M. (1989). Sensitive periods in development: structural characteristics and causal interpretations. *Psychological Bulletin, 105*, 179–197.

Bosma, H.A., Graafsma, T.L.G., Grotevant, H.D., & deLevita, D.J. (Eds.) (1994). *Identity and development*. Thousand Oaks, CA: Sage.

Bowlby, J. (1951). *Maternal care and mental health*. Geneva: World Health Organization.

Bowlby, J. (1958). The nature of the child's tie to his mother. *International Journal of Psychoanalysis, 3*, 1–23.

Bowlby, J. (1969/1982). *Attachment and loss*; vol. 1: *Attachment*. London: Hogarth Press.

Bowlby, J. (1990). *Charles Darwin: a biography*. London: Hutchinson.

Bracken, B.A. (Ed.) (1996). *Handbook of self-concept*. New York: Wiley.

Braten, S. (Ed.) (1998). *Intersubjective communication and emotion in early ontogeny*. Cambridge: Cambridge University Press.

Bretherton, I. (1992). The origins of attachment theory: John Bowlby and Mary Ainsworth. *Developmental Psychology, 28*, 759–775.

Bretherton, I., Golby, B., & Cho, E. (1997). Attachment and the transmission of values. In J.E. Grusec & L. Kuczynski (Eds.), *Parenting and children's internalization of values*. New York: Wiley.

Briggs, J.L. (1970). *Never in anger*. Cambridge, MA: Harvard University Press.

Bronfenbrenner, U. (1979). *The ecology of human development*. Cambridge, MA: Harvard University Press.

Bronfenbrenner, U. (1988). Interacting systems in human development. In N. Bolger, A. Caspi, G. Downey, & M. Moorehouse (Eds.), *Persons in contexts: developmental processes*. Cambridge: Cambridge University Press.

Bronfenbrenner, U., & Morris, P.A. (1998). The ecology of developmental processes. In W. Damon (Ed.), *Handbook of child psychology*, vol. 1 (R.M. Lerner, Ed.). New York: Wiley.

Brown, A.L., Bransford, J.D., Ferrara, R.A., & Campione, J.G. (1983). In P.H. Mussen (Ed.), *Handbook of child psychology: cognitive development*. New York: Wiley.

Brown, R. (1973). *A first language*. Cambridge, MA: Harvard University Press.

Bruner, J.S. (1959). Inhelder and Piaget's 'The Growth of Logical Thinking'. *British Journal of Psychology*, *50*, 365.

Bruner, J.S. (1977). Early social interaction and language acquisition. In H.R. Schaffer (Ed.), *Studies in mother–infant interaction*. London: Academic Press.

Bruner, J.S. (1983). *Child's talk*. New York: Norton.

Bryant, P.E. (1990). Empirical evidence for causes of development. In G. Butterworth & P.E. Bryant (Eds.), *Causes of development*. Hillsdale, NJ: Erlbaum.

Bugental, D.B., & Goodnow, J.J. (1998). Socialization processes. In W. Damon (Ed.), *Handbook of child psychology*, vol. 3 (N. Eisenberg, Ed.). New York: Wiley.

Bugental, D.B., & Johnston, C. (2000). Parental and child cognitions in the context of the family. *Annual Review of Psychology*, *51*, 315–344.

Bukowski, W.M., & Cillessen, A.N.H. (Eds.) (1998). *Sociometric theory then and now: building on six decades of measuring children's experience with the peer group*. New Directions in Child Development, No. 80. San Francisco: Jossey–Bass.

Bullowa, M. (1979). *Before speech: the beginnings of interpersonal communication*. Cambridge: Cambridge University Press.

Buss, D.M. (1999). *Evolutionary psychology: the new science of the mind*. Boston, MA: Allyn and Bacon.

Bussey, K., & Bandura, A. (1999). Social cognitive theory of gender development and differentiation. *Psychological Review*, *106*, 676–713.

Cairns, R.B. (1998). The making of developmental psychology. In W. Damon (Ed.), *Handbook of child psychology* (5th ed.), vol. 1 (R.M. Lerner, Ed.). New York: Wiley.

Campos, J.D., Barrett, K.L., Lamb, M.E., Goldsmith, H.H., & Stenberg, C. (1983). Socioemotional development. In P. Mussen (Ed.), *Handbook of child psychology*, vol. 2 (M.M. Haith, Ed.). New York: Wiley.

Capozza, D., & Brown, R. (2000). *Social identity processes: trends in theory and research*. London: Sage.

Carlsson, S.G., Fagerberg, H., Horneman, G., Hwang, C.P., Larsson, K., Rodholm, M., & Schaller, J. (1979). Effects of various amounts of contact between mother and child on the mother's nursing behavior. *Infant Behavior and Development*, *2*, 209–214.

Carpenter, M., Nagell, K., & Tomasello, M. (1998). Social cognition, joint attention and communicative competence from 9 to 15 months of age. *Monographs of the Society for Research in Child Development*, *63*, no. 4 (Serial no. 255).

Carraher, T.N., Carraher, T.W., & Schliemann, A.D. (1985). Mathematics in the streets and in the schools. *British Journal of Developmental Psychology*, *3*, 21–29.

Carver, L.J., & Bauer, P.J. (1999). When the event is more than the sum of its parts: individual differences in 9-month-old's long-term ordered memory. *Memory*, *2*, 147–174.

Case, R. (1992). *The mind's staircase: exploring the conceptual underpinnings of children's thought and knowledge*. Hillsdale, NJ: Erlbaum.

Case, R. (1998). The development of conceptual structures. In W. Damon (Ed.), *Handbook of child psychology*, vol. 2 (D. Kuhn & R.S. Siegler, Eds.). New York: Wiley.

Caspi, A. (1998). Personality development across the life course. In W. Damon (Eds.), *Handbook of child psychology*, (5th ed.), vol. 3 (N. Eisenberg, Ed.). New York: Wiley.

Caspi, A. (2000). The child is father of the man: personality continuities from childhood to adulthood. *Journal of Personality and Social Psychology, 78*, 158–172.

Caspi, A., & Moffitt, T.E. (1995). The continuity of maladaptive behavior. In D. Cicchetti & D. Cohen (Eds.), *Manual of developmental psychopathology*, vol. 2. New York: Wiley.

Caspi, A., Elder, G.H., & Bem, D.J. (1987). Moving against the world: life-course patterns of explosive children. *Developmental Psychology, 23*, 308–313.

Cassidy, J., & Shaver, P.R. (Eds) (1999). *Handbook of attachment: theory, research and clinical application*. New York: Guilford.

Chagnon, N.A. (1968). *Yanomamö: the fierce people*. New York: Holt, Rinehart & Winston.

Chapman, M. (1992). Equilibration and the dialectics of organization. In H. Beilin, & P. Pufall (Eds.), *Piaget's theory: prospects and possibilities*. Hillsdale, NJ: Erlbaum.

Chavous, T.M., Bernat, D.H., Schmeelk-Cone, K., Caldwell, C.H., Kohn-Wood., L., & Zimmerman, M.A. (2003). Racial identity and academic attainment among African American adolescents. *Child Development, 74*, 1076–1090.

Chen, X., Hastings, P., Rubin, K., Chen, H., Cen, G., & Stewart, S.L. (1998). Child rearing attitudes and behavioural inhibition in Chinese and Canadian toddlers: a cross-cultural study. *Developmental Psychology, 34*, 677–686.

Chi, M.T.H. (1978). Knowledge structures and memory development. In R.S. Siegler (Ed.), *Children's thinking: what develops?* Hillsdale, NJ: Erlbaum.

Chomsky, N. (1957). *Syntactic structures*. The Hague: Mouton.

Chomsky, N. (1965). *Aspects of the theory of syntax*. Cambridge, MA: MIT Press.

Chomsky, N. (1986). *Knowledge of language: its nature, origin and use*. New York: Praeger.

Chomsky, N. (1988). *Language and problems of knowledge*. Cambridge, MA: MIT Press.

Chomsky, N. (1991). Linguistics and cognitive science: problems and mysteries. In A. Kashar (Ed.), *The Chomskyan turn*. Cambridge, MA: Blackwell.

Cicchetti, D., Ganiban, J., & Barnett, D. (1991). Contributions from the study of high-risk populations to understanding the development of emotion regulation. In J. Garber & K.A. Dodge (Eds), *The development of emotion regulation and dysregulation*. Cambridge: Cambridge University Press.

Cillessen, A.H.N., & Bellmore, A.D. (2002). Social skills and interpersonal perception in early and middle childhood. In P.K. Smith & C.H. Hart (Eds), *Blackwell handbook of childhood social development*. Oxford: Blackwell.

Cillessen, A.N.H., & Bukowski, W.M. (Eds) (2000). *Recent advances in the measurement of accceptance and rejection in the peer system*. New Directions in Child Development, No. 88. San Francisco: Jossey–Bass.

Clarke, A., & Clarke, A. (2000). *Early experience and the life path*. London: Jessica Kingsley.

Clarke, A., & Clarke, A. (2003). *Human resilience*. London: Jessica Kingsley.

Coie, J.D., Dodge, K.A., & Coppotelli, H. (1982). Dimensions and types of social status: a cross-age perspective. *Developmental Psychology, 18*, 557–570.

Collins W.A., Maccoby, E.E., Steinberg, L., Hetherington, E.D., & Bornstein, M.H. (2000). Contemporary research on parenting: the case for nature and nurture. *American Psychologist, 55*, 218–232.

Cole, P.M., Martin, S.E., & Dennis, T.A. (2004). Emotion regulation as a scientific construct: methodological challenges and directions for child development research. *Child Development, 75*, 317–333.

Collis, G., & Schaffer, H.R. (1975). Synchronization of visual attention in mother–infant pairs. *Journal of Child Psychology and Psychiatry, 16*, 315–320.

Cooley, C.H. (1902). *Human nature and the social order*. New York: Charles Scribner.

Cox, M.J., & Paley, B. (1997). Families as systems. *Annual Review of Psychology, 48*, 243–267.

Cox, M.V. (1991). *The child's point of view* (2nd ed.). Hemel Hempstead, UK: Harvester Wheatsheaf.

Crawford, C. (1998). The theory of evolution in the study of human behavior: an introduction and overview. In C. Crawford & D.L. Krebs (Eds.), *Handbook of evolutionary psychology: ideas, issues, and applications*. Mahwah, NJ: Erlbaum.

Crawford, C., & Krebs, D.L. (Eds.) (1998). *Handbook of evolutionary psychology: ideas, issues, and applications*. Mahwah, NJ: Erlbaum.

Crick, N., & Dodge, K.A. (1994). A review and reformulation of social information processing mechanisms in children. *Psychological Bulletin, 115*, 74–101.

Cummings, E.M., Davies, P.T., & Campbell, S.B. (2000). *Developmental psychopathology and family process*. New York: Guilford.

Damon, W. (1983). *Social and personality development*. London: W.W. Norton.

Daniels, D., & Plomin, R. (1985). Differential experiences of siblings in the same family. *Developmental Psychology, 21*, 747–760.

Darwin, C. (1859). *On the origin of species*. London: John Murray.

Darwin, C. (1872). *The expressions of the emotions in man and animals*. London: John Murray.

Deater-Deckard, K., & Cahill, K. (2006). Nature and nurture in early childhood. In K. McCartney & D. Phillips (Eds.), *Blackwell handbook of early childhood development*. Oxford: Blackwell.

Deater-Deckard, K., & Petrill, S.A. (2004). Parent–child dyadic mutuality and child behavior problems: an investigation of gene-environment processes. *Journal of Child Psychology and Psychiatry, 45*, 1171–1179.

DeLoache, J.S. (2002). Early development of the understanding and use of symbolic artefacts. In U. Goswami (Ed.), Blackwell handbook of childhood cognitive development. Oxford: Blackwell.

DeLoache, J.S., & Smith, C.M. (1999). Early symbolic representation. In I.E. Sigel (Ed.), *Development of mental representation: theories and applications*. Mahwah, NJ: Erlbaum.

DeLoache, J.S., Cassidy, D.J., & Brown, A.L. (1985). Precursors of mnemonic strategies in very young children's memory. *Child Development, 56,*125–137.

Denham, S. (1998). *Emotional development in young children*. New York: Guilford.

Denham, S., von Salisch, M., Olthof, T., Kochanoff, A., & Caverly, S. (2002). Emotional and social development in childhood. In P.K. Smith, & C.H. Hart (Eds.), *Blackwell handbook of childhood social development*. Oxford: Blackwell.

Dodge, K.A. (1985). Facets of social interaction and the assessment of social competence in children. In B.H. Schneider, K.H. Rubin, & J.E. Ledingham (Eds.), *Children's peer relations: issues in assessment and intervention*. New York: Springer.

Dodge, K.A. (1986). A social information processing model of social competence in children. In M. Perlmutter (Ed.), *Minnesota Symposium on Child Psychology*, vol. 18. Hillsdale, NJ: Erlbaum.

Donaldson, M. (1978). *Children's minds*. London: Fontana.

Dunn, J., Brown, J., Slomkowski, C., Tesla,C., & Youngblade, L. (1991). Young children's understanding of other people's feelings and beliefs: individual differences and their antecedents. *Child Development, 62*, 1352–1366.

Dunn, J., & Plomin, R. (1990). *Separate lives: why siblings are so different*. New York: Basic Books.

Durkin, K. (1995). *Developmental social psychology*. Oxford: Blackwell.

Dweck, C.S. (1975). The role of expectations and attributions in the alleviation of learned helplessness. *Journal of Personality and Social Psychology, 31*, 674–685.

Eibl-Eibesfeldt, I. (1989). *Human ethology*. New York: de Gruyter.

Eisenberg, N., & Morris, A.S. (2002). Children's emotion-related regulation. In R. Kail (Ed.), *Advances in child development and behaviour*, vol. 20. Amsterdam: Academic Press.

Elder, G.H. (1974). *Children of the great depression: social change in life experience*. Chicago: University of Chicago Press.

Elder, G.H. (1985). *Life course dynamics: trajectories and transitions*. Ithaca, NY: Cornell University Press.

Elder, G.H. (1998). The life course as developmental theory. *Child Development, 69*, 1–12.

Elder, G.H., Modell, J., & Parke, R.D. (1993). *Children in time and place*: *developmental and historical insights*. Cambridge: Cambridge University Press.

Elman, J.L., Bates, E.A., Johnson, M.H., Karmiloff-Smith, A., Parisi, D., & Plunkett, K. (1996). *Rethinking innateness: a connectionist perspective on development*. Cambridge, MA: MIT Press.

Erikson, E. (1950). *Childhood and society*. New York: Norton.

Erikson, E. (1968). *Identity: youth and crisis*. New York: Norton.

Farver, J.A.M., Bhadha, B.R., & Narang, S.K. (2002). Acculturation and psychological functioning in Asian Indian adolescents. *Social Development, 11*, 11–29.

Faulkner, D., Littlejohn, K., & Woodhead, M. (Eds.) (1998). *Learning relationships in the classroom*. London: Routledge.

Feinman, S. (1982). Social referencing in infancy. *Merrill–Palmer Quarterly, 28*, 445–470.

Fenson, L., Dale, P.S., Reznick, J.S., Bates, E., Thal, D.J., & Pethick, S.J. (1994). Variability in early communicative development. *Monographs of the Society for Research in Child Development, 59*, no. 5, Serial no. 242.

Fergusson, D.M., & Horwood, L.J. (1998). Early conduct problems and later life opportunities. *Journal of Child Psychology and Psychiatry, 39*, 1097–1108.

Fergusson, D.M., & Lynskey, M.T. (1997). Physical punishment/maltreatment during childhood and adjustment in young adulthood. *Child Abuse and Neglect, 21*, 617–630.

Fergusson, D.M., Horwood, L.J., & Lynskey, M.T. (1992). Family change, parental discord and early offending. *Journal of Child Psychology and Psychiatry, 33*, 1059–1076.

Fernyhough, C. (1997). Vygotsky's sociocultural approach: theoretical issues and implications for current research. In S. Hala (Ed.), *The development of social cognition*. Hove: Psychology Press.

Fincham, F. (1983). Developmental dimensions of attribution theory. In J. Jaspars, F. Fincham & M. Hewstone (Eds.), *Attribution theory and research*. New York: Academic Press.

Fincham, F., & Hewstone, M. (2001). Attribution theory and research: from basic to applied. In M. Hewstone & W. Stoebe (Eds.), Introduction to social psychology (3rd ed.). Oxford: Blackwell.

Fischer, K.W., & Silvern, L. (1985). Stages and individual differences in cognitive development. *Annual Review of Psychology, 36*, 613–648.

Fivush, R., Haden, C., & Reese, E. (1996). Remembering, recounting and reminiscing: the development of autobiographical memory in social context. In D.C. Rubin (Ed.), *Remembering our past: studies in autobiographical memory*. Cambridge: Cambridge University Press.

Flavell, J.H. (1963). *The developmental psychology of Jean Piaget*. Princeton, NJ: Van Nostrand.

Flavell, J.H. (1971). First discussant's comments: what is memory the development of? *Human Development, 14*, 272–278.

Flavell, J.H. (1988). The development of children's knowledge about the mind: from cognitive connections to mental representations. In J.W. Astington, P.L. Harris & D.R. Olson (Eds.), *Developing theories of mind*. Cambridge: Cambridge University Press.

Flavell, J.H. (1993). The development of children's understanding of false beliefs and the appearance–reality distinction. *International Journal of Psychology, 28,* 595–604.

Flavell, J.H., & Wellman, H.M. (1977). Metamemory. In R.V. Kail & J.W. Hagen (Eds.), *Perspectives on the Development of Memory and Cognition.* Hillsdale, NJ: Erlbaum.

Flavell, J.H., Beach, D.R., & Chinsky, J.H. (1966). Spontaneous verbal rehearsal in a memory task as a function of age. *Child Development, 37,* 283–299.

Flavell, J.H., Friedrichs, A.G., & Hoyt, J.D. (1970). Developmental changes in memorization processes. *Cognitive Psychology, 1,* 324–340.

Flavell, J.H., Green, F.L., & Flavell, E.R. (1986). Development of knowledge about the appearance–reality distinction. *Monographs of the Society for Research in Child Development, 51,* no.1, Serial no. 212.

Flavell, J.H., Green, F.L., & Flavell, E.R. (1995). Young children's knowledge about thinking. *Monographs of the Society for Research in Child Development, 60,* no. 1, Serial no. 243.

Flavell, J.H., Miller, P.H., & Miller, S.A. (1993). *Cognitive Development* (3rd ed.). Englewood Cliffs, NJ: Prentice–Hall.

Fodor, J.A. (1983). *The modularity of mind.* Cambridge, MA: MIT Press.

Fogel, A. (1993). *Developing through relationships: origins of communication, self, and culture.* Chicago: University of Chicago Press.

Foot, H., & Howe, C. (1998). The psycho-educational basis of peer-assisted learning. In K. Topping & S. Ehly (Eds.), *Peer-assisted learning.* Mahwah, NJ: Erlbaum.

Forehand, R.L., & McMahon, R.J. (1981). *Helping the noncompliant child.* New York: Guilford.

Fosnot, C.F. (Ed.) (1996). *Constructivism: theory, perspectives and practice.* New York: Teachers College, Columbia University.

Frankfurt, H.G. (2005). *On bullshit.* Princeton, NJ: Princeton University Press.

Freud, S. (1930) *Civilisation and its discontents.* London: Hogarth Press.

Freud, S. (1949). *An outline of psychoanalysis.* London: Hogarth Press.

Frick, P.J., Cornell, A.H., Bodin, S.D., Dane, H.E., Barry, C.T., & Loney, B.R. (2003). Callous-unemotional traits and developmental pathways to severe conduct problems. *Developmental Psychology, 39,* 246–260.

Gallaway, C., & Richards, B. (1994). *Input and interaction in language acquisition.* Cambridge: Cambridge University Press.

Galton, F. (1869). *Hereditary genius: an enquiry into its laws and consequences.* London: Macmillan.

Gardner, H. (1984). *Frames of mind: the theory of multiple intelligences.* London: Heinemann.

Gathercole, S. (1998). The development of memory. *Journal of Child Psychology and Psychiatry, 39,* 3–28.

Gauvain, M. (2001). *The social context of cognitive development.* New York: Guilford.

Ge, X., Lorenz, F.O., Conger, R.D., Elder, G.H., & Simmons, R.L. (1994). Trajectories of stressful life events and depressive symptoms during adolescence. *Developmental Psychology, 30,* 467–483.

Geary, D.C., & Bjorklund, D.F. (2000). Evolutionary developmental psychology. *Child Development, 71,* 57–65.

Gesell, A. (1928). *Infancy and human growth.* New York: Macmillan.

Gesell, A. (1954). The ontogenesis of infant behavior. In L. Carmichael (Ed.), *Manual of child psychology.* New York: Wiley.

Gesell, A., & Amatruda, C.S. (1947). *Developmental diagnosis* (2nd ed.). New York: Hoeber.

Gesell, A., & Ilg, F.L. (1943). Infant and child in the culture of today. In A. Gesell & F.L. Ilg (Eds.), *Child development.* New York: Harper and Row.

Gewirtz, J.L., & Pelaez-Nogueras, M. (1992). B.F. Skinner's legacy in human infant behavior and development. *American Psychologist, 47,* 1411–1422.

Glantz, M.D., & Johson, J.L. (Eds.) (1999). *Resilience and development.* New York: Kluwer.

Glucksberg, S., Krauss, R.M., & Higgins, E.T. (1975). The development of communicative skills in children. In F. Horowitz (Ed.), *Review of child development research,* vol. 4. Chicago: University of Chicago Press.

Goldberg, S. (2000). *Attachment and development.* London: Arnold.

Goleman, D. (1995). *Emotional intelligence.* London: Bloomsbury.

Gomez, J.C. (1998). Do concepts of intersubjectivity apply to non-human primates? In S. Braten (Ed.), *Intersubjective communication and emotion in early ontogeny.* Cambridge: Cambridge University Press.

Goodman, R. (1991). Developmental disorders and structural brain development. In M. Rutter & P. Casaer (Eds.), *Biological risk factors for psychosocial disorders.* Cambridge: Cambridge University Press.

Goodnow, J.J. (1997). Parenting and the transmission and internalization of values: from social-cultural perspectives to within-family analysis. In J. Grusec & L. Kuczynski (Eds.), *Parenting and children's internalization of values.* New York: Wiley.

Goodnow, J., & Collins, A.W. (1990). *Development according to parents: the nature, source and consequences of parents' ideas.* Hillsdale, NJ: Erlbaum.

Gopnik, A. (1988). Conceptual and semantic development as theory change. *Mind and Language, 3,* 197–217.

Gopnik, A., & Meltzoff, A.N. (1997). *Words, thoughts and theories.* Cambridge, MA: MIT Press.

Gopnik, A., & Wellman, H.M. (1992). Why the child's theory of mind really is a theory. *Mind and Language, 7,* 145–171.

Gopnik, A., & Wellman, H.M. (1994). The theory theory. In L.A. Hirschfeld & S.A. Gelman (Eds.), *Mapping the mind: domain specificity in cognition and culture.* Cambridge: Cambridge University Press.

Gopnik, A., Meltzoff, A., & Kuhl, P. (1999). *How babies think.* London: Weidenfeld & Nicolson (in USA: *The scientist in the crib.* New York: William Morrow).

Gottlieb, G. (1997). *Synthesizing nature–nurture.* Mahwah, NJ: Erlbaum.

Gottlieb, G., Wahlsten, D., & Lickliter, R. (1998). The significance of biology for human development: a developmental psychobiological systems view. In W. Damon (Ed.), *Handbook of child psychology* (5th ed.), vol. 1 (R.M. Lerner, Ed.). New York: Wiley.

Granic, I. (2000). The self-organization of parent–child relations: beyond bidirectional models. In M.D. Lewis & I. Granic (Eds.), *Emotion, development and self-organization: dynamic systems approaches to emotional development.* Cambridge: Cambridge University Press.

Granic, I., & Dishion, T.J. (2003). Deviant talk in adolescent friendships: a step toward measuring a pathogenic attractor process. *Social Development, 12,* 314–334.

Granic, I., & Lamey, A.V. (2002). Combining dynamic and multivariate analyses to compare mother–child interactions of externalising subtypes. *Journal of Abnormal Child Psychology, 30,* 265–283.

Greenough, W.T., Black, J.E., & Wallace, C.S. (1986). Experience and brain development. *Child Development, 58,* 539–559.

Grice, H.P. (1975). Logic and conversation. In P. Cole & J. Morgan (Eds.). *Speech acts: syntax and semantics,* vol. 3. New York: Academic Press.

Grossmann, K., Thane, K., & Grossmann, K.E. (1981). Maternal tactual contact of the newborn after various postpartum conditions of mother–infant contact. *Developmental Psychology, 17,* 158–169.

Grusec, J.E. (1994). Social learning theory and developmental psychology: the legacies of Robert R. Sears and Albert Bandura. In R.D. Parke, P.A. Ornstein, J.J. Rieser, & C. Zahn-Waxler (Eds.), *A century of developmental psychology*. Washington, DC: Amercian Psychological Assocation.

Grusec, J.E., & Goodnow, J.J. (1994). Impact of parental discipline methods on the child's internalization of values: a reconceptualization of current points of view. *Developmental Psychology, 30,* 4–19.

Grusec, J.E., & Kuczynsksi, L. (Eds.) (1997). *Parenting and children's internalization of values.* New York: Wiley.

Grusec, J.E., Hastings, P., & Mammone, N. (1994). Parenting cognitions and relationship schemas. In J. Smetana (Ed.), *Beliefs about parenting: origins and developmental implications.* New Directions for Child Development, No. 66. San Francisco: Jossey–Bass.

Habermas, J. (1970). Introductory remarks to a theory of communicative competence. In H.P. Dreitzel (Ed.), *Recent sociology*, No. 2. London: Macmillan.

Haith, M.M., & Benson, J.B. (1998). Infant cognition. In W. Damon (Ed.), *Handbook of child psychology*, vol. 2 (D. Kuhn & R.S. Siegler, Eds.). New York: Wiley.

Hala, S., & Carpendale, J. (1997). All in the mind: children's understanding of mental life. In S. Hala (Ed.), *The development of social cognition.* Hove: Psychology Press.

Halberstadt, A.G., Dunsmore, J.C., & Denham, S.A. (2001). Affective social competence. *Social Development, 10,* 79–119.

Halliday, M. (1975). *Learning how to mean.* London: Arnold.

Hall, G.S. (1922). *Senescence: the last half of life.* New York: D. Appleton.

Hamilton, W.D. (1964). The genetic evolution of social behaviour. *Journal of Theoretical Biology, 7,* 1–52.

Harkness, S., & Super, C.M. (1992). Parental ethnotheories in action. In I.E. Sigel, A.V. McGillicuddy-DeLisi, & J.J. Goodnow (Eds.), *Parental belief systems: consequences for children,* (2nd ed.). Hillsdale, NJ: Erlbaum.

Harkness, S., & Super, C.H. (1996). *Parents' cultural belief systems: their origins, expressions and consequences.* New York: Guilford.

Harris, J.R. (1995). Where is the child's environment? A group socialization theory of development. *Psychological Review, 102,* 458–489.

Harris, J.R. (1998). *The nurture assumption: why children turn out the way they do.* New York: Free Press.

Harris, P.L. (1989). *Children and emotions.* Oxford: Blackwell.

Harris, P.L. (1992). From simulation to folk psychology: the case for development. *Mind and Language, 7,* 120–144.

Harris, P.L. (1994). Thinking by children and scientists: false analogies and neglected similarities. In L.A. Hirschfeld & S.A. Gelman (Eds.), *Mapping the mind.* Cambridge: Cambridge University Press.

Harter, S. (1998). The development of self-representations. In W. Damon (Ed.), *Handbook of child psychology*, vol. 3 (N. Eisenberg, Ed.). New York: Wiley.

Harter, S. (1999). *The construction of the self: a developmental perspective.* New York: Guilford Press.

Hartup, W.W. (1989). Social relationships and their developmental significance. *American Psychologist, 44,* 120–126.

Hattie, J., & Marsh, H.W. (1996). Future directions in self-concept research. In B.A. Bracken (Ed.), *Handbook of self-concept.* New York: Wiley.

Heider, F. (1958). *The psychology of interpersonal relationships.* New York: Wiley.

Helwig, C.C., & Turiel, E. (2002). Children's social and moral reasoning. In P.K. Smith & C.H. Hart (Eds.), *Blackwell handbook of childhood social development*. Oxford: Blackwell.

Hetherington, E.M., Reiss, D., & Plomin, R. (Eds.) (1994). *Separate social worlds of siblings*. Hillsdale, NJ: Erlbaum.

Higgins, E.T. (1991). Development of self-regulators and self-evaluative processes: costs, benefits and tradeoffs. In M.R. Gunnar & L.A. Sroufe (Eds.), *Self processes and development*. Hillsdale, NJ: Erlbaum.

Hinde, R.A. (1979). *Towards understanding relationships*. London: Academic Press.

Hinde, R.A. (1982). *Ethology: its nature and relation to other sciences*. Oxford: Oxford University Press.

Hinde, R.A. (1992). Human social development: an ethological/relationship perspective. In H. McGurk (Ed.), *Childhood social development: contemporary perspectives*. Hillsdale, NJ: Erlbaum.

Hinde, R.A. (1997). *Relationships: a dialectical perspective*. Hove: Psychology Press.

Hirschfeld, L.A., & Gelman, S.A. (Eds.) (1994). *Mapping the mind: domain specificity in cognition and culture*. Cambridge: Cambridge University Press.

Hoff, E. (2001). *Language Development* (2nd ed.). Belmont, CA: Wadsworth.

Hoff-Ginsberg, E., & Shatz, M. (1982). Linguistic input and the child's acquisition of language. *Psychological Bulletin, 92*, 3–26.

Hoffman, M.L. (1975). Moral internalisation, parental power and the nature of parent–child interaction. *Developmental Psychology, 11*, 228–239.

Hoffman, M.L. (1977). Moral internalisation: current theory and research. In L. Berkowitz (Ed.), *Advances in experimental social psychology*, vol. 10. New York: Academic Press.

Hoffman, M.L. (1988). Moral development. In M.H. Bornstein & M.E. Lamb (Eds.), *Developmental psychology: an advanced textbook* (2nd ed). Hillsdale, NJ: Erlbaum.

Hofstede, G. (1980). (2nd ed. 2001) *Culture's consequences: comparing values, behaviors, institutions and organizations across nations*. Beverly Hills, CA: Sage.

Hofstede, G. (1991). *Cultures and organizations: software of the mind*. London: McGraw–Hill.

Hofstede, G. (1994). Foreword. In U. Kim, H.C. Triandis, C. Kagitcibasi, S-C. Choi, & G. Yoon (Eds.), *Individualism and collectivism: theory, methods and applications*. Thousand Oaks, CA: Sage.

Holden, G.W., & Buck, M.J. (2002). Parental attitudes towards child rearing. In M.H. Bornstein (Ed.), *Handbook of parenting*, vol. 3 (2nd ed.). Mahwah, NJ: Erlbaum.

Holland Joyner, M., & Kurtz-Costes, B. (1997). Metamemory development. In N. Cowan (Ed.), *The development of memory in childhood*. Hove: Psychology Press.

Hubbard, J.A., & Coie, J.D. (1994). Emotional correlates of social competence in young children's peer relationships. *Merrill–Palmer Quarterly, 40*, 1–20.

Hudson, J.A. (1993). Understanding events: the development of script knowledge. In M. Bennett (Ed.), *The child as psychologist: an introduction to the development of social cognition*. Hemel Hempstead: Harvester Wheatsheaf.

Huesmann, L.R., Eron, L.D., & Lefkowitz, M.M. (1984). Stability of aggression over time and generations. *Developmental Psychology, 20*, 1120–1134.

Hughes, C., & Leekam, S. (2004). What are the links between theory of mind and social relations? Review, reflections and new directions for studies of typical and atypical development. *Social Development, 13*, 590–619.

Hunt, J. McV. (1961). *Intelligence and experience*. New York: Ronald Press.

Hymel, S., Vaillancourt, T., McDougall, P., & Renshaw, P.D. (2002). Peer acceptance and rejection in childhood. In P.K. Smith & C.H. Hart (Eds.), *Blackwell handbook of childhood social development*. Oxford: Blackwell.

Hymes, D. (1967). Models of the interaction of language and social setting. *Journal of Social Issues, 23*, 8–28.

Hymes, D. (1972). On communicative competence. In J.B. Pride & J. Homes (Eds), *Sociolinguistics*. Baltimore, MD: Penguin.

Jakobson, R. (1941). *Kindersprache* [Child language]. Stockholm: Almqvist & Wiksell.

James, W. (1890). *The principles of psychology*. New York: Holt.

Johnson, M.H. (1997). *Developmental cognitive neuroscience*. Oxford: Blackwell.

Johnson, M.H. (1999). Cortical plasticity in normal and abnormal cognitive development: evidence and working hypotheses. *Development and Psychopathology, 11*, 419–437.

Johnson, M.H., Munakata, Y., & Gilmore, R.O. (Eds) (2002). *Brain development and cognition: a reader*. Oxford: Blackwell.

Jones, E.E., & Davis, K.E. (1965). From acts to dispositions: the attribution process in person perception. In L. Berkowitz (Ed.), *Advances in experimental social psychology*, vol. 2. New York: Academic Press.

Kagan, J. (1997). Temperament and the reactions to the unfamiliar. *Child Development, 68*, 139–143.

Kagan, J., Snidman, N., & Arcus, D. (1998). Childhood derivatives of high and low reactivity in infancy. *Child Development, 69*, 1483–1493.

Kagitcibasi, C. (1994). A critical appraisal of individualism and collectivism: toward a new formulation. In U. Kim, H. Triandis, C. Kagitcibasi, S-C. Choi & C. Yoon (Eds.) *Individualism and collectivism: theory, method and application*. Thousand Oaks, CA: Sage.

Karmiloff-Smith, A. (1992). *Beyond modularity: a developmental perspective on cognitive science*. Cambridge, MA: MIT Press.

Kaye, K. (1982). *The mental and social life of babies: how parents create persons*. Brighton: Harvester.

Kearins, J.M. (1986). Visual and spatial memory in Aboriginal and white Australian children. *Australian Journal of Psychology, 38*, 203–214.

Keil, F.C. (2002). Cognition, content and development. In M. Bennett (Ed.), *Developmental psychology: achievements and prospects*. Philadelphia, PA: Psychology Press.

Kelley, H.H. (1973). The process of causal attribution. *American Psychologist, 28*, 107–128.

Kendler, K.S., Kessler, R.C., Walters, E.D., MacLean, C., Neale, M.C., Heath, C., & Eaves, L.J. (1995). Stressful life events, genetic liability and the onset of an episode of major depression in women. *American Journal of Psychiatry, 152*, 833–842.

Killen, M., Lee-Kim, J., McGlothlin, H., & Stangor, C. (2002). How children and adolescents evaluate gender and racial exclusion. *Monographs of the Society for Research in Child Development, 67*, no. 4, Serial no. 271.

Kim, U., Triandis, H., Kagitcibasi, C., Choi, S-C., & Yoon, C. (Eds.) (1994) *Individualism and collectivism: theory, method and application*. Thousand Oaks, CA: Sage.

Kim-Cohen, J., Moffitt, T.E., Caspi, A., & Taylor, A. (2004). Genetic and environmental processes in young children's resilience and vulnerability to socio-economic deprivation. *Child Development, 75*, 651–668.

Kitchener, R.F. (1978). Epigenesis: the role of biological models in developmental psychology. *Human Development, 21*, 141–160.

Klahr, D. (1982). Nonmonotone assessment of monotone development: an information processing analysis. In S. Strauss (Ed.), *U-shaped behavioral growth*. New York: Academic Press.

Klahr, D., & MacWhinney, B. (1998). In R. Vasta (Ed.), *Annals of child development*, vol. 6. Greenwich, CT: JAI.

Klaus, M.H., & Kennell, J.H. (1976). *Parent–infant bonding*. St Louis: Mosby.

Klaus, M.H., Kennell, J.H., & Klaus, Z. (1995). *Bonding*. New York: Addison–Wesley.

Kochanska, G. (1997). Multiple pathways to conscience for children with different temperaments: from toddlerhood to age 5. *Developmental Psychology, 33*, 228–240.

Kochanska, G., & Thompson, R.A. (1997). The emergence and development of conscience in toddlerhood and early childhood. In J.E. Grusec & L. Kuczynski (Eds.), *Parenting and children's internalization of values*. New York: Wiley.

Kochanska, G., Aksan, N., & Koenig, A.L. (1995). A longitudinal study of the roots of preschoolers' conscience: committed compliance and emerging internalisation. *Child Development, 66*, 852–868.

Kochanska, G., Coy, K.C., & Murray, K.T. (2001). The development of self-regulation in the first four years of life. *Child Development, 72*, 1091–1111.

Kohlberg, L. (1966). A cognitive developmental analysis of children's sex role concepts and attitudes. In E.E. Maccoby (Ed.), *The development of sex differences*. Stanford, CA: Stanford University Press.

Kohlberg, L. (1969). Stage and sequence: the cognitive-developmental approach to socialization. In D.A. Goslin (Ed.), *Handbook of socialization theory and research*. Chicago: Rand–McNally.

Kolb, B., & Wishaw, I.Q. (1998). Brain plasticity and behaviour. *Annual Review, 49*, 43–64.

Kopp, C.B. (1982). Antecedents of self-regulation: a developmental perspective. *Developmental Psychology, 18*, 199–214.

Kruuk, H. (2003) *Niko's nature: a life of Niko Tinbergen and the science of animal behaviour*. Oxford: Oxford University Press.

Kuczynski, L. (2003a). *Handbook of dynamics in parent–child relations*. Thousand Oaks, CA: Sage.

Kuczynski, L. (2003b). Beyond bidirectionality. In L. Kuczynski (Ed.), *Handbook of dynamics in parent–child relations*. Thousand Oaks, CA: Sage.

Kuczynski, L., & Kochanska, G. (1990). Development of children's noncompliance strategies from toddlerhood to age 5. *Developmental Psychology, 26*, 398–408.

Kuo, Z-Y. (1967). *The dynamics of behavior development* (rev. ed.). New York: Random House.

Ladd, G.W. (1999). Peer relationships and social competence during early and middle childhood. *Annual Review of Psychology, 50*, 333–359.

Ladd, G.W., Buhs, E.S., & Troop, W. (2002). Children's interpersonal skills and relationships in school settings. In P.K. Smith & C.H. Hart (Eds.), *Blackwell handbook of childhood social development*. Oxford: Blackwell.

Laible, D.J., & Thompson, R.A. (2000). Attachment and self-organization. In M.D. Lewis and I. Granic (Eds.), *Emotion, development and self-organization: dynamic systems approaches to emotional development*. Cambridge: Cambridge University Press.

Laursen, B., Pulkkinen, L., & Adams, R. (2002). The antecedents and correlates of agreeableness in adulthood. *Developmental Psychology, 38*, 591–603.

Lawrence, J.A., & Valsiner, J. (1993). Conceptual roots of internalization: from transmission to transformation. *Human Development, 36*, 150–167.

Lempers, J.D., Flavell, E.R., & Flavell, J.H. (1977). The development in very young children of tacit knowledge concerning visual perception. *Genetic Psychology Monographs, 95*, 3–53.

Lenneberg, E.H. (1967). *Biological foundations of language*. New York: Wiley

Leslie, A.M. (1988). The necessity of illusion: perception and thought in infancy. In L.Weiskrantz (Ed.), *Thought without language*. Oxford: Clarendon Press.

Leslie, A.M. (1994). ToMM, ToBY and agency. In L. Hirschfeld & S. Gelman (Eds.), *Mapping the mind: domain specificity in cognition and culture*. Cambridge: Cambridge University Press.

Levin, J.D. (1992). *Theories of the self*. Washington, DC: Taylor & Francis.

LeVine, R., Dixon, S., LeVine, S., Richman, A., Leiderman, P.H., Keefer, C.H., & Brazelton, T.B. (1994). *Child care and culture: lessons from Africa*. Cambridge: Cambridge University Press.

Lewis, M. (1994) Myself and me. In S.T. Parker, R.W. Mitchell & M.L. Boccia (Eds.), *Self-awareness in animals and humans*. Cambridge: Cambridge University Press.

Lewis, M.D. (2000). The promise of dynamic systems approaches for an integrated account of human development. *Child Development, 71*, 36–43.

Lewis, M.D., & Granic, I. (Eds.) (2000) *Emotion, development and self-organization: dynamic systems approaches to emotional development*. Cambridge: Cambridge University Press.

Lieven, E.V.M. (1994). Crosslinguistic and crosscultural aspects of language addressed to children. In C. Gallaway & B.J. Richards (Eds.), *Input and interaction in language acquisition*. Cambridge: Cambridge University Press.

Light, P., & Butterworth, G. (Eds.) (1992). *Context and cognition*. London: Harvester.

Locke, J. (1693). *Some thoughts concerning education* (4th ed.). London: A. & J. Churchill.

Locke, J.L. (1993). *The child's path to spoken language*. Cambridge, MA: Harvard University Press.

Lorenz, K. (1935). Der Kumpan in der Umwelt des Vogels [the companion in the experience of birds]. *Journal fur Ornithologie, 83*, 137–213, 289–413.

Lorenz, K. (1950). The comparative method in studying innate behaviour patterns. *Symposium of the Society for Experimental Biology, 4*, 221–268.

Lorenz, K. (1965). *Evolution and the modification of behaviour*. London: Methuen.

Maccoby, E.E., & Martin, J.A. (1983). Socialization in the context of the family: parent–child interaction. In P.H. Mussen (Ed.), *Handbook of child psychology*, vol. IV. New York: Wiley.

Mandler, J. (1998). Representation. In W. Damon (Ed.), *Handbook of child psychology*, vol. 2 (D. Kuhn & R.S. Siegler, Eds.). New York: Wiley.

Marcia, J.E. (1999). Representational thought in ego identity, psychotherapy and psychosocial developmental theory. In I.E. Siegel (Ed.), *Development of mental representation: theories and applications*. Mahwah, NJ: Erlbaum.

Mareschal, D. (2000). Connectionist modelling and infant development. In D. Muir & A. Slater (Eds.), *Infant development: essential readings*. Oxford: Blackwell.

Mareschal, D., Johnson, M.H., & Grayson, A. (2004). Brain and cognitive development. In J. Oates & A. Grayson (Eds.), *Cognitive and language development in children*. Oxford: Blackwell.

Markus, H. (1980). The self in thought and memory. In D.M. Wegner & R.R. Vallacher (Eds.). *The self in social psychology*. New York: Oxford University Press.

Markus, H.R., & Kitayama, S. (1991). Culture and the self: implications for cognition, emotion and motivation. *Psychological Review, 98*, 224–253.

Marsh, H.W. (1990). A multidimensional, hierarchical model of self-concept: theoretical and empirical justification. *Educational Psychology Review, 2*, 77–172.

Marsh, H.W., & Hattie, J. (1996). Theoretical perspectives on the structure of self-concept. In B.A. Bracken (Ed.), *Handbook of self-concept*. New York: Wiley.

Marsh, H.W., Craven, R., & Debus, R. (1998). Structure, stability and development of young children's self-concepts: a multicohort, multioccasion study. *Child Development, 69*, 1030–1053.

Martin, J.N., & Fox, N.A. (2006). Temperament. In K. McCartney & D. Phillips (Eds.), *Blackwell handbook of early childhood development*. Oxford: Blackwell.

Masataka, N. (1993). Motherese is a signed language. *Infant Behavior and Development, 15*, 453–460.

Masten, A.S., Best, K.M., & Garmezy, N. (1990). Resilience and development: contributions from the study of children who overcome adversity. *Development and Psychopathology, 2*, 425–444.

Masten, A.S., & Gewirtz, A.H. (2006) Vulnerability and resilience in early child development. In K. McCartney & D. Phillips (Eds.), *Blackwell handbook of early childhood development*. Oxford: Blackwell.

Masur, E.F., Flynn, V., & Eichorst, D.L. (2005). Maternal responsive and directive behaviours and utterances as predictors of children's lexical development. *Journal of Child Language, 32,* 63–91.

McClelland, J.L., Rumelhart, D.E., & PDP Research Group (Eds.) (1986). *Parallel distributed processing: explorations in the microstructure of cognition,* vol. 2: *Psychological and biological models.* Cambridge, MA: MIT Press.

Mead, G.H. (1934). *Mind, self and society from the standpoint of a social behaviorist.* Chicago: University of Chicago Press.

Mead, M. (1967). *Cooperation and competition among primitive peoples.* Boston, MA: Beacon Press.

Meichenbaum, D., Butler, L., & Gruson, L. (1981). Toward a conceptual model of social competence. In J.D. Wine & M.D. Smye (Eds.), *Social competence.* New York: Guilford.

Meltzoff, A.N. (2004). The case for developmental cognitive science: theories of people and things. In G. Bremner & A. Slater (Eds.), *Theories of infant development.* Oxford: Blackwell.

Meltzoff, A.N., & Moore, M.K. (1994). Imitation, memory and the representation of persons. *Infant Behavior and Development, 17,* 83–99.

Mendel, G. (1866). Versuch uber Pflanzenhybriden [experiment with plant hybrids]. *Verhandlungen des Naturforschunden Vereins in Bruenn, 4,* 3–47.

Mercer, N. (1992). Culture, context and the construction of knowledge in the classroom. In P. Light & G. Butterworth (Eds.), *Context and cognition: ways of learning and knowing.* Hemel Hempstead: Harvester Wheatsheaf.

Messer, D.J. (1994). *The development of communication: from social interaction to language.* Chichester: Wiley.

Messinger, D.S., & Fogel, A. (1998). Give and take: the development of infant gestures. *Merrill–Palmer Quarterly, 44,* 566–590.

Metzinger, T. (2003). *Being no one: the self-model theory of subjectivity.* Cambridge, MA: MIT Press.

Miller J.G., & Bersoff, D.M. (1995). Development in the context of everyday family relationships: culture, interpersonal morality and adaptation. In M. Killen & D. Hart (Eds.), *Morality in everyday life: developmental perspectives.* Cambridge: Cambridge University Press.

Miller, L.C., Lechner, R.C., & Rugs, D. (1985). Development of conversational responsiveness. *Developmental Psychology, 21,* 473–480.

Miller, P.H. (2002). *Theories of developmental psychology* (4th edn.). New York: Worth Publishers.

Miller, P.H., & Aloise, P.A. (1989). Young children's understanding of the psychological causes of behavior: a review. *Child Development, 60,* 257–285.

Miller, S.A. (1988). Parents' beliefs about children's cognitive development. *Child Development, 59,* 259–285.

Miller, S.A. (1995). Parents' attributions for their children's behavior. *Child Development, 66,* 1557–1584.

Mitchell, P. (1997). *Introduction to theory of mind.* London: Arnold.

Mize, J., Pettit, G.S., & Brown, E.G. (1995). Mothers' supervision of their children's peer play: relations with beliefs, perceptions and knowledge. *Developmental Psychology, 31,* 311–321.

Moen, P., Elder, G.H., & Luscher, K. (1995). *Examining lives in context*. Washington, DC: American Psychological Association.

Molfese, V.J., & Molfese, D. (Eds.) (2000). *Temperament and personality development across the life span*. Mahwah, NJ: Erlbaum.

Moore, C., & Dunham, P. (Eds.) (1995). *Joint attention: its origins and role in development*. Hillsdale, NJ: Erlbaum.

Moore, C., & Lemmon, K. (Eds.) (2001). *The self in time: developmental perspectives*. Mahwah, NJ: Erlbaum.

Moreno, J.L. (1934). *Who shall survive? A new approach to the problem of human interrelations*. Washington, DC: Nervous and Mental Disease Publishing Company.

Morgan, J. (1990). Input, innateness and induction in language acquisition. *Developmental Psychobiology, 23*, 661–678.

Murphy, L.B., & Moriarty, A.E. (1976). *Vulnerability, coping and growth: from infancy to adolescence*. New Haven, CT: Yale University Press.

Murray, L. (1991). Intersubjectivity, object relations theory and empirical evidence from mother–infant interactions. *Infant Mental Health Journal, 12*, 219–232.

Myers, B.J. (1984). Mother–infant bonding: the status of this critical period hypothesis. *Developmental Review, 4*, 240–274.

Neisser, U. (1988). Five kinds of self-knowledge. *Philosophical Psychology, 1*, 35–59.

Nelson, C.A. (1997). The neurobiological basis of early memory development. In N. Cowan (Ed.), *The development of memory in childhood*. Hove: Psychology Press.

Nelson, K. (1981). Social cognition in a script framework. In J.H. Flavell, & L. Ross (Eds.), *Social cognitive development: frontiers and possible futures*. New York: Cambridge University Press.

Nelson, K. (Ed.) (1986). *Event knowledge: structure and function in development*. Hillsdale, NJ: Erlbaum.

Nelson, K. (1993a). The psychological and social origins of autobiographical memory. *Psychological Science, 4*, 7–14.

Nelson, K. (1993b). Events, narratives and memory. In C.A. Nelson (Ed.), *Memory and affect*. Hillsdale, NJ: Erlbaum.

Nelson, K., & Gruendel, J. (1979). At morning it's lunchtime: a scriptal view of children's dialogues. *Discourse Processes, 2*, 73–94.

Nesdale, D. (2004). Social identity processes and children's ethnic prejudice. In M. Bennett & F. Sani (Eds.), *The development of the social self*. Hove: Psychology Press.

Neville, H.J., & Bavelier, D. (2002). Specificity and plasticity in neurocognitive development in humans. In M.H. Johnson, Y. Munakata & R.O. Gilmore (Eds.), *Brain development and cognition: a reader* (2nd ed.). Oxford: Blackwell.

Newell, A., (1973). Production systems: models of control structures. In W.G. Chase (Ed.), *Visual information processing*. New York: Academic Press.

Newell, A., & Simon, H. (1972). *Human problem solving*. Englewood Cliffs, NJ: Prentice–Hall.

NICHD Early Child Care Research Network (2004). Trajectories of physical aggression from toddlerhood to middle childhood. *Monographs of the Society for Research in Child Development, 69*, no. 4 (Serial no. 278).

Ninio, A. (1995). Expression of communicative intents in the single-word period and the vocabulary spurt. In K.E. Nelson & Z. Regar (Eds.), *Children's language*, vol. 8. Mahwah, NJ: Erlbaum.

Ninio A., & Snow, C.E. (1999). The development of pragmatics: learning to use language appropriately. In W.C. Ritchie & T.K. Bhatia (Eds.), *Handbook of child language acquisition*. New York: Academic Press.

Nucci, L.P. (1996). Morality and the personal sphere of action. In E. Reed, E. Turiel & T. Brown (Eds.), *Values and knowledge*. Hillsdale, NJ: Erlbaum.

Nucci, L.P. (2002). The development of reasoning. In U. Goswami (Ed.), *Blackwell handbook of childhood cognitive development*. Oxford: Blackwell.

Oakley, K. (2004). *Emotions: a brief history*. Oxford: Blackwell.

Ochs, E., & Schieffelin, B.B. (1984). Language acquisition and socialization: three developmental stories and their implications. In R. Shweder & R. LeVine (Eds.), *Culture theory*. Cambridge: Cambridge University Press.

O'Connor, T.G. (2002a). The 'effects' of parenting reconsidered: findings, challenges and applications. *Journal of Child Psychology and Psychiatry, 43*, 555–572.

O'Connor, T.G. (2002b). Behavioral genetic contributions to understanding dynamic process in parent-child relationships. In L. Kuczynsky (Ed.), *Handbook of dynamics in parent–child relations*. Thousand Oaks, CA: Sage.

O'Connor, T.G., Caspi, A., DeFries, J.C., & Plomin, R. (2003). Genotype-environment interaction in children's adjustment to parental separation. *Journal of Child Psychology and Psychiatry, 44*, 849–856.

Owens, R.E. (2005) *Language development* (6th ed.). Boston, MA: Allyn & Bacon.

Padilla-Walker, L.M., & Thompson, R.A. (2005). Combating conflicting messages of values: a closer look at parental strategies. *Social Development, 14*, 305–323.

Paris, S.G., & Cross, D.R. (1988). The zone of proximal development: virtues and pitfalls of a metaphorical representation of children's learning. *The Genetic Epistemologist, 16*, 27–37.

Parke, R.D., Killian, C.M., Dennis, J., Flyr, M.L., McDowell, D.J., Simpkinds, S., Kim, M., & Wild, M. (2003). Managing the external environment: the parent and child as active agents in the system. In L. Kuczynski (Ed.), *Handbook of dynamics in parent–child relations*. Thousand Oaks, CA: Sage.

Parten, M.B. (1932). Social participation among preschool children. *Journal of Abnormal and Social Psychology, 27*, 243–269.

Perner, J. (1991). *Understanding the representational mind*. Cambridge, MA: MIT Press.

Peterson, C., & Siegal, M. (1995). Deafness, conversation and theory of mind. *Journal of Child Psychology and Psychiatry, 36*, 459–474.

Piaget, J. (1929). *The child's conception of the world*. New York: Harcourt Brace Javanovich.

Piaget, J. (1932). *The moral judgement of the child*. London: Kegan Paul.

Piaget, J. (1951). *Play, dreams and imitation*. London: Routledge & Kegan Paul.

Piaget, J. (1952). *The origins of intelligence in children*. New York: Norton.

Piaget, J. (1954). *The construction of reality in the child*. New York: Basic Books.

Piaget, J. (1955). *The language and thought of the child*. New York: Meridian Books.

Piaget, J. (1972). *The principles of genetic epistemology*. London: Routledge & Kegan Paul.

Piaget, J. (1985). *The equilibration of cognitive structures: the central problem of intellectual development*. Chicago: University of Chicago Press.

Pinker, S. (1994). *The language instinct*. London: Penguin.

Pinker, S. (1997). *How the mind works*. London: Penguin.

Pinker, S. (2002). *The blank slate: the modern denial of human nature*. London: Allen Lane.

Pipp, S. (1993). Infants' knowledge of self, other and relationships. In U. Neisser (Ed.), *The perceived self*. Cambridge: Cambridge University Press.

Plomin, R. (1994). *Genetics and experience: the interplay between nature and nurture*. Thousand Oakes, CA: Sage.

Plomin, R., & Daniels, D. (1987). Why are children in the same family so different from each other? *Behavioral and Brain Sciences, 10*, 1–16.

Plomin, R., DeFries, J.C., McClearn, G.E., & McGuffin, P. (2001). *Behavioral genetics* (4th ed.). New York: Worth.

Plunkett, K. (1995). Connectionist approaches to language acquisition. In P. Fletcher & B. MacWhinney (Eds.), *The handbook of child language*. Oxford: Blackwell.

Plunkett, K. (2000). Development in a connectionist framework: rethinking the nature–nurture debate. In K. Lee (Ed.), *Childhood cognitive development: the essential readings*. Oxford: Blackwell.

Plunkett, K., Karmiloff-Smith, A., Bates, E., Elman, J., & Johnson, M.H. (1997). Connectionism and development psychology. *Journal of Child Psychology and Psychiatry*, *38*, 53–80.

Premack, D., & Woodruff, G. (1978). Does the chimpanzee have a theory of mind? *Behavioral and Brain Sciences*, *1*, 515–526.

Quinlan, P.T. (Ed.) (2003). *Connectionist models of development: developmental processes in real and artificial networks*. Hove: Psychology Press.

Reddy, V. (1999). Prelinguistic communication. In M. Barrett (Ed.), *The development of language*. Hove: Psychology Press.

Reddy, V., Hay, D., Murray, L., & Trevarthen, C. (1997). Communication in infancy: mutual regulation of affect and attention. In G. Bremner, A. Slater & G. Butterworth (Eds.), *Infant development: recent advances*. Hove: Psychology Press.

Reese, E. (2002). Autobiographical memory development: the state of the art. *Social Development*, *11*, 124–142.

Rhee, E., Uleman, J.S., & Lee, H.K. (1996). Variations in collectivism and individualism by ingroup and culture: confirmatory factor analysis. *Journal of Personality and Social Psychology*, *71*, 1037–1054.

Rode, S.S., Chang, P.N., Fisch, R.O., & Sroule, L.A. (1981). Attachment patterns of infants separated at birth. *Development Psychology*, *17*, 188–191.

Rogoff, B. (1990). *Apprenticeship in thinking: cognitive development in social context*. Oxford: Oxford University Press.

Rogoff, B. (1998). Cognition as a collaborative process. In W. Damon (Ed.), *Handbook of child psychology*, vol. 2 (D. Kuhn & R.S. Siegler, Eds.). New York: Wiley.

Rogoff, B. (2003). *The cultural nature of human development*. Oxford: Oxford University Press.

Rogoff, B., Mistry, J., Goncu, A., & Mosier, C. (1993). Guided participation in cultural activities by toddlers and caregivers. *Monographs of the Society for Research in Child Development*, *58*, no. 8 (Serial no. 236).

Rose, H., & Rose, S. (Eds.) (2000). *Alas, poor Darwin: arguments against evolutionary psychology*. New York: Harmony Books.

Rose-Krasnor, L. (1997). The nature of social competence: a theoretical review. *Social Development*, *6*, 111–135.

Rothbart, M.K., & Bates, J.E. (1998). Temperament. In W. Damon (Ed.), *Handbook of child psychology*, vol. 3, (N. Eisenberg, Ed.). New York: Wiley.

Rousseau, J.J. (1762/1948). *Emile, or education*. London: J.M. Dent.

Rowe, D.C., & Plomin, R. (1981). The importance of nonshared environmental influences in behavioural development. *Developmental Psychology*, *17*, 517–531.

Rowe, S.M., & Wertsch, J.W. (2002). Vygotsky's model of cognitive development. In U. Goswami (Ed.), *Blackwell handbook of childhood cognitive development*. Oxford: Blackwell.

Rubin, K.H., Bukowski, W., & Parker, J.G. (1998). Peer interactions, relationships, and groups. In W. Damon (Ed.), *Handbook of child psychology*, vol. 3 (N. Eisenberg, Ed.). New York: Wiley.

Rubin, K.H., Burgess, K.B., & Coplan, R.J. (2002). Social withdrawal and shyness. In P.K. Smith & C.H. Hart (Eds.), *Blackwell handbook of childhood social development*. Oxford: Blackwell.

Ruble, D., & Martin, C. (1998). Gender development. In W. Damon (Ed.), *Handbook of child psychology*, vol. 3 (N. Eisenberg, Ed.). New York: Wiley.

Ruble, D., Alavarez, J., Bachman, M., Cameron, J., Fuligni, A., Coll, C.G., & Rhee, E. (2004). In M. Bennett & F. Sani (Eds.), *The development of the social self*. Hove: Psychology Press.

Rummelhart, D.D., McClelland, J.L., & PDP Research Group (Eds.) (1986). *Parallel distribution processing: explorations in the microstructure of cognition*, vol. 1: *Foundations*. Cambridge, MA: MIT Press.

Russell, A., & Russell, G. (1992). Child effects in socialization research: some conceptual and data analysis issues. *Social Development, 1*, 163–184.

Russell, A., Mize, J., & Bissaker, K. (2002). Parent–child relationships. In P.K. Smith & C.H. Hart (Eds.), *Blackwell handbook of childhood social development*. Oxford: Blackwell.

Rutter, M. (1987a). Continuities and discontinuities from infancy. In J.D. Osofsky (Ed.), *Handbook of infant development* (2nd ed.). New York: Wiley.

Rutter, M. (1987b). Psychosocial resilience and protective mechanisms. *American Journal of Othopsychiatry, 57*, 316–331

Rutter, M. (1996). Transitions and turning points in developmental psychopathology: as applied to the age span between childhood and mid-adulthood. *International Journal of Behavioral Development, 19*, 603–626.

Rutter, M. (1999). Autism: a two-way interplay between research and clinical practice. *Journal of Child Psychology and Psychiatry, 40*, 169–188.

Rutter, M. (2002). Nature, nurture and development: from evangelism through science toward policy and practice. *Child Development, 73*, 1–21.

Rutter, M., & the English and Romanian Adoptees (ERA) Study Team (1998). Developmental catch-up and deficit following adoption after severe early privation. *Journal of Child Psychology and Psychiatry, 39*, 465–476.

Rutter, M., Kreppner, J.M., & O'Connor, T.G. (2001). Specificity and heterogeneity in children's responses to profound institutional privation. *British Journal of Psychiatry, 179*, 97–103.

Rutter, M., Quinton, D., & Hill, D.J. (1990). Adult outcome of institution-reared children: males and females compared. In L.N. Robins & M. Rutter (Eds.), *Straight and devious pathways from childhood to adulthood*. Cambridge: Cambridge University Press.

Rutter, M., & Rutter, M. (1993). *Developing minds: challenge and continuity across the life span*. London: Penguin.

Rutter, M., & Schopler, E. (1987). Autism and pervasive developmental disorders: concepts and diagnostic issues. *Journal of Autism and Developmental Disorders, 17*, 159–186.

Saarni, C. (1984). An observational study of children's attempts to monitor their expressive behavior. *Child Development, 55*, 1504–1531.

Saarni, C. (1999). *The development of emotional competence*. New York: Guilford Press.

Sameroff, A. (1975). Transactional models in early social relations. *Human Development, 18*, 65–79.

Sanson, C., Hemphill, S.A., & Smart, D. (2002). Temperament and social development. In P.K. Smith & C.H. Hart (Eds.), *Blackwell handbook of childhood social development*. Oxford: Blackwell.

Sanson, A., Hemphill, S.A., & Smart, D. (2004). Connections between temperament and social development: a review. *Social Development, 13*, 142–170.

Scarr, S. (1992). Developmental theories for the 1990s: development and individual differences. *Child Development, 63*, 1–19.

Scarr, S., & McCartney, K. (1983). How people make their own environments: a theory of genotype-environmental effects. *Child Development, 54*, 424–435.

Schaffer, H.R. (1977). *Studies in mother–infant interaction*. London: Academic Press.

Schaffer, H.R. (1979). Acquiring the concept of the dialogue. In M.H. Bornstein & W. Kessen (Eds.), *Psychological development from infancy: image to intention*. Hillsdale, NJ: Erlbaum.

Schaffer, H.R. (1984). *The child's entry into a social world*. London: Academic Press.

Schaffer, H.R. (1989). Language development in context. In S. von Tetzchner, L.S. Siegel & L. Smith (Eds.), *The social and cognitive aspects of normal and atypical language development*. New York: Springer-Verlag.

Schaffer, H.R. (1992). Joint involvement episodes as context for development. In H. McGurk (Ed.), *Childhood social development*. Hove: Erlbaum.

Schaffer, H.R. (1996). *Social development*. Oxford: Blackwell.

Schaffer, H.R. (1999). Understanding socialization: from unidirectional to bidirectional conceptions. In M. Bennett (Ed.), *Developmental psychology: achievements and prospects*. London: Psychology Press.

Schaffer, H.R. (2002). The early experience assumption: past, present and future. In W. Hartup & R. Silbereisen (Eds.), *Growing points in developmental science*. Hove: Psychology Press.

Schaffer, H.R. (2004). *Introducing child psychology*. Blackwell: Oxford.

Schaffer, H.R., & Crook, C.K. (1980). Child compliance and maternal control techniques. *Developmental Psychology, 16*, 54–61.

Schaffer, H.R., & Emerson, P.E. (1964). The development of social attachments in infancy. *Monographs of the Society for Research in Child Development, 29*, no. 3, Serial no. 94.

Schaffer, H.R., Collis, G.M., & Parsons, G. (1977). Vocal interchange and visual regard in verbal and pre-verbal children. In H.R. Schaffer (Ed.), *Studies in mother–infant interaction*. London: Academic Press.

Schaffer, H.R., Hepburn, A., & Collis, G. (1983). Verbal and nonverbal aspects of mothers' directives. *Child Language, 10*, 337–355.

Schaie, K.W. (2002). The impact of longitudinal studies on understanding development from young adulthood to old age. In W.W. Hartup and R.K. Silbereisen (Eds.), *Growing points in developmental psychology*. Hove: Psychology Press.

Schank, R.C., & Abelson, R.P. (1977). *Scripts, plans, goals and understanding*. Hillsdale, NJ: Erlbaum.

Schiefelbusch R.L. (1986). *Language competence: assessment and intervention*. London: Taylor & Francis.

Schiefelbusch, R.L., & Pickar, J. (Eds.) (1984). *The acquisition of communicative competence*. Baltimore: University Park Press.

Schneider, W., & Pressley, M. (1997). *Memory development between 2 and 20* (2nd ed.). Mahwah, NJ: Erlbaum.

Schneirla, T.C. (1957). The concept of development in comparative psychology. In D.B. Harris (Ed.), *The concept of development*. Minneapolis: University of Minnesota Press.

Searle, J. (1969). *Speech acts: an essay in the philosophy of language*. Cambridge: Cambridge University Press.

Sears, R.R., Maccoby, E.E., & Levin, H. (1957). *Patterns of child rearing*. Evanston, IL: Row, Peterson.

Seligman, M.E.P. (1975). *Helplessness: on depression, development and death*. San Francisco: W.H. Freeman.

Sellers, R.M., Shelton, J.M., Cooke, D., Chavours, T.M., Rowley, S., & Smith, M. (1998). A multidimensional model of racial identity: assumptions, findings and future directions.

In R.L. Jones (Ed.), *African American identity development: theory, research and intervention*. Hampton, VA: Cobb and Henry.

Shatz, M., & Gelman, R. (1973). The development of communication skills: modifications in the speech of young children as a function of listener. *Monographs of the Society for Research in Child Development, 38*, no. 5, Serial no.152.

Shimizu, H., & LeVine, R.A. (Eds.) (2001). *Japanese frames of mind: cultural perspectives on human development*. Cambridge: Cambridge University Press.

Shiner, R., & Caspi, A. (2003). Personality differences in childhood and adolescence: measurement, development and consequences. *Journal of Child Psychology and Psychiatry, 44*, 2–32.

Shwe, H.I., & Markman, E.M. (1997). Young children's appreciation of the mental impact of their communicative signals. *Developmental Psychology, 33*, 630–636.

Siegler, R.S. (1996). *Emerging minds: the process of change in children's thinking*. New York: Oxford University Press.

Siegler, R.S. (1998). *Children's thinking* (3rd ed.). Upper Saddle River, NJ: Prentice–Hall.

Sigel, I.E. (Ed.) (1985). *Parental belief systems: the psychological consequences for children*. Hillsdale, NJ: Erlbaum.

Sigel, I.E. (Ed.) (1999). *Development of mental representation: theories and applications*. Mahwah, NJ: Erlbaum.

Sigel, I.E., & McGillicuddy-DeLisi, A.V. (2002). Parental beliefs and cognitions: the dynamic belief systems model. In M.H. Bornstein (Ed.), *Handbook of parenting*, vol. 3 (2nd edn.). Mahwah, NJ: Erlbaum.

Sigman, M., & Kasari, C. (1995). Joint attention across contexts in normal and autistic children. In C. Moore & P.J. Dunham (Eds.), *Joint attention: its origins and role in development*. Hillsdale, NJ: Erlbaum.

Skinner, B.F. (1957). *Verbal behavior*. New York: Appleton–Century–Crofts.

Slater, A., Carrick, R., Bell, C., & Roberts, E. (1999). Can measures of information processing predict intellectual ability? In A. Slater & D. Muir (Eds.), *The Blackwell reader in developmental psychology*. Oxford: Blackwell.

Slater, P.J.B. (1985). *An introduction to ethology*. Cambridge: Cambridge University Press.

Slobin, D.I. (1986). Cross-linguistic evidence for the language-making capacity. In D.I. Slobin (Ed.), *The cross-linguistic study of language acquisition*. Hillsdale, NJ: Erlbaum.

Slomkowski, D.L., Nelson, K., Dunn, J., & Plomin, R. (1992). Temperament and language: relations from toddlerhood to middle childhood. *Developmental Psychology, 28*, 1090–1095.

Sluckin, W. (1972). *Imprinting and early learning* (2nd ed.). London: Methuen.

Sluckin, W., Herbert, M., & Sluckin, A. (1983). *Maternal bonding*. Oxford: Blackwell.

Smetana, J. (1993). Understanding of social rules. In M. Bennett (Ed.), *The development of social cognition*. New York: Guilford.

Smith, J., & Baltes, P.B. (1999). Life-span perspectives on development. In M.H. Bornstein & M.E. Lamb (Eds.), *Developmental psychology: an advanced textbook* (4th ed.). Mahwah, NJ: Erlbaum.

Smith, L. (2002). Piaget's model. In U. Goswami (Ed.), *Blackwell handbook of childhood cognitive development*. Oxford: Blackwell.

Smith, L.B. (1995). Self-organizing processes in learning to learn words. In C.A. Nelson (Ed.), *New perspectives on learning and development*. Minnesota Symposium on Child Psychology, vol. 28. New York: Academic Press.

Smith, P.K. (1990). Ethology, socio-biology and developmental psychology: in memory of Niko Tinbergen and Konrad Lorenz. *British Journal of Developmental Psychology, 8*, 187–200.

Smith, P.K., & Connolly, K. (1972). Patterns of play and social interaction in preschool children. In N.G. Blurton-Jones (Ed.), *Ethological studies of child behaviour*. Cambridge: Cambridge University Press.

Snow, C.E. (1972). Mothers' speech to children learning language. *Child Development, 43*, 549–565.

Snow, C.E. (1994). Issues in the study of input: fine tuning, universality, individual and developmental differences and necessary causes. In P. Fletcher & B. MacWhinney (Eds.), *The handbook of child language*. Oxford: Blackwell.

Snow, C.E., Pan, B.A., Imbens-Bailey, A., & Herman, J. (1996). Learning how to say what one means: a longitudinal study of children's speech act use. *Social Development, 5*, 56–84.

Sodian, B., & Schneider, W. (1999). Memory strategy development: gradual increase, sudden insight or roller coaster? In F.E. Weinert & W. Schneider (Eds.), *Individual development from 3 to 12: findings from the Munich Longitudinal Study*. Cambridge: Cambridge University Press.

Soh, S., & Leong, F.T.L. (2002). Validity of vertical and horizontal individualism and collectivisim in Singapore. *Journal of Cross-Cultural Psychology, 33*, 3–15.

Spalding, D.A. (1873). Instinct, with original observations on young animals. *Macmillan's Magazine, 27*, 282–293.

Spelke, E.S. (1991). Physical knowledge in infancy: reflections on Piaget's theory. In S. Carey & R. Gelman (Eds.), *The epigenesis of mind: essays in biology and cognition*. Hillsdale, NJ: Erlbaum

Spelke, E.S., & Newport, E.L. (1998). Nativism, empiricism and the development of knowledge. In W. Damon (Ed.), *Handbook of child psychology*, vol. 1 (Ed. R.M. Lerner). New York: Wiley.

Spencer, J.T., & Thelen, E. (2003). Introduction: Why this question and why now? Special Issue: Connectionist and dynamic systems approaches to development. *Developmental Science, 6*, 375–376.

Spitz, R.A. (1957). *No and yes: on the genesis of human communication*. Madison, CT: International Universities Press.

Stern, D.N. (1985). *The interpersonal world of the infant*. New York: Basic Books.

Sternglanz, S.H., Gray, J.L., & Murakami, M. (1977). Adult preference for infantile facial features: an ethological approach. *Animal Behaviour, 25*, 108–115.

Stiles, J., Bates, E.A., Thal, D., Tranner, D.A., & Reilly, J. (2002). Linguistic and spatial cognitive development in children with pre- and perinatal focal brain injury. In M.H. Johnson, Y. Munakata & R.O. Gilmore (Eds.), *Brain development and cognition: a reader*. Oxford: Blackwell.

Stone, C.A. (1993). What is missing in the metaphor of scaffolding? In E.A. Forman, N. Minick & C.A. Stone (Eds.), *Contexts for learning*. Oxford: Oxford University Press.

Super, C.M., & Harkness, S. (1986). The developmental niche: a conceptualisation at the interface of child and culture. *International Journal of Behavioral Development, 9*, 545–569.

Super, C.M., & Harkness, S. (1997). The cultural structuring of child development. In J.W. Berry, Y.H. Pootinga & J. Pandey (Eds.), *Handbook of cross-cultural psychology*, vol. 1: *Theory and method*. Boston, MA: Allyn and Bacon.

Svejda, M.J., Campos, J.J., & Emde, R.N. (1980). Mother–infant 'bonding': failure to generalize. *Child Development, 51*, 775–779.

Tager-Flusberg, H., Calkins, S., Nolin, T., Baumberger, T., Anderson, M., & Chadwick-Dias, A. (1990). A longitudinal study of language acquisition in autistic and Down syndrome children. *Journal of Autism and Developmental Disorders, 1*, 1–21.

Tajfel, H. (Ed.) (1978). *Differentiation between social groups*. London: Academic Press.

Tajfel, H., & Turner, J.C. (1979). An integrative theory of intergroup conflict. In W.G. Austin & S. Worchel (Eds.), *The social psychology of intergroup relations*. Monterey, CA: Brooks/Cole.

Thelen, E. (2002). Motor development as foundation and future of developmental psychology. In W.W. Hartup and R.K. Silbereisen (Eds.), *Growing points in developmental science*. Hove: Psychology Press.

Thelen, E., & Adolph, K.E. (1994). Arnold L. Gesell: the paradox of nature and nurture. In R.D. Parke, P.A. Ornstein, J.J. Rieser & C. Zahn-Waxler (Eds.), *A century of developmental psychology*. Washington, DC: American Psychological Association.

Thelen, E., & Smith, L.B. (1994). *A dynamic systems approach to the development of cognition and action*. Cambridge, MA: MIT Press.

Thomas, A., & Chess, S. (1977). *Temperament and development*. New York: Bremner/Mazel.

Thomas, M.S.C., & Karmiloff-Smith, A. (2002). Modelling typical and atypical cognitive development: computational constrains on mechanisms of change. In U. Goswami (Ed.), *Blackwell handbook of childhood cognitive development*. Oxford: Blackwell.

Thomas, A., Chess, S., Birch, H.G. Hertzig, M.E., & Korn, S. (1963). *Behavioral individuality in early childhood*. New York: New York University Press.

Thompson, R.A. (1994). Emotional regulation: a theme in search of definition. *Monographs of the Society for Research in Child Development*, 59, no. 2–3 (Serial no. 240).

Tinbergen, N. (1951). *The study of instinct*. Oxford: Clarendon Press.

Tizard, B., & Hughes, M. (2002). *Young children learning* (2nd ed.). Oxford: Blackwell.

Tobin, J.J., Wu, Y.H., & Davidson, D.H. (1989). *Preschool in three cultures: Japan, China and the United States*. New Haven, CT: Yale University Press.

Tomasello, M. (1993). On the interpersonal origins of the self-concept. In U. Neisser (Ed.), *The perceived self: ecological and interpersonal sources of self-knowledge*. Cambridge: Cambridge University Press.

Tomasello, M., & Farrar, M.J. (1986). Joint attention and early language. *Child Development*, 57, 1454–1463.

Trevarthen, C. (1977). Descriptive analyses of infant communicative behaviour. In H.R. Schaffer (Ed.), *Studies in mother–infant interaction*. London: Academic Press.

Trevarthen, C. (1979). Communication and cooperation in early infancy: a description of primary intersubjectivity. In M. Bullowa (Ed.), *Before speech: the beginnings of interpersonal communication*. Cambridge: Cambridge University Press.

Trevarthen, C. (1980). The foundations of intersubjectivity: development of interpersonal and cooperative understanding in infants. In D.R. Olson (Ed.), *The social foundations of language and thought*. New York: W.W. Norton.

Trevarthen, C. (1988). Universal co-operative motives: how infants begin to know the language and culture of their parents. In G. Jahoda & I.M. Lewis (Eds.), *Acquiring culture*. London: Croom Helm.

Trevarthen, C., & Hubley, P. (1978). Secondary intersubjectivity: confidence, confiding and acts of meaning in the first year. In A. Lock (Ed.), *Action, gesture and symbol: the emergence of language*. London: Academic Press.

Triandis, H.C. (1990). Cross-cultural studies of individualism and collectivism. In J. Berman (Ed.), *Nebraska Symposium on Motivation*. Lincoln, NB: University of Nebraska Press.

Triandis, H.C. (1995). *Individualism and collectivism*. Boulder, CO: Westview Press.

Triandis, H.C., Leung, K., Villareal, M.V., & Clark, F.L. (1985). Allocentric versus idiocentric tendencies: convergent and discriminant validation. *Journal of Research in Personality, 19*, 395–415.

Trivers, R.L. (1972). Parental investment and sexual selection. In B. Campbell (Ed.), *Sexual selection and the descent of man, 1871–1971*. Chicago: Aldine.

Turiel, E. (1983). *The development of social knowledge: morality and convention*. Cambridge: Cambridge University Press.

Turiel, E. (1998). The development of morality. In W. Damon (Ed.), *Handbook of child psychology*, vol. 3 (N. Eisenberg, Ed.). New York: Wiley.

Turkheimer, E., & Waldron, M. (2000). Nonshared environment: a theoretical, methodological and quantitative review. *Psychological Bulletin, 126,* 78–108.

Turner, J.C., Hogg, M.A., Oakes, P.J., Reicher, S.D., & Wetherall, M.S. (1987). *Rediscovering the social group: a self-categorization theory*. Oxford: Blackwell.

van Geert, P. (1993). A dynamic systems model of cognitive growth. In L.B. Smith and E. Thelen (Eds.), *A dynamic systems approach to development: applications*. Cambridge, MA: MIT Press.

von Bertalanffy, L. (1933). *Modern theories of development: an introduction to theoretical biology*. Oxford: Oxford University Press.

von Bertalanffy, L. (1968). *General systems theory: foundations, development, applications*. New York: G. Braziller.

Vygotsky, L.S. (1962). *Thought and language*. Cambridge, MA: MIT Press.

Vygotsky, L.S. (1978). *Mind in society: the development of higher psychological processes*. Cambridge, MA: Harvard University Press.

Wachs, T.D., & Kohnstamm, G.A. (Eds.) (2001). *Temperament in context*. Mahwah, NJ: Erlbaum.

Waddington, C.H. (1957). *The strategies of the genes*. London: Allen & Unwin.

Wang, S., & Tamis-LeMonda, C. (2003). Do child-rearing values in Taiwan and the United States reflect cultural values of collectivism and individualism? *Journal of Cross-Cultural Psychology, 34,* 629–642.

Warren, A.R., & McCloskey, A. (1997). Language in social contexts. In J. Berko Gleason (Ed.), *The development of language* (4th ed.). Boston, MA: Allyn Bacon.

Warren, A.R., & Tate, C.S (1992). Egocentrism in children's telephone conversations. In R.M. Diaz & L.E. Berk (Eds.), *Private speech: from social interaction to self-regulation*. Hillsdale, NJ: Erlbaum.

Waters, E., & Sroufe, L.A. (1983). Social competence as a developmental construct. *Developmental Review, 3,* 79–97.

Watson, J.B. (1928). *Psychological care of infant and child*. New York: Norton.

Weiner, B. (1986). *An attributional theory of motivation and emotion*. New York: Springer Verlag.

Weinstein, E.A. (1969). The development of interpersonal competence. In D. Goslin (Ed.), *Handbook of socialization theory and research*. Chicago: Rand McNally.

Wellman, H.M. (1988). The early development of memory strategies. In F.E. Weinert & M. Perlmutter (Eds.), *Memory development: universal changes and individual differences*. Hillsdale, NJ: Erlbaum.

Wellman, H.M. (1990). *The child's theory of mind*. Cambridge, MA: MIT Press.

Wellman, H.M., & Gelman, S.A. (1992). Cognitive development: foundational theories of core domains. *Annual Review of Psychology, 43,* 337–375.

Wellman, H.M., & Gelman, S.A. (1998). Knowledge acquisition in foundational domains. In W. Damon (Ed.), *Handbook of child psychology*, vol. 2 (D. Kuhn & R.S. Siegler, Eds.). New York: Wiley.

Wellman, H.M., Cross, D., & Watson, J. (2001). Meta-analysis of theory-of-mind development: the truth about false beliefs. *Child Development, 72*, 655–684.

Werker, J.F., & Desjardins, R.N. (1995). Listening to speech in the first year of life: experiential influences on phoneme perception. *Current Directions in Psychological Science, 4*, 76–81.

Werner, E.E. (1993). Risk, resilience and recovery: perspectives from the Kauai longitudinal study. *Development and Psychopathology, 5*, 503–515.

Werner, E.E., & Smith, R.S. (1982). *Vulnerable but invincible: a longitudinal study of resilient children and adolescents*. New York: McGraw–Hill.

White, R. (1959). Motivation reconsidered: the concept of competence. *Psychological Review, 66*, 297–333.

Wilson, E.O. (1975). *Sociobiology: the new synthesis*. Cambridge, MA: Harvard University Press.

Wilson, E.O. (1978). *On human nature*. Cambridge, MA: Harvard University Press.

Wimmer, H., & Perner, J. (1983). Beliefs about beliefs: representation and constraining function of wrong beliefs in young children's understanding of deception. *Cognition, 13*, 103–128.

Winnicott, D.W. (1958). *From paediatrics to psychoanalysis*. London: Hogarth.

Wolff, P.H. (1987). *The development of behavioral states and the expression of emotions in early infancy*. Chicago: University of Chicago Press.

Wood, D., Bruner, J., & Ross, G. (1976). The role of tutoring in problem solving. *Journal of Child Psychology and Psychiatry, 17*, 89–100.

Wynn, K. (1992). Addition and subtraction by human infants. *Nature, 358*, 749–750.

INDEX

All concepts described in the book are given in bold lettering